Susanna and Alice: Quaker Rebels

The Story of Susanna Parry and Her Cousin Alice Paul

Leslie Mulford Denis

an imprint of Sunbury Press, Inc.
Mechanicsburg, PA USA

an imprint of Sunbury Press, Inc.
Mechanicsburg, PA USA

Copyright © 2022 by Leslie Mulford Denis.
Cover Copyright © 2022 by Sunbury Press, Inc.

Sunbury Press supports copyright. Copyright fuels creativity, encourages diverse voices, promotes free speech, and creates a vibrant culture. Thank you for buying an authorized edition of this book and for complying with copyright laws. Except for the quotation of short passages for the purpose of criticism and review, no part of this publication may be reproduced, scanned, or distributed in any form without permission. You are supporting writers and allowing Sunbury Press to continue to publish books for every reader. For information contact Sunbury Press, Inc., Subsidiary Rights Dept., PO Box 548, Boiling Springs, PA 17007 USA or legal@sunburypress.com.

For information about special discounts for bulk purchases, please contact Sunbury Press Orders Dept. at (855) 338-8359 or orders@sunburypress.com.

To request one of our authors for speaking engagements or book signings, please contact Sunbury Press Publicity Dept. at publicity@sunburypress.com.

FIRST OXFORD SOUTHERN EDITION: April 2022

Set in Adobe Garamond | Interior design by Crystal Devine | Cover by Tyler Handa | Edited by Sarah Peachey.

Publisher's Cataloging-in-Publication Data
Names: Denis, Leslie Mulford, author.
Title: Susanna and Alice: Quaker rebels: the story of Susanna Parry and her cousin Alice Paul.
Description: First trade paperback edition. | Mechanicsburg, PA : Oxford Southern, 2022.
Summary: With revolutionary spirit, two cousins challenge Quaker propriety and become New Women. One is notorious—Alice Paul, who wins suffrage for women and writes the Equal Rights Amendment—the other is completely unknown, spinster Susanna Parry who fights societal norms and parental control to be with the woman she loves.
Identifiers: ISBN : 978-1-62006-873-1 (softcover).
Subjects: BIOGRAPHY & AUTOBIOGRAPHY / Women | HISTORY / Women | BIOGRAPHY & AUTOBIOGRAPHY / Social Activists.

Product of the United States of America
0 1 1 2 3 5 8 13 21 34 55

Continue the Enlightenment!

Cover photos – Top left: Susanna Parry; Top right: Alice Paul, c. 1918 (Library of Congress); Bottom: Silent Sentinels with protest banners in front of the White House, 1917 (Library of Congress).

For Little Star, with gratitude and love.

"I look forward to when we get real equality and everybody can be what he or she wants to be, so that we'll have a very much more perfect world in which to live. I haven't any doubt about it at all."

—Alice Paul to Amelia Fry, recorded in
Conversations with Alice Paul: An Autobiography, 1974

CONTENTS

Introduction: Jigsaw Pieces   vii

CHAPTERS

1. Their America   1
2. Century's End, Their Beginning   10
3. New Century, New Women   23
4. Coming of Age   41
5. Young Hearts Take Flight   49
6. All Things Must Pass   59
7. Setting Sail in Her Voice   74
8. The Susanna Tour Begins: Italy   82
9. Travels Continue: Switzerland, Germany, The Netherlands, Belgium   98
10. Paris   111
11. Coming Home   116
12. A New Chapter   125
13. 1914   141
14. Waging War   173
15. Prisoners of War   180
16. The Best and Worst of Times   186
17. Battle in the Shadowlands   192
18. Through Depression and War   203
19. Little Star, Norwegian Eyes   212
20. Passing the Torch   231

Epilogue: Looking Back   235

Acknowledgments	240
Bibliography	242
Notes	245
Index	249
About the Author	255

INTRODUCTION

JIGSAW PIECES

Decades ago, when I lived in Boston, one of my favorite weekend activities was visiting the Museum of Fine Arts to see the Impressionists and Post-Impressionists. My favorite painting was Paul Gauguin's haunting *Where do we come from? What are we? Where are we going?* The enormous masterpiece of symbolism depicted Tahitians in all stages of the life cycle, from a baby on the far right to an old woman on the far left, paused and pensive as if caught up in a dream. The title painted in the upper left-hand corner lets us know what they were thinking about: the three questions about the mystery of human existence. Without fail, I too would pause in front of the painting, mesmerized, meditating upon those very questions: Where do I come from? What am I? Where am I going?

The older I get, the less I seem to know about what I am and where I'm going. However, I've known since childhood where I come from. At gatherings, family members would speak about our lineage, the bloodlines of ancestry, telling the stories, keeping the history alive. This was particularly true of my mother's family—the Parry clan. Mother and her sisters were descended from a long line of Quakers, the most famous of which was seamstress Betsy Ross, who, according to legend, made the first American flag. Also in the Parry bloodline, although not a direct relation, was the infamous Alice Paul, suffragette and women's rights activist who founded the National Woman's Party and fought tirelessly and single-mindedly all her adult life for a woman's right to full equality under the law.

The forefather who links me to Alice Paul was my great-great-grandfather, the Honorable William Parry, a distinguished judge and a founding father of Swarthmore College in Pennsylvania. He married Alice Stokes, and they had two daughters (one of whom died at age fourteen) and five sons. Son Oliver, my great-grandfather, married Lydia Satterthwaite (the Betsy Ross connection), and they had two children: a daughter, Mary, and son, Edwin Satterthwaite Parry—my grandfather. Edwin S. Parry lived in Riverton, New Jersey, with his wife, Mary Bond Parry, and their three daughters: Dora, Lydia, and the eldest Charlotte, my mother. Although my grandfather earned his living in advertising, he was also a writer who published a book entitled *Betsy Ross Quaker Rebel* about his much-revered great-great-grandmother, Elizabeth Claypoole, whose name as a child was Betsy Griscom, then Betsy Ross in her first marriage, then Betsy Ashburn in her second. After her first two husbands died in the Revolution, she married my great-great-great-great-grandfather John Claypoole. Betsy Ross was the original rebel in the family, being "read out" or banished by her Quaker meeting because she chose to marry not a Quaker but, God help her, an Episcopalian. Her other two husbands weren't Quakers either. The title of this book is a nod to my grandfather's book about Quaker rebel Betsy Ross. The subjects of this book are two of my grandfather's cousins: Susanna Parry and Alice Paul, who were, like Betsy Ross, Quaker rebels, challenging the cultural norms and laws of their day.

Judge William Parry's daughter Tacie married William Mickle Paul. She and her husband lived in Mt. Laurel, New Jersey, and had four children—sons William and Parry, daughter Helen, and eldest daughter Alice Paul. Alice would become a suffragette and feminist, would have little place in her life for men, and would never marry. Judge William's son Howard married the wealthy Elizabeth Haines. They lived in Riverton, New Jersey, and had two daughters, Susanna and Beulah, who, like their cousin Alice Paul, never married and lived together for most of their lives on the family estate.

The three cousins of my grandfather—Susanna Parry, Beulah Parry, and Alice Paul, were still alive when I was a child. I regret never having met Alice. I have only dim recollections of seeing Susanna and Beulah at the Fourth of July parades in Riverton. I remember Susanna as very tall, quiet, stately—a handsome woman. On the other hand, Beulah appeared shorter and plump with dark bushy eyebrows. My sister Susan said she was always afraid of Beulah. From what I heard family members say about Susanna and Beulah, I gathered they were two old maid Quakers who lived together inseparably, had a whole lot of money, and in their youth traveled throughout Europe. They were always spoken of together: Susanna-and-Beulah. I never thought of them as individuals, each with a rich life of her own. How quick we are to label, define, and diminish other people, especially the elderly. How often do we fail to see others fully because we don't take the time to learn their stories?

When the last Susannah-and-Beulah sister died in 1979, family members were invited to an estate sale at the Parry home in Riverton. Mom went with her sisters, returning with several items: a pink blanket for a single bed with beautifully hand-stitched satin binding, under which I slept for many years and still have today; a lovely, simple gold bracelet, which another sister has; and a beautifully framed print of a picture by Pieter de Hooch—"Dutch Interior"—signed on the back by Beulah and dated 1908, which hung in my bedroom in the family home and remains with me to this day. It traveled through the decades from apartment to apartment, then across the ocean to France, returning to the U.S., then back again to France, a precious keepsake of these enigmatic, distant cousins.

The wheel of time turned, as it must, and Mom, her sisters, their husbands—the whole generation—died. My generation of Parry cousins has gathered from time to time at weddings and, with increasing frequency, at funerals. After the heartbreaking funeral of a cousin, we decided that we should make an effort to get together, while we're still able, for happy occasions, as we used to in our childhood at Christmas, the Fourth of July, and summer vacations on Long Beach Island, New Jersey. To that end, my cousin Ed hosted a Parry family reunion at his home in Oxford, Maryland, a few years ago, which was wonderful fun and well attended by the cousins and their children and grandchildren. We brought old family photo albums to share and swapped stories of our ancestors, hoping the next generation would care enough to listen.

On the last day of the reunion, the Parry cousins got together one last time at Ed's for lunch and Sunday afternoon football. Ed came downstairs with an old wooden box full of dusty bundles of letters, put them on the floor in front of us, and told the story. He also went to Susanna's and Beulah's estate sale some forty years before. As other relatives poured over the jewelry, furnishings, and other things of more monetary value, something told him to go into the attic, where he found a box of old correspondence, which the auctioneer let him have at no charge—after all, they were just old letters. Ed had kept the box in his attic ever since, never having had the time to open even one of the bundles tied up in string like dusty gift packages.

I was drawn to the box like a child to a birthday present and plopped myself down in front of it to explore the contents. My adventure had begun. Having always been interested in genealogy, especially the family stories, I was a miner for gold who had just hit the motherload. In those dusty bundles were letters written to Parry family members, mostly Susanna, along with postcards, engraved invitations, dance cards, and other keepsakes. Obviously, the bundles had not been opened for a very long time, if ever, and some of the postmarks were very old, before 1900. Many were from the early 1900s when Susannah and Beulah were students at Swarthmore College. Many were from Susanna herself, written to her stateside family during her travels in Europe on two occasions—the first time when she and her sister Beulah traveled with their aunt on a first-class grand tour of Europe, the second time when she studied at Woodbrooke Quaker Study Centre in England, as her cousin Alice had done. Most of the letters in the collection were written in pen-and-ink script and full of Quakerisms: "thee, thy, thine" and "First Day" through "Seventh Day" as days of the week. What I was looking at was a pile of puzzle pieces, the jumbled chronicle of three generations of a Quaker family, and more broadly, of a way of life that has long disappeared.

One item that I uncovered in that initial exploration was a newspaper clipping about the arrest and incarceration of Alice Paul during a suffrage demonstration. With Ed's blessing, my cousin Lee took the clipping to donate to the Alice Paul Institute at her birthplace in Mt. Laurel, New Jersey. Lee said she had heard from her mother and grandmother that Alice Paul was a pariah in the family, considered "a kook" because she was obsessed with women's suffrage and equal rights. Family members would talk of her, if at all, in hushed tones. Not the conventional prim and proper Quaker lady, she was audacious, passionate, confrontational, possibly crazy, and certainly an embarrassment to the family name. A misunderstood and unappreciated heroine: I wanted to learn more.

When it was time to leave the family reunion, I had looked at only a few of the letters, postcards, and newspaper clippings. I was covered in dust and mold from the family treasure trove but delighted, in a daze, having caught a new glimpse of my family's history, my where-do-I-come-from.

The wheel turned again. A year and a half later, wanting to escape the deep snows of Maine winters, my husband, Laurent, and I moved to the Eastern Shore of Maryland. After unpacking and settling in, I looked for a new project. With my interest in Parry family history rekindled after our reunion, I restored what the family had always called "the Parry desk" and supposedly belonged to my mother's grandfather Oliver Parry. As it turned out, the desk was older than we thought, dating from the late 1700s. Given that Oliver Parry was born in 1851, the desk certainly belonged to his father, Judge William Parry, born in 1817—the blood link between me, Alice, Susanna, and Beulah.

Shortly after Laurent and I had settled in our new home, cousin Ed visited us to welcome us to the Eastern Shore. Knowing that I had restored William Parry's desk, Ed brought a much-treasured housewarming gift—a framed portrait of William Parry which had belonged to his mother and had hung in his office for many years, which he was now passing on to me for safe keeping. The picture now hangs proudly over William Parry's desk.

Ed also brought another gift: the box of Susanna's correspondence that he had shown the family at the reunion. He said he was certain that I was the right caretaker of the papers and let me hold on to them for perusal and safekeeping. Of course, I wanted to catalog the contents. What a challenge: the letters needed to be cleaned, sorted, arranged in chronological order, read, and chronicled. Daunting, but doable. I started the task that winter, which was unusually cold and snowy for the Eastern Shore, keeping me housebound for days on end.

My dining room became genealogy central. I opened the bundles on the dining room table and put all the pieces in chronological order. Some of the bundles had been chewed in the corners by mice, some very old and probably hadn't been read in over one hundred years. The dust and mold irritated the respiratory passages. I probably should have worn a mask but didn't and would the next time. I survived the job with a couple of weeks of sneezing. The most unpleasant part was not the sneezing but resisting the temptation to read the letters as I sorted them. I wanted first to put them in chronological order and then read the entire collection from beginning to end. I wanted to experience Susanna's story as it unfolded.

Finally, all the papers were in order—over four hundred letters, postcards, graduation and wedding invitations, birth announcements, and other keepsakes dating from 1879 to 1971. It took me over a year to read and chronicle them all. What emerged was the saga of one branch of the Parry family, particularly of one leaf on the branch—Susanna. What I learned in the reading was that Susanna and Beulah were educated, well-to-do, well-traveled, and well-connected Quaker ladies who never married yet had full lives blessed with friendship, family, and generous service to others. What I also learned, sometimes between the lines, was the story of Susanna's youthful rebellion, her struggle against the cultural norms of the nineteenth century, her desire to free herself from bondage to tradition and become a twentieth-century "New Woman." She did not fully succeed. Nonetheless, the story of this unknown Quaker rebel, who was in some ways ordinary, in some ways extraordinary, needed to be told.

I was pleased to find some letters and cards from Alice Paul in Susanna's correspondence and learn that they were very close cousins and spent a great deal of time together in their youth and old age. Because Alice was rarely spoken about in the family, I needed to research this American icon of feminist rebellion and activism. I am shocked when I ask women if they know who Alice Paul was: most don't. For this reason, I want to tell Alice's story as well as Susanna's because hers was a life that all women

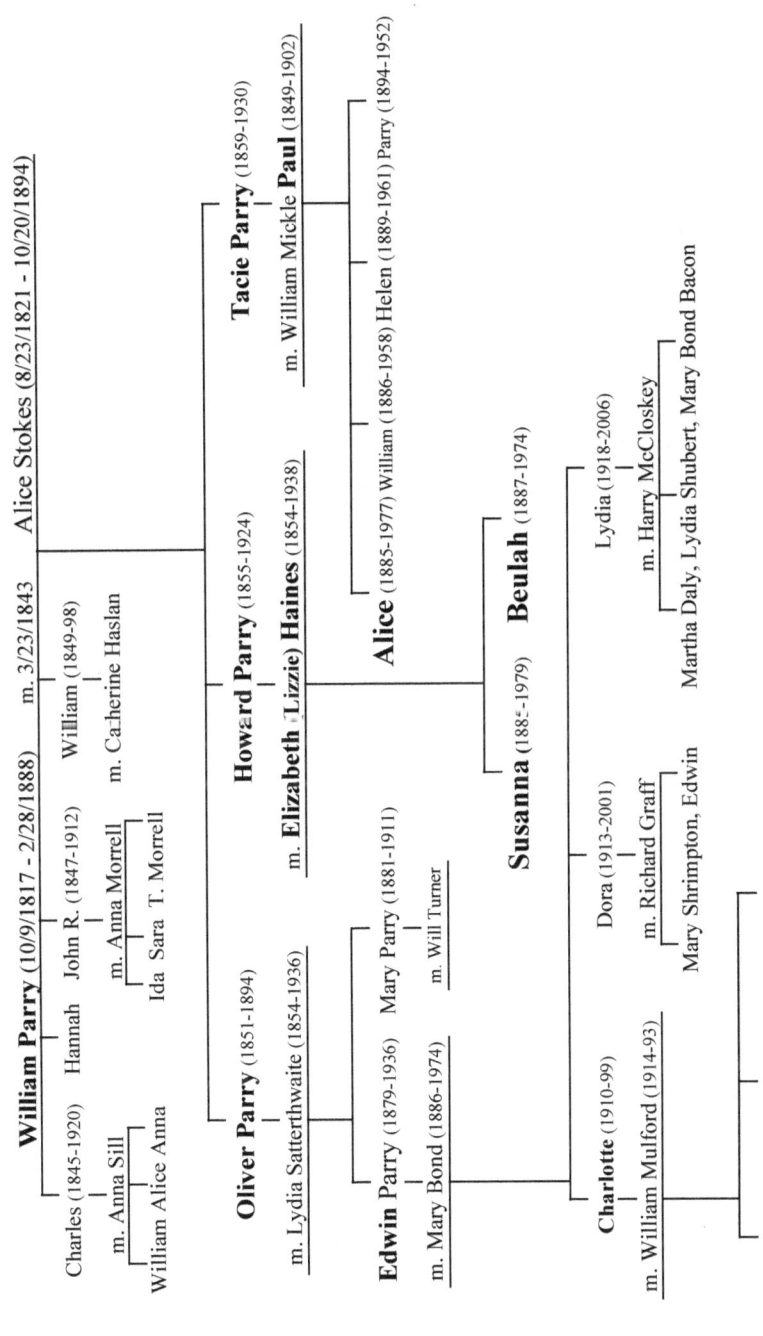

Branches of the Parry Family Tree

should not just know about but celebrate, especially as the ratification of the Nineteenth Amendment celebrated its one hundredth anniversary in 2020. A woman's right to vote became guaranteed by federal law because Alice, with the help of many others, dared to persevere, brave censure, and sometimes endure prison, hunger strikes, and forced feedings. Getting the vote was just the first step for Alice. Her goal was full equality for women, and she dedicated her life to that end: she established the National Woman's Party, penned the Equal Rights Amendment, and lobbied for women's rights internationally.

The letters of the Susanna Collection are rich in details of daily life. This book is a chronicle not only of Susanna's and Alice's lives but also of the Progressive Era of their youth—America at the turn of the new century, a period rich in political, cultural, scientific, and technological change, and rich in the promise of a better world. Everything in those years was new: Progressive reforms in politics, Art Nouveau and Modernism in art and literature, jazz music, the telephone, automobiles, and for Susanna and Alice, the possibility of becoming "New Women."

As children, my sister Charlotte and I had an annual ritual at Christmastime of putting together Mom's childhood jigsaw puzzle. The completed puzzle was a lovely old-fashioned skating scene of boys and girls having fun on the ice. We spent happy hours around the card table putting together the jumbled wooden puzzle pieces, cut by jigsaw, many in unforgettable, whimsical shapes—a heart, a key, a snowflake, a lady's profile. It was a thrilling breakthrough when a skater's face would be pieced together, or a fur muff warming delicate hands, or a petticoated skirt cut coquettishly high above the skates. We didn't have a picture to go by, but we didn't need one: we knew the scene by heart.

I have loved puzzles ever since. In these pages, I have pieced together scenes from the lives of two twentieth-century Quaker rebels, Susanna Parry and her cousin Alice Paul, the largest puzzle I have ever tackled. Its pieces were made not of wood but of paper—thousands of dusty pages that only mites and mice had touched in two generations. From these letters, the story of Susanna emerges, and with this book, I hope to pass on her story to future generations. I also hope to kindle new interest in the story of Alice Paul. Little is known of her private life because she intentionally destroyed traces of it, wanting to be remembered only for her work on behalf of women's rights. I tried to learn enough about her life to chronicle both women's stories simultaneously. I know from the collection that they kept in touch throughout their lives. Although they shared many carefree childhood memories, they lived radically different lives as adults. However, the kind hand of coincidence brought them together again in their final days.

A dusty box of long-hidden letters led me on a genealogical adventure during which I discovered that Susanna Parry and Alice Paul, Quaker cousins and Progressive Era New Women, struggled for their emancipation, and in Alice's case, the emancipation of all women. Alice's struggle was very public in her day and the object of much current attention. However, Susanna's youthful struggle has remained untold until now. None of my cousins knew about it. No one in my parents' generation knew about it. It remained unspoken, tucked away between the pages of old letters bundled up and kept secret in Susanna's attic—until the spirit led my cousin to go up to the attic at her estate sale, retrieve the box, and pass it on to me decades later. And now I share the story with you.

This is the story of two Quaker rebels fighting for women's emancipation. Both had the audacity to seek freedom and change. Both confronted strong opposition. Both showed great courage in the face of resistance. And both, in defeat, carried on.

CHAPTER 1

THEIR AMERICA

*S*usanna and Alice were both born in 1885 in southern New Jersey to well-to-do Hicksite Quaker families. They were cousins: Susanna's father, Howard Parry, and Alice's mother, Tacie Parry Paul, were brother and sister, children of the venerable and wealthy Judge William Parry. They were born into an America far different from ours. Most of us would have difficulty imagining the daily life of Americans at the end of the nineteenth century. Most homes did not yet have electricity: Although Thomas Edison had developed lights powered by electric current in 1879, generating stations and power grids had not yet reached all Americans. To communicate with friends and family, they couldn't pick up a telephone or send an e-mail but had to visit in person or write letters: Although Alexander Graham Bell had patented the telephone in 1876, it would take time for the telephone system to extend nationwide. For entertainment, they had to read, go for a walk or a horse-and-buggy ride, or get together with friends and family to dine or play cards or parlor games: There were no movies, television, or radio. To travel from one place to another, they had to walk, ride a bike, hitch up a horse, or for long voyages, take a ferry, train, or ship: There were no cars or buses, no subways, no planes. They had to tough it out if they had a headache: Aspirin wasn't produced yet. If they became sick with the flu or pneumonia or just about any disease, they were in trouble: Vaccines and antibiotics hadn't been developed yet, except for anthrax (1881) and rabies (1885). At the beginning of the twentieth century, the average life expectancy was forty-seven years; the leading causes of death in the U.S.

were pneumonia and tuberculosis.[1] Susanna and Alice were born into a different world: There were no atomic bombs or nuclear warheads; there had not yet been a world war.

POLITICS

The political scene at the turn of the last century was in some ways different from ours, in many ways the same. In 1885, America was still recovering from the heartbreak of the Civil War, which had ended just twenty years before, having claimed the lives of over 600,000 Americans. Reconstruction, the program of bringing the southern states back into the American fold, had been difficult, as was life for formerly enslaved people.

The two decades after the end of the Civil War were marked by staggering change: many presidents and much political and economic turmoil. We aren't the only generation to know political instability: assassinations, contested elections, presidential impeachment, corruption, strife, and economic depression.

Southern-born Vice President Andrew Johnson became president upon Lincoln's death. His tenure was tainted by scandal when he tried to undo all the good that Lincoln had done. An avowed white supremacist, Johnson waged war on the Republican majority in Congress. He unsuccessfully opposed the Fourteenth Amendment of 1868, which gave citizenship and other rights to the formerly enslaved. Congress passed the Tenure of Office Act to stop the outraged Johnson from firing members of his administration. When Johnson fired Secretary of War Edwin Stanton in 1868, the House impeached him; he escaped conviction in the Senate by only one vote. However, his presidential influence had ended.

General Ulysses S. Grant, who led the implementation of Reconstruction, succeeded Johnson as president in the election of 1868 and served two consecutive terms from 1869 to 1877. Grant created the Department of Justice and presided over Reconstruction by promoting the Fifteenth Amendment, extending the vote to black men (ratified in 1870) and prosecuting the Ku Klux Klan, using military force when necessary to protect the formerly enslaved. However, during Grant's second term, white supremacist "Redeemers" won control of the state governments in the South through violence and voter fraud. This period was also darkened by the Panic of 1873 and the resulting economic depression, unemployment, bankruptcies, and a weakened dollar. Grant tried to support the dollar by introducing the Gold Standard. Although he escaped scandal, his administration was fraught with corruption, and he would not serve another term.

Rutherford B. Hayes won a much-contested election in 1876, losing the popular vote and only narrowly winning the Electoral College. To gain the needed southern votes, he withdrew federal support of formerly enslaved people, ending Reconstruction and beginning the era of Jim Crow—sanctioned racial discrimination and violence.

James Garfield became president in 1880 but would serve only a few months in office. He died in 1881 after unhygienic surgery on a gunshot wound led to infection. During his short time as president, he reinforced the Navy, rid the Post Office of corruption, advocated education and civil rights, and called for Civil Service reform.

After Garfield's assassination, Vice President Chester A. Arthur became president and served for one term. He strengthened the Navy and took up Garfield's cause of Civil Service reform, signing the Pendleton Civil Service Reform Act.

Democrat Grover Cleveland won the election of 1884 and became the only president to serve two nonconsecutive terms. His first term was from 1885 to 1889. Although he won the popular vote in 1888, he lost the Electoral College. However, he won the 1892 election. Cleveland, admired for his integrity, fought corruption and sought fiscal conservatism. He was America's president when Susanna and Alice were born.

WOMEN'S RIGHTS

In the turbulent decades preceding the births of Susanna and Alice, women began their fight for autonomy and the vote. Three prominent leaders of the nineteenth-century suffrage movement were Lucretia Mott and Susan B. Anthony—Hicksite Quakers like Susanna and Alice—and Elizabeth Cady Stanton. At the time of the Seneca Falls Meeting of 1848, women were, at best, second-class citizens and, in many ways, were slaves to their husbands. They couldn't vote, had little access to a college education, and couldn't testify in court. Married women couldn't own property, keep their earnings if they worked, or write checks. Divorced or separated women couldn't obtain custody of their children. At the Seneca Falls Meeting, Stanton's "Declaration of Rights and Sentiments" proposed that women be given the right to vote, which shocked the crowd. Frederick Douglass was one of the few who spoke in favor of women's suffrage.

At the Women's Rights Convention of 1854, which took place at the New York state legislature, suffragists went further, demanding the vote and the right to own property. The legislature rejected the right to vote but allowed women to keep their earnings and have custody of their children in some cases. In 1860, the New York state legislature passed the Married Women's Property Act, which allowed married women to keep their wages, sue in court, and share custody of children. This was progress but a state law applicable only to women residing in New York.

Anthony and Stanton formed the American Equal Rights Association for Universal Suffrage in 1863 after Lincoln's Emancipation Proclamation failed to include women.

In 1872, Anthony was arrested for registering and voting in an election. Because she was a woman, she was not allowed to testify in her own defense; she was found guilty and fined $100, which she never paid.

In 1878, California Senator Aaron Sargent proposed an amendment to the U.S. Constitution to allow women to vote. When arguing the proposal before the Senate, he was jeered at by the all-male senators, and the proposal didn't make it out of committee. The proposal for suffrage would be reintroduced and rejected over the next four decades. In 1885, the year Susanna and Alice were born, few women had been given the right to vote, except in the territories of Wyoming (1869), Utah (1870), and Washington (1883).

Women in 1885 had little access to quality careers. Before the Civil War, most women didn't work. They remained at home, raised their children, and cared for their husbands. By the mid-nineteenth century, lower-class women worked in textile mills and agriculture. About the only other option was prostitution. However, because of the shortage of available men during and after the Civil War, more women began working in factories and domestic service in the latter half of the nineteenth century. More rewarding careers became possible as institutions of higher education began to open their doors to women. Ohio's Oberlin College began admitting women in 1833, Massachusetts' Mount Holyoke in 1837, Georgia Female College (later Wesleyan) in 1839, Virginia's Hollins University in 1842, Michigan's Hillsdale College in 1844, North Carolina's Charlotte Female Institute (now Queens University) in 1857, Virginia's Union Women's College (now Averett University) in 1859, New York's Vassar in 1861, and Pennsylvania's Swarthmore College in 1864.

Swarthmore, near Philadelphia, was founded in 1864 by Hicksite Quakers. One of Swarthmore's founders was Susanna's and Alice's grandfather, Judge William Parry, whose daughter Tacie attended Swarthmore but had to leave in her senior year when she married William Mickle Paul. Her firstborn was Alice Paul. Both Alice and her cousin Susanna graduated from Swarthmore. Alice graduated with high honors and would earn an array of graduate degrees impressive in any era. She was one of the most educated women of her time, awarded a Master's in Sociology and Political Science from the University of Pennsylvania in 1907; a Ph.D. in Economics, Sociology, and Political Science from the University of Pennsylvania in 1912; a Legum Baccalaureus law degree from American University in 1922; a Master's of Law degree from American University in 1927; and a Doctorate in Civil Law from American University in 1928.

AMERICAN QUAKERS

Understanding the world that Susanna and Alice were born into requires knowledge of the Quakers, also known as the Religious Society of Friends, particularly the lifestyle of the Hicksite Quakers at the end of the nineteenth century. The Quaker movement was born in England in the mid-seventeenth century when a group of Christian dissenters—rebels—broke away from the Church of England. Their leader, George Fox, claimed that clergy were not necessary for a spiritual life because everyone had direct access to Christ inside of themselves, which they referred to as "the inner light." Understandably, the Church of England considered this doctrine heretical. The American colonies also saw Quakers as heretics and persecuted them with banishment, imprisonment, and sometimes death, as in Mary Dyer, who was hanged to death on the Boston Common in 1660. King Charles II soon after forbade Massachusetts from executing Quakers. Beginning in the 1680s, Quakers emigrated elsewhere in America and established communities in Rhode Island, "West" Jersey, and Pennsylvania, the latter two founded by affluent Quaker William Penn.

In the "Great Separation" of 1827, the Quakers divided along ideological and sociological differences. The Orthodox Quakers were affluent urban dwellers who wanted to assimilate themselves more closely to the mainstream culture, adjusting their religious practices to approach those of the Protestant churches. The Hicksite Quakers, named after Elias Hicks, were far less urbane, more agricultural, and generally less wealthy. Suspicious of capitalism, they considered the Orthodox Quakers far too worldly. They wanted nothing of Protestant ritual in their faith and held fast to the original belief in their direct access to God's light within themselves.

The Orthodox Quakers shunned the Hicksites, and the feeling was mutual. The Hicksites remained isolated from the Orthodox Quakers and much of mainstream society. Consequently, the Hicksites' spiritual, educational, and social life was primarily limited to interaction with family members and other Hicksites. To broaden their sense of community, Hicksite Friends from Philadelphia, Baltimore, New York, Ohio, and Indiana gathered together at yearly "Meetings." Following traditional Quaker practices, they devoted their lives to purifying their speech and behavior to reflect the light of God. They were honest, did not drink, dressed plainly, shunned loud and unseemly behavior, opposed war, and engaged in progressive activism such as prison reform and the abolition of slavery. They believed in the spiritual (if not legal) equality of men and women and encouraged each member of the community to be led by the "inner light" to find their calling to social service. This last point is central to the paths taken by Susanna and Alice. Susanna found her vocation of philanthropy later in life, while Alice found hers as a young adult, then devoted the rest of her life and all her energy and thought to her calling: obtaining complete equality for women under the law.

Although the Parrys were Hicksites, they were by no means poor or removed from the world. Quite the contrary. The cousins' grandfather, Judge William Parry, owned hundreds of acres of land in Cinnaminson, New Jersey, and married into a wealthy and illustrious family of Rancocas, New Jersey, in marrying Alice Stokes. A lover of land and nature, Judge William established the Pomona Nursery and developed new and improved varieties of fruit trees. He was also a member of the New Jersey legislature, where he was instrumental in passing legislation that ended the railroad monopoly in the state. William Parry was also a civil engineer who designed and oversaw the construction of thirty turnpikes in New Jersey. Along with Lucretia Mott, he was also one of the founders of Swarthmore College; he wanted his grandchildren to attend Swarthmore for at least a year to give their college education a strong Quaker foundation.

Susanna's father was Judge Parry's son Howard. He followed in his father's footsteps as a civil engineer specializing in road construction. Like his father, he wore many professional hats. He was a prominent banker, an incorporator of the Burlington County Trust Company, and a director of the Moorestown National Bank. He was also one of the founders of the Riverton-Palmyra Water Company. He, too, had strong ties to the land as a surveyor and real estate agent. And like his father, he too married into money by marrying the very wealthy Elizabeth Haines.

Alice's mother was Judge Parry's daughter Tacie, who surely brought with her a sizeable dowry when she married William Mickle Paul, who was wealthy in his own right. He was president of the Moorestown National Bank, vice president of the Riverton-Palmyra Water Company (which Susanna's father had founded), and an entrepreneur, investing in such enterprises as the Tacony Palmyra Ferry Company and the Squirrel Inn on Squirrel Island, Maine, where Susanna and Alice would vacation together. He, too, had strong ties to the land as a real estate investor and owner of a large working farm—over 170 acres—in Mt. Laurel, New Jersey.

Judge William Parry, c. 1870.

The Parry Family, c 1883. Top Row (right to left): Lydia Satterthwaite and Oliver Parry, Elizabeth (Lizzie) Haines and Howard Parry, Tacie Parry and William Mickle Paul, Catherine Haslan and William Parry. Bottom Row (right to left): Charles and Anna Sill Parry, Alice Stokes and Judge William Parry, Anne Morrell and John R. Parry.

The strong common ties of the Hicksite Quaker families of Susanna and Alice kept them in close contact throughout their lives. Susanna and Alice, born the same year, were particularly close as children—favorite cousins and schoolmates at Swarthmore College. Although they were more distant as adults because of Alice's much frowned upon involvement in the suffrage movement, they remained in contact through letters and would spend their final days together. I was very excited to find letters from Alice to Susanna in the collection. Unfortunately, I know of no existing letters from Susanna to Alice because Alice intentionally destroyed traces of her personal life, wanting to be remembered only for her work on behalf of women.

CHAPTER 2

CENTURY'S END, THEIR BEGINNING

*T*he earliest entries in the Susanna Collection appropriately mark the beginning of Susanna's story. The first is an invitation to her parents' wedding: Elizabeth (Lizzie) Haines to Howard Parry on October 5, 1884. The next entry, dated almost a year to the day of the wedding, is a letter from Lizzie's sister Susanna (often referred to in this story as Auntie Sue) announcing the home birth of her niece, our Susanna. With no telephone to spread the news, Auntie Sue wrote a brief note to the Haines family on October 6, 1885: "Our little girl is two hours old. . . . Dr. says baby is remarkably pretty, weighs 8 lbs—both mother & baby seem to be doing well thus far—We are all so thankful it's over."

Interesting that Auntie Sue called baby Susanna "our little girl." Sue would later marry a man who already had five children and would never have children of her own. As the letters in the collection show, she would devote much attention, influence, and even control over Susanna and her sister, Beulah. The children should not have been subjected to two mothers at the same time; one was often more than enough.

Alice Paul, Susanna's cousin, was born at the beginning of the same year on January 11, 1885.

The next letter in the Susanna Collection is from 1890. In the five years since Susanna's birth, America had witnessed a multitude of significant changes in politics, technology, and medicine. (See the chronology of events.) The Parry family had also experienced significant family events: two births and a death. On March 15, 1887, Susanna's sister and lifelong companion, Beulah Parry, was born. On February 28, 1888, the venerable Judge William Parry died, the patriarch of the Parry family and grandfather of Susanna and Alice. In 1889, Helen Paul was born, Alice's sister, lifelong supporter, and sometimes companion.

On December 13, 1890, Auntie Sue, the well-traveled and very privileged Sue Haines, sent a letter to her beloved nieces, the toddlers Susanna and Beulah. Auntie said she had heard that the children had gone to their Uncle Oliver's for Thanksgiving. Oliver, brother of the children's father, Howard, and father of the children's older cousin, Edwin (my grandfather), would die four years later of typhoid fever.

Auntie Sue wrote her nieces (and her sister Lizzie, their mother) that she would be taking a steamer back to America in a couple of weeks. When the steamer arrived in New York Harbor, people on Fire Island would see the steamer passing and notify the morning papers; a telegraph would then be sent to the family announcing her arrival. How much easier communications are today, with instantaneous international e-mails and telephone calls.

Auntie Sue told her young nieces that she would take them to Europe when they got older. Between the lines of this letter, she notified her sister of her plans for the girls' education. Unlike her, they would be able to speak French; like her, they would be privileged international travelers: "When you get older and can talk like the French people can Auntie wants you to come here & see all the pretty things & strange people Auntie has seen—but you must know how to talk like the French people do or you will not enjoy it half as well as you might & only a few people can understand what you say. Auntie does not even know how to ask for a drink of water when she is with the French people, isn't that too bad!" As the letters from the collection show, Auntie would make good on this promise to her nieces: The summer after Susanna's graduation from Swarthmore, the three would travel extensively and extravagantly through Europe for three months.

Susanna (left), Lizzie (center), and Beulah Parry, c. 1898.

From left to right: Alice, Helen, and William Paul, 1894. (Courtesy of the Alice Paul Institute, www.alicepaul.org)

Edwin (left) and Mary Parry, c. 1890.

The next entries in the Susanna Collection are two tiny, sweet letters to Susanna from her cousin Mary, my grandfather Edwin's younger sister. In the first one from 1892, when Susanna was seven years old, eleven-year-old Mary talked about their dolls and bicycles, then told an amusing account of chasing mice in her house: "Mamma used to give me a penny for every mouse I caught in a trap but we have so many cats that we do not have many mice now. From thy cousin Mary A. Parry."

Two years later, in February 1894, cousin Mary sent Susanna and Beulah a child-sized letter containing an adorable sketch of a young witch scolding a rabbit. She thanked her cousins for the two oranges they sent her, then related the visit of Aunt Anna Parry (Anna Sill Parry, wife of Judge William Parry's son Charles) and their little cousin Anna. She then described how she took sick after that visit: "I had the rheumatism in my foot so bad I could not stand up, but Papa carried me down the stairs and it pained all day. On Seventh Day and First Day it did not pain but I could not use it. But yesterday and today I could walk." Future letters would show that cousin Mary remained sickly all her short life and died at a very young thirty-one years old. I had never heard anyone in

Sketch by Mary Parry, 1894.

the family speak of my grandfather's sister Mary and was grateful to find traces of this lost relative in the collection.

The next item in the collection is an invitation to the wedding of Susanna Haines (Auntie Sue) to Joseph L. Haines on November 22, 1894, about a year after the death of his first wife. The wedding took place at Auntie Sue's home in Riverton, New Jersey. Joseph, who lived in Carroll County, Maryland, had inherited his father's land and the houses on it but was accomplished in his own right—a civil engineer who surveyed for the Western Maryland Railroad and was very interested in county and state politics. Joseph lived with his first wife and their five children at the "Forest Home" family residence in Maryland. Auntie Sue would live at Forest Home after the marriage. I can't imagine how difficult that would be for Sue, becoming stepmother to five grieving children. Sue and Joseph would not have children, and it is clear from the letters in the collection that Auntie Sue would always feel far closer to Susanna and Beulah than to her stepchildren.

The next entries in the collection are 1896 and 1897 letters to Lizzie, Susanna's mother, from Auntie Sue. America had experienced more technological innovations, political changes, and economic hardships by that time. (See the chronology of events.) From 1890 to 1897, the Parry family suffered emotional blows. In the middle of the economic depression, on October 16, 1894, Oliver Parry, father of Susanna's and Alice's cousin Mary and my grandfather Edwin, died of typhoid fever at forty-three years old. Before being cut down in his prime, Oliver was already an accomplished citizen: he developed a 300-acre tract of land in Willingboro, New Jersey, into three self-sustaining farms, was chairman of Willingboro's Township Committee, was a director of the Burlington County Safe Deposit and Trust Company, and was being considered as a candidate for state senator. An effective vaccine had not yet been developed for typhoid, a deadly bacterial disease spread by poor sanitation and hygiene still present today in underdeveloped countries. Oliver's death was soon followed by a second painful loss: the death of Oliver's mother, matriarch Alice Stokes Parry, Judge William Parry's widow, grandmother to Susanna and Alice, and Alice's namesake. I can't imagine the grief of Susanna's father and Alice's mother—losing a brother and mother in the same year.

The two 1896 letters to Susanna's mother, Lizzie, from Auntie Sue are painfully annoying. In the first, written in May from her Maryland estate at Forest Home, Sue talked on and on about material things: her new gold tooth, rugs she bought, going to the dressmaker. However, I enjoyed reading "Am glad you are pleased with William Parry's picture." This is surely a reference to the framed portrait of Judge William Parry given to me by my cousin Ed, which now hangs over William Parry's desk—a missing puzzle piece found and put in place.

Auntie Sue's October 1896 letter was just like the last one, page after page about absolutely nothing of importance: dresses being made, social visits, house renovations, gossip. I suspect Lizzie might have rolled her eyes a bit. One section of the letter discussed politics and is more interesting. With the country reeling from the depression that followed the Panic of 1893, Auntie Sue's husband, Joe, had decided to enter politics. Joe had "gone to a political meeting tonight & we are expecting to entertain Congressman Baker overnight." She wrote of election fever: "If only McKinley is elected—if he is not Joe talks as though we could all be ruined." As we know, McKinley would indeed be elected and would lead the country out of depression. We aren't the only generation to have feared economic collapse and lived through it.

The November 1897 letter from Auntie Sue to Lizzie was no better than the last ones: endless inanities—teas, tablecloths, fried oysters, dresses, and curtains. Then in a very bossy tone, she told her sister—in great detail and underlined for emphasis—how she should decorate her dining room: "<u>Don't think of putting a carpet there</u>." I wondered what gave her the right to tell her sister how to decorate her own house. Research on Susanna's family home at 809 Main Street in Riverton shed some light on the matter: the house was the childhood home of Lizzie and Auntie Sue, inherited by both sisters. Since Auntie Sue was part owner of the house, she apparently felt she had the right to tell Lizzie how to decorate it. Good times between sisters.

In December 1897, Susanna and Beulah received a letter from their seven-year-old cousin Sara Parry, daughter of their Uncle John R. Parry and Aunt Anna Morrell Parry from Orlando, Florida. These Parry relatives were Susanna's and Beulah's Florida connection; they would visit them in Orlando, come to enjoy Florida's winter warmth, and eventually buy a secondary residence in Coral Gables.

Florida was sparsely populated at the end of the century. It had become the twenty-seventh state only recently in 1845, one of the slave states which had seceded from the Union. It had taken several wars against the Seminole Indians between 1817 and 1858 to ready the state for occupation. Orlando had remained undeveloped until after the Civil War, when its population exploded during Reconstruction. From 1875 to 1895, Orlando became the center of Florida's citrus industry, and between the Spanish American War and the end of World War I, it became a popular resort. The entire state experienced a land boom in the 1920s. One of the developments in the 1920s was Coral Gables, 240 miles south of Orlando, one of America's first planned communities and forerunner of the modern gated communities. It is here that Susanna and Beulah would decades hence purchase a secondary residence.

On January 26, 1898, my grandfather Edwin's sister Mary Parry sent her cousin Susanna a note of thanks for Susanna's Christmas gift of little vases and a calendar. Then she said, "Eddie asked me to thank you for him." I was taken aback when I read this: how strange to think of my grandfather Edwin as "Eddie." I never met Grandfather Parry, who died of pneumonia in 1936 at the early age of fifty-five, four years before the industrialization of penicillin. From my mother's descriptions, he was a reserved, kind, and exceedingly proper Quaker man—certainly not an Eddie. This reminded me that all seniors—myself included—started out as children, with toys and nicknames and the pranks of youth. The elderly should more patiently tolerate the antics of the young, and the young should realize that the elderly were not so long ago just like them—energetic, boisterous, sometimes reckless, and full of hope for the future.

In May 1898, Susanna's mother, Lizzie, received a packet of letters from two of her husband's cousins who had been living in California for several years. With true pioneer spirit, their families had moved out west to become ranchers at Rancho Balu'arte, seventy-five miles from "The Valley." California (along with Texas and New Mexico) had become annexed to the United States at the end of the Mexican-American War in 1846. Gold was discovered there in 1848, sparking the gold rush of 1848 to 1855, luring hundreds of thousands of men from the U.S. and around the world. California became a state in 1850. Although few struck it rich, many prospectors brought their families to California to settle down, most of them to farm. Stagecoach service brought passengers and mail to the Golden State from 1857 to 1861, the first transcontinental telegraph connected the east with the west in 1861, and the first transcontinental railroad arrived in 1869.

The letter from cousin Fannie (Francenia Haines Dale) is very touching. Her son, Arthur—her only child—was in the Mt. Tamalpais Military Academy in San Rafael, getting ready to go to war—which she, as a Quaker, opposed: "He wants to go to the war. Of course, I do not wish it, should feel very badly to have him go. But if his country really seemed to need him I should not say no. I do hope there will be a speedy termination of the war, as I think war is so wicked." Fannie could be a mother in any century, not wanting to lose her son to war.

The war Fannie's son wanted to fight in was the Spanish-American War, which did, as she hoped, have a "speedy termination." America's involvement in this ten-week war was sparked by Cuba's fight for independence from Spain and the sinking of the U.S. Navy battleship *Maine* in Havana Harbor. The U.S. made attacks in the Caribbean and Spain's Pacific possessions, Theodore Roosevelt led his Rough Riders to victory in the battle of San Juan (Kettle) Hill, the Spanish fleet was destroyed, and the war ended with the 1898 Treaty of Paris, ending Spain's claim as a world power and giving the U.S. temporary control of Cuba and ownership of Puerto Rico, Guam, and the Philippines. With this rapid victory in its first engagement in world affairs, America rose on the international scene as the self-proclaimed "Defender of Democracy." The Progressive Era had begun, and war hero Theodore Roosevelt would soon become president and fight for reform.

Intervention came at a cost. A tax on telephone lines financed the Spanish-American War. Only the wealthy owned telephones at that time. Auntie Sue was one of the privileged few, as she mentioned a telephone in one of her letters. This telephone tax was not eliminated after the war but continued for almost a century.

In 1898, the Spanish-American War was not the only source of anxiety for the Parry family. Another Parry brother died at the early age of forty-nine: William (Will), brother of Susanna's father and Alice's mother. A letter from the second California cousin, Fannie's sister Lettie (Laetitia Haines Cook), expressed the sorrow of Will's death. "It is so hard to feel Cousin Will is no more among you, I cannot come into the full realization untill [sic] I visit among you all again & then the great void will be felt as we were so very congenial & we were such good friends." Who among us hasn't felt "the great void" after losing a beloved family member?

I found some comic relief in another annoying letter to Lizzie from Auntie Sue in August 1898. She started off well enough by thanking Lizzie and the girls for birthday gifts, but she then let fly a meddling tirade on how terribly her sister was decorating her home: "Thee seems to be running more & more to cheap things until I fear the house will wear a cheap look. The parlor paper has so darkened the room to me—what thee has in it does not show to any advantage and the affect [*sic*] is gloomy. However that can be changed without much cost . . ." I'm glad my sisters never criticized my taste like that (at least not to my face). I wonder how Lizzie responded.

The last entry in the collection from the nineteenth century is an 1899 letter to Lizzie from Anna Parry in Orlando. Her nine-year-old daughter Sara had been very ill with whooping cough: "The dear little girl has been very sick but is about well again." The other two children "have hard cough" but were still going to school. Not the best idea to send the coughing children to school: the bacterial disease whooping cough (pertussis—also known as the one-hundred-day cough) is highly contagious. Beulah received a letter from the children a few days after, and indeed all the children had whooping cough. A pertussis vaccine would not be developed until the 1930s and would be widely used in the 1940s when combined with diphtheria and tetanus toxoids to create the DTP vaccine. The children said they were sorry to hear there was scarlet fever in Beulah's school, and they hoped she wouldn't get it. Scarlet fever, a bacterial disease caused by streptococcus, was a major cause of childhood death. In 1924, George Dick would develop a vaccine, replaced in the 1940s by penicillin.

Nineteenth-century America ended with the independent Republic of Hawaii becoming a U.S. territory in 1898 and yet another war: the Philippine-American War, which lasted from 1899 to 1902. After the Treaty of Paris, when defeated Spain granted the U.S. possession of the Philippines, the First Philippine Republic declared war against the U.S., continuing their fight for independence. The U.S. was victorious but would grant the Philippines a path toward independence in 1916 with the Philippine Autonomy Act, followed by the Philippine Independence Act in 1934. The Treaty of Manila would finalize their independence after the Japanese occupation during World War II.

As the last years of the nineteenth century bristled with advances in science and technology and global political unrest, cousins Susanna Parry and Alice Paul grew out of their childhood, and they became college students as the new century dawned. They would soon be transformed by Progressive Era changes and become New Women.

Changes in Politics, Science, and Technology from 1885–1899

1885 Alexander Graham Bell incorporated AT&T; Bell invented the telephone in 1876, revolutionizing communications, then introduced the gramophone the following year, bringing music into the American home and changing entertainment forever.

1886 Karl Benz built and patented the first modern automobile, the Benz Patent Motorwagon. However, affordable cars would not be mass-produced until after 1900.

Cigar maker Samuel Gompers founded the American Federation of Labor, a coalition of unions. Although a strong advocate of unions, Gompers opposed socialism and had a somewhat conservative approach to labor relations.

Herman Hollerith constructed the first electromechanical sorting and adding machine called the "tabulator," used to tally the 1890 census. Hollerith's Tabulating Machine Company would merge with two other companies in 1924 to become International Business Machines.

Apache warrior-chief Geronimo surrendered, clearing the way for increased westward expansion.

1887 Louis Pasteur, the founder of bacteriology, established the Pasteur Institute in France. Pasteur accomplished epic advancements in disease prevention—creating vaccines for rabies and anthrax and developing his pasteurization process—despite ridicule and opposition from his peers. His heroic persistence saved countless lives. In England, Dr. Joseph Lister, a Quaker, inspired by Pasteur's work, saw the need for antiseptic surgery and became the Father of Modern Surgery.

Congress passed the Interstate Commerce Act. The Interstate Commerce Commission (ICC) ensured that railroad rates were reasonable, outlawing rebates to the big transporters.

1888 A new American president was elected to succeed Grover Cleveland: Benjamin Harrison, who would serve from 1889 to 1893. During his tenure, he signed the Sherman Antitrust Act, established the national forest reserves, and modernized the Navy. However, he also imposed high protective trade tariffs, which were very unpopular and would lead to his defeat in the 1892 election.

1889 The first North American electric power transmission line was activated in Oregon.

President Harrison appointed Theodore Roosevelt as Civil Service Commissioner. From 1889 to 1894, Roosevelt demanded adherence to Civil Service laws and sought Civil Service reform to combat the spoils system of cronyism in hiring.

1890	The United Mine Workers Union was founded.
	Congress passed the Sherman Antitrust Act, an attempt to break up monopolies.
1891	Thomas Edison revolutionized entertainment by producing the first motion picture camera.
1892	Telephone service was opened between New York and Chicago.
	At the Pasteur Institute, Russian bacteriologist Waldemar Haffkine developed an anti-cholera vaccine, partially successful in treating this disease which caused multiple pandemics in the nineteenth century and is still present today.
	In Nebraska, farmers created the Populist Party, which called for a graduated income tax, eight-hour workday, government ownership of railroads, and direct election of U.S. senators. The Populists did not succeed in the 1892 election but gave voice to working-class grievances.
	America elected a new president to replace Benjamin Harrison: Grover Cleveland, who had previously served as president from 1885 to 1889. Unfortunately for Cleveland and the Democratic party, the Panic of 1893 led to a depression and strikes, which crippled his presidency. He would not serve another term.
1893	Westinghouse and Tesla provided electricity for the Chicago World's Fair.
1894	Theodore Roosevelt was appointed New York City Police Commissioner. He continued the anti-corruption agenda he began as New York state assemblyman (1882 to 1884). His successes angered the Republican bosses.
1896	British bacteriologist Almroth Wright of the Army Medical School developed an effective vaccine against typhoid to protect soldiers fighting in the Boer War in South Africa. However, it would take years for a vaccine to become available to the public.
	French physicist Henri Becquerel discovered radioactivity. The following year, English physicist J. J. Thomson discovered the negatively charged electron, which he would show to be part of the atom in 1899. The atomic age had begun.
	The first large-scale central generating system was built at Niagara Falls, followed by other generating systems, leading to the first national power grid.
	William McKinley was elected to replace Grover Cleveland. He would serve from 1897 to 1901, when he would be assassinated at the beginning of his second term. He would lead the country out of depression and into much-needed economic growth, raising protective tariffs and signing the Gold Standard Act in 1900.

1897 President McKinley appointed Theodore Roosevelt as Assistant Secretary of the Navy, bowing to the pressure of the corrupt Republican machine which wanted Roosevelt out of the New York Police Department.

Englishman Charles Parsons developed the steam turbine engine to improve ship propulsion.

1898 William Howard Taft, as a federal judge sitting in the Sixth District Court, fought against unsafe railroad practices and unfair contracts prohibiting railroad workers from suing in cases of accident or death. He also ruled against Addyston Pipe and Steel, breaking up the pipe trust.

The Spanish-American war was triggered by Cuba's fight for independence from Spain and the sinking of the battleship *Maine*, ending in America's victory over Spain; the Treaty of Paris gave the U.S. temporary control of Cuba and possession of Puerto Rico, Guam, and the Philippines. The Philippines, in turn, would seek independence and declare war on the U.S. in 1899, the war ending in 1902 with the U.S. victorious but eventually giving the Philippines a path toward independence.

War hero and Rough Rider Theodore Roosevelt was elected Governor of New York. In his short term of office, he promoted conservation and pressured Republican bosses to pass labor reforms. He most angered machine Republicans by passing the Ford Franchise-Tax Bill; they, in turn, would get him out of the Governor's office by persuading McKinley to choose him as his running mate in 1900.

1899 The Bayer Company began selling aspirin, made from the bark of a willow tree, for reducing fever. Aspirin remains one of the most widely used anti-inflammatory pain medicines to this day.

CHAPTER 3

NEW CENTURY, NEW WOMEN

As the new century dawned, change swept through America and Europe. In England, Queen Victoria, who had reigned since 1837, died in 1901, and Victorian confines loosened when her son Edward VII took the throne. King Edward was the prince of the upper-class elite whose extravagant taste was inspired by the art and fashion of the Continent. They cared little for the struggling workers in the coal mines and textile mills whose labor had made them rich when England transitioned from a farming to an industrialized economy. The abominable working and living conditions of the workers sparked the rise of labor unions and socialists, culminating in the birth of the Labour Party.

Although industrialism had brought unprecedented economic growth and an improved standard of living for many in America, as well as England, the unconstrained rise of industrial giants led to a growing gap between the rich and the poor in the so-called Gilded Age of industrial robber barons, resulting in an increasingly loud call for the regulation of large corporations and the elimination of political corruption. Progressive reformers in both the private and public sectors differed in the causes they took on and the solutions they proposed, but they held the common belief that government had a social responsibility to right the wrongs.

By the end of the nineteenth century, America emerged as a global economic power with massive resources and industrial might. The nation had triumphantly entered the world stage as the "Defender of Democracy" by freeing Cuba from Spanish oppression. Theodore Roosevelt, who had prepared the Navy for war as Secretary of the Navy in 1896, led the Rough Riders to victory in Cuba in 1898, won the governor's seat in New York afterward, then became McKinley's vice president in 1900. When a Polish-American anarchist shot McKinley on September 6, 1901, the forty-two-year-old Roosevelt became the youngest American president ever, with an ambitious progressive agenda.

THEODORE ROOSEVELT: CHAMPION OF PROGRESSIVE REFORM

Theodore Roosevelt developed a reputation as an accomplished reformer throughout his career: as an anti-corruption New York state assemblyman (1882 to 1884); as Civil Service Commissioner under Presidents Cleveland and Harrison (1889 to 1894), where he sought Civil Service reform to eliminate the spoils system of cronyism in hiring; as Commissioner of the New York Police Department (1894 to 1897) where he undertook surprise inspections of cops on the beat and vigorously enforced the Sunday closing laws, angering the Republican bosses who wanted to get him out of New York and pressured McKinley to appoint him Assistant Secretary of the Navy in 1897.

After establishing himself as a fearless war hero in 1898, having led the Rough Riders to victory over Spain in the battle of San Juan (Kettle) Hill, Roosevelt was elected Governor of New York in 1898. In his short term as governor, he pressured the Republican bosses to pass worker reforms, including limited workdays for women and children, an eight-hour workday for state employees, mandated air brakes on freight trains, and other safety measures. He also promoted state conservation, protecting endangered birds and preserving forest lands. He infuriated the political machine when he passed the Ford Franchise-Tax Bill, although he allowed Republicans to water it down to assure its passage. In so doing, he proved himself to be a practical politician, willing to compromise. Nonetheless, the Republicans wanted him out of the way and persuaded McKinley to choose him as his running mate in 1900. They thought

Roosevelt would be buried in the vice presidency, powerless to attack the *laissez-faire* cooperation of big business and government. They were right about the ineffectiveness of the vice presidency, but Roosevelt didn't remain vice president for long, becoming president in less than a year when McKinley was assassinated.

During his two terms in office, President Roosevelt used his "bully pulpit" and the muckraking exposés of investigative journalists to drum up popular support for his reform program, whose aim was to give all Americans a "square deal." He became the champion of the Progressive Era, using the federal government to curb the power of large trusts, notably the railroads; protect consumers against contaminated food and drugs; and preserve the country's natural resources from industrial exploitation.

Roosevelt was a progressive powerhouse but far more moderate than the Populists and Socialists. He didn't want government to redistribute wealth, but he did want it to address the social problems that industrialization had created. He understood that the growth and prosperity created by big business were essential to a healthy economy, that trusts could lower consumer prices through economies of scale, but he also recognized that unfair trusts preyed upon and eliminated their competition. He didn't want to break up all the trusts, but he did want government regulation to find and prosecute the ones that fixed prices and otherwise acted unfairly.

President Roosevelt's progressive accomplishments during his first years in office are impressive. In 1902, he arbitrated a successful resolution of the coal miners' strike in Pennsylvania and passed the Newlands Reclamation Act to federally fund reservoirs, dams, and irrigation projects to transform the arid western landscape, making new land available to small farmers. In 1903, he created the Department of Commerce and Labor to improve the lives of workers and the Department's Bureau of Corporations to inspect corporate finances. Also in 1903, he signed the Elkins Act, increasing the power of the Interstate Commerce Commission to regulate the railroads and abolish unfair railroad rebates—legislation inspired by Ida Tarbell's exposés on Standard Oil.

In 1904, Roosevelt finally broke up the Northern Securities Trust, a conglomerate of large rail and shipping lines in the northwest (including the Northern Pacific Railway and the Great Northern Railway). Formed by E. H. Harriman, James Hill, and J.P. Morgan, the monopoly ruthlessly controlled prices to eliminate its competition. The antitrust suit began in 1902 and referenced Judge William Howard Taft's Addyston Pipe and Steel opinion of 1898. Roosevelt next targeted the Beef Trust, whose Armour & Co. and Swift & Co. colluded to fix prices and eliminate competition. Also in 1904, Roosevelt began what he considered one of his best accomplishments: the construction of the Panama Canal.

Roosevelt took on yet another trust in 1905: Rockefeller's Standard Oil monopoly. When huge oil reserves were discovered in Kansas and Oklahoma in 1904, Standard Oil swooped in and took over, promising to pay market price for oil produced by independents. They lied. Standard Oil monopolized the refineries and pipelines and set the prices paid to independents below market. Roosevelt directed the Bureau of Corporations to investigate. *McClure's* investigative journalist Ida Tarbell also went to Kansas, having already written a series of articles about the abuses of Standard Oil in Pennsylvania. Tarbell's article advised independent producers to build their own pipelines and told Congress to regulate all pipelines. The Bureau of Corporation's report accused Standard Oil of colluding with the railroads to overcharge independents and give rebates to Standard Oil in violation of the Elkins Act, and it accused Standard of being a monopoly in violation of the Sherman Antitrust Act. Unfortunately, although Standard was found guilty of accepting rebates, an appeals court overturned the decision a year later. The wheel of justice turned slowly, but it finally caught up with Standard in 1909, when the attorney general charged Standard with monopoly and ordered the dissolution of the trust; the decision was upheld in federal court and affirmed by the Supreme Court in 1911.

In 1906, Roosevelt signed landmark legislation protecting consumers. Socialist Upton Sinclair's sensational novel *The Jungle* exposed the horrific conditions of Chicago's meat processing industry, which endangered workers and consumers. Although Roosevelt disagreed with the socialist proselytizing of the novel, he believed Sinclair had exposed a threat to the general welfare that needed to be eliminated. Government inspectors corroborated Sinclair's accusations, and the Beveridge Meat Inspection Act was passed, requiring the federal inspection and labeling of all meat. The next consumer protection act was the Pure Food and Drug Act which mandated proper labels on food and drugs.

Also in 1906, Roosevelt signed the Hepburn Act, which gave further power to the ICC to regulate railroad rates. When the 1903 Elkins Act proved ineffective in controlling railroad rates, the Populists called for a government takeover of the railroads. Roosevelt, however, took a more moderate approach, calling for stronger ICC regulatory power. Roosevelt knew that conservative Republicans would resist, so he sought help from investigative journalists to expose railroad corruption and stir up a public outcry loud enough to sway lawmakers to pass the bill. *McClure's* reporter Ray Stannard Baker produced a series of convincing articles, "The Railroads on Trial." The House passed the bill after Roosevelt compromised and agreed to keep protective tariffs, and the Senate passed the bill after Roosevelt agreed to add an amendment allowing judicial review of ICC rates. (Judges tended to be pro-railroad.)

In addition to curbing the power of the trusts and protecting consumers from contaminated food and drugs, President Roosevelt also protected America's natural resources. An avid outdoorsman and conservationist, Roosevelt established the National Conservation Commission and the U.S. Forest Service (creating fifty national forests), expanded national parks, created bird and game reserves, and protected over 200 million acres of federal land from exploitation. With his boundless energy and impressive accomplishments, Roosevelt at times seemed larger than life; he was certainly Mount Rushmore-worthy.

Because Roosevelt had promised not to seek a third term when he ran for office in 1904, he became something of a lame duck toward the end of his second term and had increasing difficulties pushing reforms through Congress. In addition, the public was growing tired of muckraking journalism, and magazines turned their focus away from exposés about industrial and political corruption, preferring to entertain their readers instead of informing them about social issues. S. S. McClure, plagued by marital indiscretions and bad business decisions, lost the best of his muckraking journalists; Ida Tarbell, Lincoln Steffens, and Ray Stannard Baker left *McClure's* and started their own publication, *The American Magazine*. Investigative journalists continued to expose corruption, but American muckraking journalism, which had helped drive progressive reform, was never quite the same.

Roosevelt's dismantling of the trusts and regulating big business came under attack in 1907 when the country suffered a financial crisis which Wall Street called the "Roosevelt Panic." The failure of Knickerbocker Trust Company, one of New York's largest banks, sparked a general panic. With no centralized banking system to prevent catastrophe, help came from J. P. Morgan, who assembled a group of leading bankers; with help from the U.S. Treasury, the banking group raised enough money to save the most important banks. Part of the plan to prevent widespread financial collapse involved Roosevelt's agreeing not to file an antitrust lawsuit against U.S. Steel when it purchased all the shares of Tennessee Coal and Iron to save the big brokerage firm Moore & Schley from collapse. This angered progressives, but Roosevelt felt he had no choice but to compromise to avoid a national financial collapse.

With his political power waning, Roosevelt feared that conservatives would try to repeal his progressive legislation once he was out of office. To protect his legacy, he wanted the next president to be a progressive champion as he had been. Roosevelt chose and groomed his close friend William Howard Taft as his successor in the election of 1908, and Taft easily won. Taft tried to take up his predecessor's progressive agenda but without great success. Although Taft did initiate ninety antitrust lawsuits, he wasn't particularly popular, lacking Roosevelt's charisma, oratorical skills, and effective use of the press. Taft infuriated Roosevelt when he fired the head of forestry services, Gifford Pinchot, who had accused Secretary of the Interior Richard Ballinger of failing to protect forest lands and natural resources, undercutting Roosevelt's conservation achievements. Taft also ineffectively handled the passage of the watered-down Payne-Aldrich Tariff Act, making concessions to conservative Republicans, which angered the progressive "insurgents."

In a 1910 speech in Kansas, increasingly progressive Roosevelt broke with conservative Republicans in calling for a "New Nationalism" favoring increased corporate control, a ban on corporate political contributions, and a broad program of social reform. Completely breaking with his former friend President Taft, who had become increasingly conservative, Roosevelt decided to run for a third term in 1912, allowed under the Constitution, which had not yet passed the Twenty-Second Amendment limiting presidential terms. When the Republicans failed to nominate Roosevelt as their candidate, he formed his own party, the Progressive Party, also known as the Bull Moose Party, because Roosevelt claimed he felt "strong as a bull moose." The Progressive Party platform was based on Roosevelt's Square Deal and proposed classic progressive reforms: reduction of tariffs; a minimum wage law; an eight-hour workday; limits to and disclosure of political campaign contributions; social insurance for the elderly, disabled, and unemployed; an inheritance tax; direct election of senators; and unlike the platforms of Republican and Democrats—women's suffrage. (The Socialist Party also endorsed women's suffrage.) Suffragist and social activist Jane Addams gave a speech at the Progressive Party convention, seconding Roosevelt's nomination. With the Republican Party now split, both Roosevelt and Taft lost to southern-born Democrat Woodrow Wilson. Wilson received 42% of the popular vote, Roosevelt 27%, Taft 23%, and Socialist Eugene Debs 6%.

Wilson began his presidency with progressive economic reforms. In 1913, the Federal Reserve Act created a national banking system to stabilize banking, and the Sixteenth Amendment authorized Congress to levy an income tax on the wealthy to help fund the government and eliminate its dependence on tariffs. In 1914, the Clayton Antitrust Act strengthened the Sherman Antitrust Act of 1890, and the Federal Trade Commission was created to enforce antitrust laws. However, the political pendulum swung away from progressive reform when Wilson stubbornly resisted women's relentless call for the vote. His engaging the country in World War I when he declared war on Germany in 1917 "to save the world for democracy" marked the end of the Progressive Era and American innocence.

SOCIAL ACTIVISTS

The era of progressive reform was a remarkable and formative period in American history. In the last two decades of the nineteenth century, industries had developed without restraint at the expense of their immigrant workers. Millions of new immigrants working in the mines, mills, and factories suffered in poverty and tenement squalor while the owners became outrageously and conspicuously rich. In this so-called Gilded Age, less than one percent of the population owned almost all the country's wealth, and they were intent on keeping it. In reaction to the growing rift between the rich and the poor, dedicated progressive politicians, investigative journalists, church groups, and philanthropists believed they could fundamentally reform society, and made real progress for a few Camelotian years. Progressives with a "yes, we can" belief in their ability to effect social change worked tirelessly on multiple fronts: to control big business and eliminate corrupt politicians; to improve the working and living conditions of workers and eliminate child labor; to prohibit the production and sale of alcohol, which burdened the working class with alcoholism and domestic abuse; to fight against racial discrimination, race riots, and the horrors of lynching, resulting in the 1909 founding of the National Association for the Advancement of Colored People; and—central to our story—to improve the lives of women.

Immigrant working women struggled under abuses on the job and at home, forced to work long hours in unsafe factories by day and often subjected to abusive drunken husbands by night. Many who had neither husbands nor jobs turned to prostitution to survive. All immigrants endured squalid and unhealthy living conditions in the slums. Quakers were at the heart of the battle to improve the quality of life of immigrant workers. Social activist and Quaker Jane Addams, awarded the Nobel Peace Prize in 1931 for her life's work, called for labor laws, unemployment insurance, and women's suffrage. In 1889, she founded Hull House in Chicago, the country's first settlement house for unmarried immigrant women, providing food, shelter, childcare, job training, and a path to citizenship. By 1914, there were over 400 settlement houses in the U.S.[1] Our Quaker cousins Susanna and Alice were trained for this work in England at Woodbrooke, the school for social activism and community service founded by the Cadburys, a wealthy Quaker family and leaders of the English chocolate industry.

Alice Paul quickly realized that her calling went far beyond work in settlement houses. While studying settlement work in England, she was

Jane Addams, c. 1896–1900. (James Addams Collection, Swarthmore College Peace Collection)

inspired and trained by militant suffragettes Emmeline and Christabel Pankhurst, then returned to the States to become a leader of the suffrage movement. She was one of a new generation of suffragists, carrying the torch formerly carried by Elizabeth Cady Stanton, who died in 1902, and Susan B. Anthony, who died in 1906. Whereas most earlier suffragists after the Civil War had called for the vote to be given to women at the state level, Alice followed Susan B. Anthony's lead and insisted that the vote be given to all women by an amendment to the U.S. Constitution. At the electric center of Progressive Era reforms, Alice shared the optimism of her fellow activists, convinced that she would succeed in obtaining universal suffrage for women. She would eventually succeed, but at great personal cost.

The Progressive Era saw not only the social activism of the Quakers and suffragists but also the rise of the Socialist Party in America. Immigrant labor activists had already established the Socialist Labor Party in 1877. The Socialist Party of America—the party of labor—was founded in 1901 and championed by charismatic Eugene Debs, who co-founded the Industrial Workers of the World and was the Socialist Party's candidate in five presidential elections from the beginning of the century to 1920. Debs devoted his life to the fight for reforms to improve workers' lives: an eight-hour workday, sick leave, workers' compensation, social security, and pension plans. Debs wasn't the only socialist politician elected to office in the Progressive Era: In 1910, Victor Berger won Wisconsin's Fifth Congressional District seat—the first socialist to serve in the U.S. Congress; and socialist mayors were elected in increasing numbers, peaking to 74 in 1911. Created in 1911, *The Masses*, a Socialist monthly magazine edited by Max Eastman, was stunning in visuals and literary content, whose contributors included Sherwood Anderson, Jack London, Amy Lowell, Carl Sandburg, and Upton Sinclair. *The Masses* was kept afloat by the wealthy Alva Belmont, who also generously supported the cause of women's suffrage in England and the U.S. and who co-founded the National Woman's Party with Alice Paul.

In the Progressive Era, Alva Belmont was a fascinating figure transitioning from socialite to socialist. In her first marriage, she was Alva Vanderbilt, wife of the incredibly wealthy grandson of railroad tycoon Cornelius Vanderbilt. A poster child for the nouveau riche, she was known for outrageous conspicuous consumption, building a chateau on Fifth Avenue and throwing lavish balls, hoping to gain acceptance by New York's established elite. After divorcing the philandering Vanderbilt in 1895, she married Vanderbilt's friend Oliver Belmont. After Oliver died suddenly in 1908, she went to England, was inspired by the Pankhursts, and from then on, devoted her fortune and energy to the suffrage movement, a story which echoes that of our Alice.

Alva Belmont was one of many wealthy, influential philanthropists who used their wealth for the common good. John D. Rockefeller, Jr. gave over a billion dollars of his father's oil money to humanitarian projects such as Lincoln Center, the Museum of Modern Art, Colonial Williamsburg, Yosemite National Park, and the land for the site of the United Nations. Similarly, Andrew Carnegie, who had made a fortune in the steel industry, gave a large part of his fortune to charities at home and abroad; his article "The Gospel of Wealth", a treatise of *noblesse oblige*, called on the wealthy to put their money to good use by giving to libraries, museums, hospitals, universities, and the like. As we shall see, Susanna, although no Rockefeller or Carnegie, had a substantial fortune; she and her sister, Beulah, gave generously to Quakers in need and the cause of higher education. Alice gave all her money, time, and energy to advance the cause of women.

The rise of the socialists would be abruptly curtailed when President Wilson declared war on Germany and passed the Espionage Act of 1917, which permitted government repression of anyone who opposed the country's involvement in the war. Socialists, who opposed U.S. involvement in the war, were routed and jailed, including Eugene Debs, who ran for president from the prison into which he was thrown when he protested the country's participation in World War I. *The Masses* was forced to shut down, and by 1920, only two socialist mayors were elected.

The struggles against corruption and social injustice weren't the only things new on the American and European scene in the early years of the Progressive Era. All aspects of culture were alive with change, especially in the arts.

LITERATURE

Naturalism, in which the behavior and fate of characters are determined by their sordid environment, originated at the end of the nineteenth century in France, with novelist Emile Zola's *L'Assommoir* (1877), depicting the destruction caused by alcoholism, and *Germinal* (1885), portraying the struggle of coal miners. Naturalist and Realist writers in America focused on the evils of industrialism. Theodore Dreiser's *Sister Carrie* (1900) chronicles the corruption of an innocent country girl who loses her factory job, resorts to prostitution, and yields to the shallow lure of materialism. Frank Norris's *The Octopus: A Story of California* (1901) exposes the abusive power of the railroad monopolies in his story of the Pacific and Southwestern Railroad's mistreatment of wheat farmers in the San Joaquin Valley; Norris's *The Pit: A Story of Chicago* (1903) details wheat speculation and greed in the trading pits of Chicago. Upton Sinclair's *The Jungle* (1906) exposes the horrors of Chicago's meatpacking industry. In a completely different setting, Edith Wharton's *The House of Mirth* (1905) explores the moral bankruptcy of the New York City elite during the Gilded Age.

The Modernist poets of the first two decades of the twentieth century broke with literary traditions with new subject matter and styles. In "The Lovesong of J. Alfred Prufrock" (1915), T. S. Eliot's masterpiece of alienation and despair, irregular meters mirror a fractured world.

In England, emboldened by the new field of psychoanalysis, D. H. Lawrence broke through multiple sexual taboos—the Oedipus complex, extramarital sex, and homosexuality—in his novels set in the dehumanized industrialized world: *Sons and Lovers* (1913), *The Rainbow* (1915), and *Women in Love* (1920). American Henry James explored the inner landscape of his characters caught in the clash of the old and new worlds in masterpieces like *The Ambassadors* (1902) and *The Golden Bowl* (1904).

Early feminist works portray the dilemma of women caught between the conformity of traditional marriage and their desire for independence. In Kate Chopin's *The Awakening* (1899), Edna Pontellier, at last, finds sexual satisfaction in extramarital affairs but commits suicide when she can no longer be with the man she loves. In Charlotte Perkin Gilman's *The Yellow Wallpaper* (1892), when the narrator's husband and male doctor confine her to a "rest cure" and deprive her of the creative outlet of writing, she finds her only solace in insanity.

INVESTIGATIVE JOURNALISM

The rise of investigative journalism at the beginning of the twentieth century was one of the most powerful engines that propelled progressive reform, second only, perhaps, to the dynamo Theodore Roosevelt. Journalists in the early 1900s raised middle-class awareness of social problems, exposing corruption, malfeasance, and worker exploitation in politics and big business. S. S. (Sam) McClure was a pioneer in this movement, assembling an astounding team of investigative journalists—the so-called muckrakers—whose irreproachable reporting and the ability to tell a compelling story reached a wide audience. Roosevelt greatly admired and depended upon these journalists to advance his Progressive agenda and actively collaborated with them.

Jacob Riis raised public awareness of the plight of the working poor in his photojournalistic exposé, documenting the negligence of landlords and the horrors of slum life. First published as an article in *Scribner's Magazine*, it was published in book form in 1890: *How the Other Half Lives: Studies among the Tenements of New York*.

Ida Tarbell was a star among the Progressive Era's investigative journalists, best known for her two series of articles in *McClure's*, beginning in 1902, exposing the corruption of John D. Rockefeller, whose Standard Oil Company colluded with the railroads to raise transportation rates of independent oil producers while giving rebates to Standard, driving out the independent producers and creating a giant monopoly. Tarbell's father was one of the independent oil producers ruined by Standard Oil. Her exposés inspired the Elkins Act of 1903, which increased the power of the Interstate Commerce Commission to regulate the railroads and later inspired the antitrust suit that broke up Rockefeller's monopoly.

Lincoln Steffens' six-part series in *McClure's*, "Tweed Days in St. Louis", exposed the widespread corruption of political machines in municipal government. The articles were reprinted as a book, *Shame of the Cities*, in 1904.

S. S. McClure was willing to expose labor corruption as well as corruption in big business and politics. In the November 1903 issue of *McClure's*, Ray Stannard Baker's "The Trust's New Tool – The Labor Boss" exposed the collusion of labor boss Sam Parks with the Fuller Construction Company. Parks told his union workers to strike at the projects of Fuller Construction's competition, then extort payments to stop the strikes, destroying Fuller's competition. Parks was indicted and arrested.

MUSIC AND DANCE

John Philip Sousa closed the nineteenth century with his nationalistic march "The Stars and Stripes Forever." The twentieth century, however, would kick off with a new form of syncopated music: ragtime, beginning with Scott Joplin's "Maple Leaf Rag" (1899), all the rage in the first two decades of the new century with such hits as Irving Berlin's "Alexander's Ragtime Band" (1911).

Dance followed suit. The waltz had to step aside to make room on the dance floor for the foxtrot, made popular in the mid-teens by Irene and Vernon Castle, followed by the turkey trot, bunny hug, and ultimately, the Charleston in the Roaring Twenties. Concurrently, black Americans were developing a new kind of dance: tap dance.

Classical music and dance also broke with tradition in the first decades of the new century. The most notable example is *The Rite of Spring*, composed by Russian Igor Stravinsky for Diaghilev's *Ballets Russes* and choreographed by the great Vaslav Nijinsky. When the work opened in Paris on May 29, 1913, it was so avant-garde and iconoclastic that it caused a near-riot in the theater in reaction to the music's dissonance and frenzied rhythms and the ballet's depiction of primitive rituals and the sacrificial "Chosen One" dancing herself to death. This was no *Swan Lake*. The controversial ballet was not performed again until 1920. Today, Stravinsky's composition is considered one of the greatest orchestral works of the twentieth century.

Free-spirited American Isadora Duncan liberated herself from the confines of classical ballet and gave birth to Modern Dance at the turn of the century, replacing toe shoes, tutus, and pirouettes with bare feet, Greek tunics, and freeform movements. Having opened schools in Berlin (1904) and Paris (1914), she left Europe at the outbreak of the First World War and moved back to the United States for her American Tour (1915 to 1918). Pioneering Duncan also enjoyed celebrity (and censure) as the prima donna of the Bohemian set, a bisexual New Woman who bore children out of wedlock and became a Soviet citizen at the end of her life.

ART

At the turn of the twentieth century, artists explored new themes and techniques. At the end of the 1800s, Impressionists in France—Monet, Degas, Pissarro, Renoir—caused scandal with their new way of seeing and painting: their broken brushstrokes and subject matter were not lofty scenes but depictions of the everyday life of ordinary people. The Post-Impressionists—Cezanne, Van Gogh, Gauguin—went further toward abstraction, the Symbolists (Rousseau, Redon) even further, and Expressionists further still with Munch's *The Scream* (1893). Picasso's *Les Demoiselles d'Avignon* (1907) gave the art world something completely different: Cubism, with its abstract complexity and exaggerated fragmentation. In the U.S., the "Ash Can School," like literature's naturalists, exposed the ugly side of industrialism with scenes of dingy slum life.

An altogether new art form inspired by the Lumière brothers in France arrived on the American scene in 1902 with the country's first movie theater: Thomas Tally's Electric Theater in Los Angeles, whose first film of merit was shown a year later: Edwin S. Porter's *The Great Train Robbery*. Entertainment would never be the same.

TECHNOLOGY

Technological inventions modernized the first years of the twentieth century. In 1900, cable elevators were introduced and the first international telephone call was made over a telegraph cable from Key West, Florida, to Havana, Cuba. In 1901, Italian Guglielmo Marconi used electromagnetic waves, which he called radio waves, to transmit Morse code across the Atlantic. In 1902, the first artificial fiber was patented—rayon yarn.

A historic change flew into view and the American spirit in 1903. Bicycle mechanics Wilbur and Orville Wright achieved the first solo powered flight in Kitty Hawk, North Carolina. The "twelve-second flight changed the world, lifting it to new heights of freedom and giving mankind access to places it had never dreamed of reaching. . . . The Wrights created one of the greatest cultural forces since the development of writing, for their invention effectively became the World Wide Web of that era, bringing people, languages, ideas, and values together. It also ushered in an age of globalization."[2] In 1906, the brothers patented their airplane control system and, beginning in 1908, manufactured planes for the U.S. Army. Wilbur died of typhoid in 1912.

In 1907, American Lee DeForest invented the triode vacuum tube to amplify weak radio signals. He made the amplifier far more powerful in 1912. In 1918, Edwin Armstrong introduced the receiver-amplifier—the superheterodyne circuit—making modern radio and television possible.

In 1907, Belgian-American chemist Leo Baekeland patented the first fully synthetic plastic: Bakelite, which could be molded into different shapes to suit various applications. The age of plastics had begun.

Another big advance in 1908: Henry Ford produced his affordable "Tin Lizzie"—the Model T—so that almost everyone in America could be on the go toward expanded horizons. In 1913, his efficient moving assembly line speeded up automobile production and lowered the cost to consumers. Modern industrial automation was born.

Housewives' lives were made easier in 1910 with the first electric washing machine; in 1913, with the first electric refrigerator for home use; and in 1915, when Pyrex glass was introduced.

In 1914, the opening of the Panama Canal linked the Atlantic and Pacific oceans. This achievement would be celebrated in the 1915 World's Fair in San Francisco—the Panama-Pacific International Exposition. The east and west coasts would be further connected in 1915 when the first transcontinental telephone call was made from New York City to San Francisco.

SCIENCE

Science redefined the physical world at the beginning of the new century.

In 1903, Marie and Pierre Curie won the Nobel Prize for Physics for their discovery of radioactivity.

Einstein's Specific Theory of Relativity ($E=mc^2$) exploded on the scene in 1905, explaining the relationship of mass and energy and identifying time as a dimension related to space.

In 1911, Ernest Marsden, Ernest Rutherford, and Hans Geiger discovered the structure of the atom.

In 1915, Einstein's General Theory of Relativity described gravity in terms of the curvature of space-time. (Einstein would receive the Nobel Prize in Physics in 1922.)

In 1917, U. S. astronomer George Hale built the world's largest reflecting telescope on Mount Wilson in California. The following year, American Harlow Shapely described the size and composition of the Milky Way galaxy.

MEDICINE

In medicine, three major advances occurred in 1901: Walter Reed discovered that a virus caused yellow fever; Jokichi Takamine isolated the first hormone, adrenalin; and Austrian Karl Landsteiner identified three different types of human blood—A, B, and O—opening the way for life-saving blood transfusions.

In 1906, German neurologist Alois Alzheimer discovered a disease that progressively destroys brain functioning.

In 1908, the first chlorination of public drinking water in Jersey City, New Jersey, was the most significant advance in fighting the spread of dreaded typhoid.

In 1910, German bacteriologist Paul Ehrlich became the father of chemotherapy in using a derivative of arsenic to treat syphilis.

In 1911, Casimir Funk discovered "B"—the first of the elements needed for good health, which he named vitamins. Vitamin A was discovered in 1913.

In 1913, mammography was first used to diagnose breast cancer.

PSYCHOLOGY

A new branch of medicine emerged at the beginning of the new century—psychology—with the 1900 publication of Sigmund Freud's *The Interpretation of Dreams*. In 1905, Freud's explosive *Three Essays on the Theory of Sexuality* claimed that any fixation on sexuality was harmful: If expressed openly, it led to perversion; if repressed, it led to neurosis. Damned if you did, and damned if you didn't.

Freud's theories, as controversial and often silly as they were (penis envy—really?), at least brought sexual desire into mainstream conversation, a reflection of radically changing morals. Sexuality at the turn of the century was, like art and dance and music and literature, breaking with convention. "New Marriage" arrived on the scene, with divorce more commonplace among the elite and "open" marriage among the more bohemian. Homosexuality in men, although perhaps not talked about much in America (especially among Quakers), was well known on the Continent and in England, for example, with the brilliant and scandalous Oscar Wilde. Less known was the new kind of women who appeared in the late nineteenth century: "Passing Women"—women "passing" as men, cross-dressing to escape the wide-ranging restrictions of mainstream society.[3]

A less controversial "New Woman" also arrived on the scene, as described by Carroll Smith-Rosenberg:

> Who was the New Woman? Initially, Henry James' literary conceit. Affluent, educated, and intelligent, she boldly asserted her right to share in America's heritage of individualism and self-reliance. Heedless of social conventions and social consequences, she announced herself captain of her own destiny. She was Daisy Miller. She was Isabelle Archer. I have appropriated the term to refer to a cohort of middle- and upper-middle-class American women born between the late 1850s and the early 1900s, who were educated, ambitious, and, most frequently, single. By the early twentieth century, they had established places for themselves within the new professions and within government and reform agencies. Asserting their right to a public voice and visible power, they demanded rights and privileges customarily accorded only to white middle-class men. Their emergence within middle-class rhetoric signaled the symbolic death of that earlier female subject, the refined and confined Victorian lady. . . . The New Woman challenged existing gender relations and the distribution of power.[4]

This perfectly defines Alice Paul and, in many ways, Susanna Parry—both upper-middle-class, both educated, both challenging convention, both New Women.

CHAPTER 4

COMING OF AGE

*I*n 1900, Alice and Susanna were fifteen years old, soon to leave home to attend Swarthmore College, soon to change with the changing world, soon to become New Women. They were among the few young women who attended college at that time (less than 5% of eligible girls). They were on a path different from most American women, so it is no surprise that they would remain untraditional as adults. The image of young womanhood was radically changing. "Studies of the first two generations of college-educated women showed that a significant proportion remained unwed, suggesting that higher education undermined traditional ideas about a woman's role. Indeed, college graduates sought meaningful, though often unpaid, work in the public sphere. Their visibility led observers to dub them 'new women.'"[1]

Alice was the first of our cousins to leave home. The Parry family received an invitation to attend the graduation of Alice Paul from Friends' High School in Moorestown, New Jersey, on June 6, 1901. Alice was listed in the program as presenting her essay on Florence Nightingale. One of the best students, she had been awarded a college scholarship given to the top student from Quaker high schools. Alice would be an exceptional student at Swarthmore, the country's only Hicksite college, co-founded by her grandfather Judge William Parry. Because the Quakers believed in gender equality (at least spiritually, if not economically and legally), young Quaker women were encouraged to pursue higher education, and Swarthmore admitted equal numbers of women and men. Alice's mother, Tacie, was one of the first women to attend the

Alice Paul's graduation photograph, Moorestown Friends School, 1901. (Courtesy of the Alice Paul Institute, www.alicepaul.org)

college, but she had to drop out in her senior year when she married William Paul because married women were not allowed to attend. Tacie's daughter Alice, however, would graduate from Swarthmore with honors.

Although we know relatively little about Alice before her involvement in the suffrage movement, we have a pretty good idea from existing photos, the research of others, and a revealing journal from her first year at Swarthmore: she was a rather pretty girl with brown hair, an oval face, and striking large blue eyes, but she was self-conscious about her "buck" teeth.[2] As a Quaker child, she and her cousin Susanna undoubtedly had lives structured around going to school, attending the weekly meeting on

First Day, and gathering with the family. Susanna and Alice were favorite cousins, close in age and sense of humor. We know that as a girl, Alice accompanied her mother, Tacie, to women's suffrage meetings and that Tacie was probably involved in preparations for the State Suffrage Convention of 1900. Although Tacie had planted the suffrage seed, Alice was not as a girl impassioned by the quest for the vote; instead, she enjoyed athletics and reading, especially Dickens.[3]

Alice wasn't the only member of the extended Parry family to graduate in 1901. Susanna's family also received an invitation to the June 26 commencement exercises of Amherst College, Class of 1901, for the graduation of Susanna's cousin, my grandfather Edwin Satterthwaite Parry. He would later marry Mary Bond, whose father also went to Amherst, class of 1863.

On November 3, 1901, Auntie Sue wrote to Susanna's mother that Joe, Sue's husband, was running for elected office in Maryland, attending many committee meetings and speaking engagements. He didn't think he had a chance of winning and refused to buy votes. She complained how his being elected would be a terrible inconvenience to her, then concluded the letter with her usual chatter about clothes and home decorations. A follow-up letter on November 13 informed Lizzie that Joe had not been elected and enclosed some newspaper clippings about election fraud, charging that the Democrats tampered with the ballot boxes by removing Republican ballots, making an accurate vote count impossible.

Alice started her freshman year at Swarthmore in the fall of 1901. She took the train to Swarthmore with her cousin Mary Parry, my grandfather Edwin's sister, a sophomore. Although most women students chose the arts as a major, assuming their occupational fate would be domesticity or social work, Alice chose a different path and declared biology as her major.

In the spring of 1902, as Alice was finishing her first year of college, her father, William Paul, died at age fifty-three of pneumonia. The research implies that his death, in some ways, liberated the family. Alice's mother, Tacie, took control of the large family estate and loosened the reins a bit at home. She bought a piano for the family, which had been prohibited by the strict Quaker father, as well as the latest new-fangled device—the telephone. Not at all broken by the death of a father who had been far too busy to cultivate a bond with his eldest daughter, Alice didn't take time off from Swarthmore to grieve. She carried on, apparently quite at home and happy in school.

Alice must have been inspired by Swarthmore's progressive Dean of Women, the sixty-year-old widow Elizabeth Bond. "In Alice's time at the college, Bond led a woman-centered life; she not only served as dean but enjoyed an intimate friendship with Swarthmore's librarian Sarah Nowell."[4] "She introduced music and dancing to Swarthmore, as well as literary readings . . . endlessly enthusiastic for reform movements like woman suffrage, she often urged students, 'Ally thyself with some great cause.'"[5] Elizabeth Bond was a New Woman role model and would also be Susanna's Dean of Women.

At Swarthmore, the Hicksite Quaker administration discouraged excessive opposite-sex socializing. Boys and girls couldn't walk around town together. Although music was allowed on campus, only single-sex dancing was allowed except for the rare formal dances which brought boys and girls together; consequently, women often enjoyed each other's company in the waltz and the trendy two-step. In discouraging opposite-sex activities, the administration was, in effect, encouraging same-sex relations. By the time Susanna and Alice were students, the administration saw same-sex socializing as a growing problem and sought to restrict "unseemly attachments" between female students: "The dean warned against improper displays, like 'girls promenading in public places with arms wrapped about one another' . . . but some rules proved hard to enforce, including those that stipulated girls walk outdoors in groups rather than in pairs."[6]

Despite the restrictions placed on women students and the warnings against forming close attachments, it appears that they were somewhat commonplace between college-aged New Women. Martha Vicinus explores the same-sex crushes that occurred in boarding schools at the turn of the century, examining the phenomenon of "smashing" and "crushing" between young women away from familial restrictions.[7] This was apparently Alice's case at Swarthmore.

Intimate friendships still animated many undergraduates' experiences—indeed their lives—in this era; the crushes on older girls or women commonplace at home developed greater intensity in a dormitory setting. Alice . . . spent the most time with her special friends, including Rena Miller, Anne Holmes (Rena's roommate), Ethel Close, and a few others . . .[8] Close friends commonly shared a bed on campuses at the turn of the twentieth century. Alice carefully noted her sleeping companions, as if she was logging her own popularity or lack thereof. She often slept with Rena during their first months and with Anne or Ethel later in the years. Alice wrote nothing beyond the fact of the bed sharing . . . However, the young Quaker's love of athleticism hints that other forms of physicality came easily to her too.[9]

In the first months of her freshman year, Alice got into trouble with her parents because of her hijinks with her adored new girlfriend Rena, with whom she would sneak off campus at night to go into town and other such pranks. Her parents were informed of their daughter's unruly behavior, and they reined her in. Alice, only sixteen years old and well aware of her complete dependence on her parents, heeded their warning and adjusted her behavior, curtailing her outings with the reckless Rena and turning instead to the more acceptable Ethel Close.[10] This is a fascinating parallel with what Susanna would have to endure in her Swarthmore years: like Alice, Susanna would have no choice but to obey her parents and distance herself from her college girlfriend, but unlike Alice's case, the incident would break her heart.

Alice appears to have had dalliances with college girlfriends, later with women in the suffrage movement, and even occasional dates with men, but she never formed lasting intimate relationships. Although many women in the movement adored her, Alice had only one obsession to which she gave her heart: the fight for equal rights for women. Not so with Susanna, as we shall see.

Alice's keeping track of her sleeping partners with notches-on-the-bedpost notations in her journal is amusing but also quite scientific. She was, after all, a biology major. Susanna would also declare biology as her major, perhaps so she could attend classes with her favorite cousin, perhaps so she too could take a path different from the liberal arts majority. Perhaps the Susanna Collection is her scientific way of documenting her experiences, her way of collecting evidence for discovery one day by a distant cousin from a future generation.

In the collection, I found an undated letter Alice wrote to her favorite cousin in the fall of her sophomore year at Swarthmore in 1902. Susanna, at the time, was a senior at Friends' Central in Philadelphia, a Quaker high school. It was a delightful find because the Alice Paul remembered by history was a serious, intimidating, hard-working suffragist with no time for anything but the fight for women's rights. Here we see young student Alice enjoying frivolous college antics. She revealed a great sense of humor, her involvement in playing basketball, and her special enjoyment of the company of her "dearest" and "very attractive" new roommate:

> My dear Susan—
> I've hardly recovered from the shock I received when thy letter came. Miracles still happen it seems. I am having an awfully nice time here and have the dearest room mate. She is eighteen years old and very attractive. Thee knows that the girl with whom I expected to room this year wrote me that she couldn't come back so I was put with a Freshman. The Freshmen had a class meeting to-night and while they were there we stole all the shoes of all the Freshman girls and piled them up in an empty closet where they would never dream of looking. We surely had fun and the Freshmen are wild. . . .
>
> Yesterday we played Princeton football and were beaten only 18-0. Isn't that fine! Princeton has about the finest team in the country this year and we expected to be beaten about 50-0. The team came home on the 9:04 train and the boys all dressed up in their night shirts and formed a parade and marched all around the college and then around the village with horns and drums etc. When the train came in they got a truck and hauled all the fellows up on it. It surely was a ridiculous sight to see all these boys flying around in their night gowns. . . .
>
> I invested in an alarm clock the other day and the first two nights my room mate and I lay awake nearly all night because of the awful

ticking so now we pile all our sofa pillows on top it and consequently don't hear a sound when the alarm goes off. We surely have hard times. We play basket ball every afternoon and in November the class games are coming off. This year we play outdoors—before we have always played in the gym.

There are three Friends' Central girls here this year and several boys entered too. How is thee enjoying the Senior dignity? Has thee had to speak yet before the school? That is what I always associate with the Seniors at Friends Central.

Ever lovingly Alice

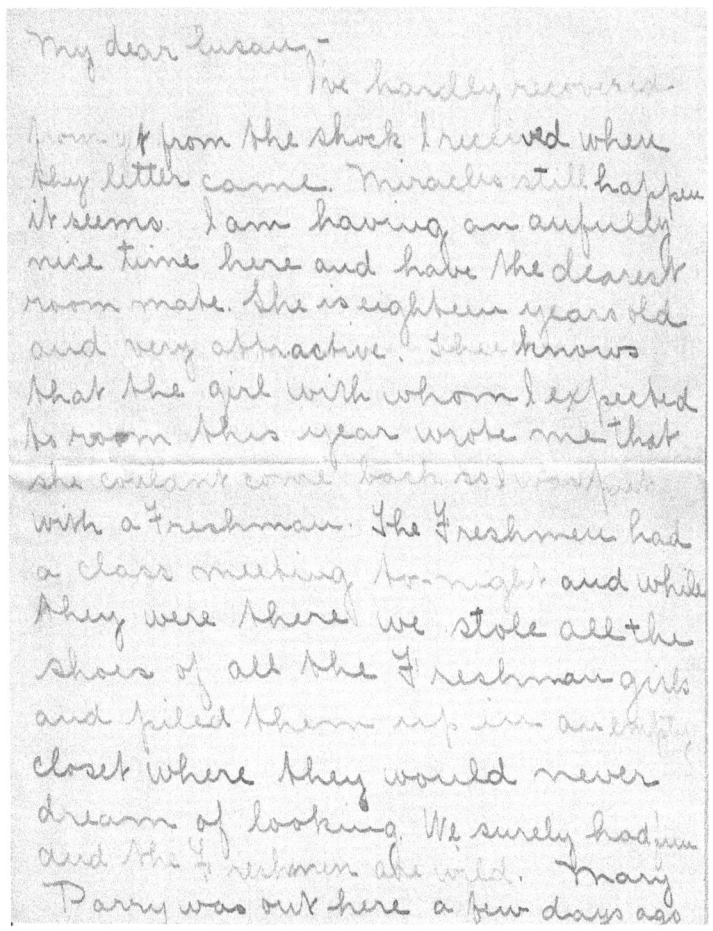

Letter from Swarthmore College Sophomore Alice Paul, 1902.

The collection contains a June 18, 1903, Class Day Program from the Friends' Central, with Susanna H. Parry included in The Girls' Roll. She would start her studies at Swarthmore College in the fall, where her cousin Alice would be a junior.

On October 6, 1903—her eighteenth birthday, Susanna received a check for $25—almost $700 in today's money—and notes from Uncle Joe and Aunt Sue. Aunt Sue's note is very sweet, for once her words not at all shallow and critical: "My dear little girl . . . is our little girl no longer, but inexpressibly dear." Uncle Joe's note is a tender and beautiful treatise on coming of age and love: ". . . thee has passed thy infancy, thy childhood & thy girlhood, to become what is the last & best of God's creation—a woman . . . For 18 years, we have loved thee but not all unselfishly as there is that in love which enriches both the giver & the receiver. May we then in the fullness of our love wish for thee a life that is real, one that is earnest & upheld by that love which brightens as the eye grows dim & strengthens when the steps are slow & halting."

Susanna started college just as she was coming of age. Her life would soon be forever changed when she received a letter from a friend of a friend at Swarthmore in May 1904. Shortly thereafter, her cousin Alice's life would be changed when she went to study in England and happened to attend a lecture by suffragette Christabel Pankhurst. Our Quaker rebels were about to find the passions which drove their lives.

CHAPTER 5

YOUNG HEARTS TAKE FLIGHT

At the end of her first year at Swarthmore, Susanna received a May 22, 1904, letter of introduction addressed to "My Dear Miss Parry" from E. of Baltimore, Maryland. E. had heard from a mutual friend that Susanna had been looking for a roommate for the next academic year. Because she, too, was looking for a roommate, she thought they could room together. She ended on a humorous note, saying that if Susanna were interested in her as a roommate, "I will write thee a full description of myself if thee wants it. I won't put it in now—for fear that it would be disastrous."

So begins the story of Susanna and E. They did indeed room together starting in the fall of 1904. The collection has little correspondence—none of consequence—for the remainder of 1904 and the beginning of 1905.

I have tried to protect the identity of E. by not disclosing her full first name or last initial, as some of the occurrences revealed in the collection might offend E.'s descendants. This is not an issue with Susanna, as she never married or had children, nor did her sister, Beulah: there is no one left in her bloodline to offend. Susanna saved the letters about her relationship with E., intentionally not destroying them although keeping them hidden, bundled up in her attic. When in her later years she built a new home and moved her affairs from one house to another, she moved the box of letters as well, perhaps hoping that someday the letters would be discovered and the story of her relationship with E. would be told. That day has come.

On February 10, 1905, Susanna received a letter from a Swarthmore friend Mary in Collection Hall, telling "Susie" to hurry back because everyone missed her. I assume Susanna was away from college because of illness. Obviously, Susanna had made some good friends at school. The postscript is revealing: "P.S. I'm just dying for somebody to hug. So hurry back." Apparently, Susanna—"Susie"—was affectionate and well-liked.

In March 1905, the Parrys received an invitation from Lydia S. Parry, my great-grandmother, the Betsy Ross connection in my bloodline. Lydia was the widow of Oliver Parry, Susanna's and Alice's uncle, who died at the young age of forty-three in 1894 of typhoid fever; she was also the mother of Susanna and Alice's cousins—my grandfather Edwin and his sister Mary, who as a child drew the little sketch of a witch and wrote the amusing account of catching mice. The wheel of time had turned since then. Lydia's invitation was to the marriage of Mary to William Turner at the Parry house on Main Street and Highway in Riverton, right down the street from Susanna's house. Sadly, Mary, who was always a sickly child, would die at the young age of thirty-one, seven years after her marriage.

The next entry of note in the collection is an April 15, 1905, booklet of the *Proceedings of the Annual Meeting of the Somerville Literary Society* held in Somerville Hall at Swarthmore. Among the active members were Susanna, her roommate E., Alice Paul, and her friend Mabel Vernon, who would later be one of Alice's chief organizers at the National Woman's Party. These were educated, articulate, literary New Women.

Alice was an outstandingly brilliant student, a member of Phi Beta Kappa.[1] She was the "Ivy Poet" at her graduation in 1905 and delivered the pre-commencement poem on Class Day, having been coached by Mabel Vernon. Professors at Swarthmore had greatly influenced Alice with progressive and socialist leanings which supported women's suffrage, racial equality, and social activism—Jesse Holmes and Robert C. Brooks. Professor of Political Science Brooks steered Alice away from a teaching career and obtained for her a year's College Settlement Scholarship (1905 to 1906) in a settlement house in New York City's Lower East Side, where she would work in the settlement house as well as attend the New York

School of Philanthropy[2] which would later become Columbia University's School of Social Work. Here she would be inspired and energized by the community of other New Women working for social reform.

The next stunning entry in the collection is an invitation for Susanna from her younger sister, Beulah. The invitation itself was run-of-the-mill, one of several Susanna received for June graduations. This one was for Beulah's June 16, 1905, Commencement Exercises at the Friends' Central School of Philadelphia. The invitation isn't shocking but the envelope is: Beulah had addressed the invitation to "Susanna H. Parry and Wife." Was the "Wife" E., Susanna's roommate? Were Susanna and E. a couple of sorts? Or was Beulah simply jealous and somewhat mean-spirited about the closeness of the two female roommates? Answers would soon be given.

Beulah Parry's high school graduation photograph, Friends' Central School of Philadelphia, 1905.

A June 26, 1905, letter to Susanna from her Swarthmore friend Helen Price revealed that Susanna recently hosted a house party and that E. had been there: "E. said . . . that they had a fine time." The letter also revealed that E.'s parents had taken their daughter to Europe for the summer and that E. would not be back at Swarthmore in time for the beginning of the fall term. Helen wondered if she could stay in Susanna's room the first week since work was being done in her building. The timing of E.'s European tour with the parents is curious, given that privileged students customarily enjoyed such a trip after they graduated. Could E.'s parents—perhaps with the encouragement of Howard and Lizzie Parry—have taken E. across the ocean for the summer to separate the two roommates and allow the relationship to cool?

Apparently so. The next long letter, dated June 21, 1905, was postmarked in Gibraltar and written to Susanna by E. in mid-ocean. She wrote beautifully and had a great power of observation and a wry sense of humor. The letter was addressed to "Dearest Wifie." So, Beulah was on to something after all. E. began by describing the ocean liner's departure from New York: "Soon the ropes were loosened, & we slowly steamed down the bay, leaving our friends with many others, standing on the wharf, and becoming less and less distinct as we moved until they were finally nothing but a mass of moving colors, then a blot. I did have a queer little twinge as I thought of what I was leaving, but it's all in the game, so—au revoir all silliness until my wife teaches it to me again next winter." This certainly seems to imply that E.'s parents were taking her to Europe to take her away from the "silliness" of what they perceived as her excessive attachment to Susanna. It also appears that E. indeed saw Susanna as her partner. The letter went on to describe activities onboard and how she missed her dance partner Susanna: "The motion is great—even better than the merry-go-round & it certainly is invigorating. I had a wild desire to dance to the music this morning as the waves are doing, but I had neither my slippers nor—thee dear, so how could I?" At Swarthmore, boys and girls weren't ordinarily allowed to dance together so that girls would take each other as partners; apparently, Susanna and E. were quite a couple on the dance floor. (Alice also loved dancing with her girlfriends when she was at Swarthmore. In her freshman year, "at the

Halloween dance, she waltzed and two-stepped with Rena, Ethel, and eleven other girls, tucking her dance card into her diary to treasure."[3])

E. gave Susanna her itinerary: Switzerland, Belgium, France, England, then sailing for home at the end of September. She closed the letter "I am as ever/Thy loving wife/E."

E.'s July 6, 1905, letter from Rome to "Dearest Wifie" waxed poetic about the beauty of Naples and said that the two must spend some time there while on their honeymoon: "Naples was perfect—except the beggars—and when thee & I take our long-deferred wedding trip we must spend two weeks in the Hotel Royal, which overlooks that Bay of Azure hue."

That these turn-of-the-century women called each other "Wife" and "Wifie" and talked of their honeymoon in Naples might catch the reader by surprise as it did me. However, in this era of the twentieth century New Woman, taking a schoolmate as a wife was common. Jean Baker examines such same-sex relationships in *Sisters: The Lives of America's Suffragists*, revealing that Alice Paul also had a "wife" at Swarthmore: "In the playful custom of special girlfriends she took a wife, in that kind of intimate relationship between adolescent girls that had no necessary sexual connotation."[4] No *necessary* sexual connotation, perhaps, but given Alice's penchant for sports and dancing, physical contact couldn't be ruled out.

Baker's study addresses a nineteenth-century suffragist's relationships with other women: Susan B. Anthony, who partnered in intense, short-term relationships with protégées, such as Anna Dickinson. Interestingly, women expressing physical affection with each other in public was widespread in the nineteenth century and not yet frowned upon because, at that time, women weren't esteemed and their feelings were ignored and discounted. Women were seen by most—even themselves—not as independent sentient sexual beings with desires of their own but mere objects of the desires of men, breeders, or prostitutes. No wonder some women in the nineteenth century turned to each other for physical and emotional affection, which in some cases was sexual: "women established romantic friendships with other women marked by courting, flirting, pet nicknames, and baby talk, and when apart, rhetorical sighs of attachment and devotion. In their female world of love and ritual, women of the nineteenth century engaged in petting, kissing, and hand holding without outsiders paying much attention. In the conventional wisdom of the day, women were considered asexual and passionless. With society's negligent blessing, they could engage in emotionally and sexually gratifying relationships as kindred spirits who, beyond the prying eyes of family or friends, may or may not have been involved in the homoerotic genital contact that forms today's definition of lesbianism."[5]

At the beginning of the twentieth century, in the dawn of psychoanalysis, such behavior was suspect: "by the end of the nineteenth century, same-sex passion in the United States had lost its innocence; no longer an acceptable form of affection for women, it was considered perverted."[6]

Alice and Susanna had a foot in each century. They were born in 1885, children of very traditional Quaker families, yet adolescents in college in the first decade of the 1900s. Were their relationships with other women sexual or simply affectionate? I couldn't care less. What they did with their female partners behind closed doors was completely their business and not the focus of this work. My goal is to identify each woman's driving passion—her heart. In the case of Alice, from the time of her involvement with the Pankhursts' suffragettes in England, her driving passion was the struggle to obtain equal rights for all women, beginning with suffrage. As for Susanna, the letters reveal that the "marriage" between Susanna and E. was no mere adolescent dalliance, no passing fancy, at least for Susanna. Susanna's was an affair of the heart, and at the end of the day, the sex of the people we love is not part of the equation: the heart knows no gender.

Alice and Susanna were not pioneers as women partnering with women. Intimate relationships between socially prominent women go back centuries. Two of the most interesting examples are the famous Ladies of Llangollen, two upper-class women living together for decades in the late 1700s, early 1800s. Sarah Ponsonby and Lady Eleanor Butler met in boarding school and fell in love. To live together, the soulmates were forced to leave their families in Ireland, settling in at their beloved "Plas Newydd" in North Wales, living there for over fifty years and entertaining the illustrious and artistic.

"Ladies of Llangollen," lithograph by J. H. Lynch, c. 1840.

The Ladies of Llangollen passed their same-sex torch to two well-known avant-garde contemporaries of Alice and Susanna: After the 1906 San Francisco earthquake, Alice B. Toklas moved to Paris and met writer and celebrity Gertrude Stein. They would become one of history's most famous lesbian couples.

Henry James wrote about a same-sex couple among Boston's elite at the end of the nineteenth century in *The Bostonians* (1886). In the novel, upper-class feminist Olive Chancellor takes beautiful spiritualist Verena Tarrant under her wing and into her nest on posh Charles Street. At the end of the story, Verena leaves Olive brokenhearted when she elopes with

Olive's cousin Basil Ransom. Olive is completely invested in her exclusive love for Verena, but not so for Verena, who moves on to a traditional relationship. This parallels Susanna's story, as we shall see. The monogamous relationship between Olive and Verena in *The Bostonians* became so well known that the cohabitation of women living in complete independence from men became known as a "Boston marriage." In James's novel, the relationship is not explicitly sexual, and the emotional devotion is not fully mutual; the couple does not endure. However, such Boston marriages would intensify and strengthen in the new century.

Fast forward several decades and west of Boston to Wellesley College in the late nineteenth and early twentieth century, where Boston marriages were so common that they became known as Wellesley marriages, typically between female faculty members who had to leave their positions if they married traditionally with a man. At the same time in England, similar relationships between women were common among boarding school teachers and workers in settlement houses, many of them committed, enduring, and sexually passionate unions in the age of the New Woman. Martha Vicinus's research explores this boarding school tradition in turn-of-the-century England. "Like countless women before them, many of these women teachers and settlement-house residents formed passionate relationships with one another. Unlike those earlier women, many of these New Woman, eschewing men, felt they had married each other for life."[7]

A bittersweet letter, written by E. from London on August 23, 1905, suggested that the love between the two roommates, although very real, was yet impossible: "My own Dear Sue . . . not a day passes without my feeling a great sense of gain—(& loss) in knowing & loving thee as I do. Merely a case of so near & yet so far, isn't it?" She closed the letter "With love untold --/E." E. implied that their couple could not endure and that they should not talk openly about their love.

In the summer of 1905, Susanna received numerous letters from Swarthmore friends. Obviously, she was well-liked and had intelligent and playful friends, most of whom displayed a good sense of youthful humor in their letters. A July 25 letter from Philadelphian Anna Pettit revealed an unusual nickname for Susanna, who was addressed as "My dear Squeeze." Susanna was apparently not reluctant to express affection physically.

On September 2, 1905, Alice Paul wrote Susanna a letter from Moorestown (Mt. Laurel), inviting her cousin to join her at Squirrel Inn on the Hudson as a guest of her Aunt Hannah Paul, the proprietor. With Alice's late father's financial support, Aunt Hannah had opened Squirrel Inn in the Catskills as a Quaker resort. Susanna was apparently Alice's favorite cousin and one of her closest friends, as Susanna was the one she chose to invite to her Aunt's inn on her vacation before starting her settlement work in New York. "Aunt Hannah has been good enough to invite any friend of mine whom I might ask to go with me as her guest . . . up the Hudson. I am going to start a week from this Tuesday—September 12th and stay till the 25th. Of course thee could come back sooner if thee wanted to be at college when it opened. I do hope thee will want to go. Sorry I couldn't come down to ask thee but our horse is still too lame to drive. /Lovingly,/Alice" (No horse power when the horse was lame, no phone call or e-mail possible, so a letter mailed).

The next letter from Alice Paul to Susanna—one of my favorites in the collection—was written from New York City on October 9, 1905, a wonderful letter written by a young Quaker woman who was thrilled to have escaped from her family and sleepy Moorestown, now out in the world at large in the exciting neighborhood of the New York settlement house at 95 Rivington Street. She thanked her cousin for having sold off some of the things she had left at Swarthmore, then described her fascinating, active life, including a visit from her Swarthmore friend and sleeping companion Ethel Close. "Ethel remained her closest companion, and she came every Sunday to play the house piano for guests and share Alice's bed."[8]

> Thank thee very much for selling my furniture and sending me the money. I'm sorry to have put thee to so much trouble about it. I'll have thee for agent again—anybody who could sell that clothes pole has decided mercantile [sic] ability . . . This is the most interesting place in the world—it is glorious. I am going to have thee up here later in the winter—if thee will come. To day is the

'Day of Atonement' for the Jews—the synagogue has been crowded since morning—we are next door to the synagogue. Yesterday I went to meeting with Ethel Close. In the afternoon we went to the Metropolitan Art Museum. Saturday night we went to an Italian theatre and afterwards to a Salvation Army meeting. . . . We are in the heart of the Jewish Quarters—It seems like a foreign city—not a word of English is heard on the streets—the newspapers are all in Yiddish. . . . Chinatown is a few blocks distant. We went to the Chinese theatre, restaurant and Josh temple the other night. It is a fascinating place. I do so want thee to see all these places. I go to the School of Philanthropy every morning but Sunday—and three afternoons—the other three afternoons I teach sewing, basketball, and gym at the settlement. I've never been happier in my life. Thank thee for the films—lots of love to thee, Alice

The films referenced must have been pictures or negatives of their stay together at Squirrel Inn. Alice so wanted to share her new, different, and exciting world with her friend and cousin Susanna. However, knowing Susanna's protective and controlling family, I guess that Susanna was never allowed to visit Alice in the ghetto. Perhaps Susanna wasn't even interested in making a trip to New York, as, by that time, E. had returned from Europe and was back with her "Wifie" at Swarthmore.

CHAPTER 6

ALL THINGS MUST PASS

Susanna began 1906 by getting sick—apparently very sick, cared for at home in Riverton. She received a handful of letters from Swarthmore friends letting her know how much she was missed. Girlfriends Nome and Tommy sent letters to "My Dear Squeeze," telling her that they missed her and that others were sick as well, including E., who was in the "nursery" with a sore throat. They said folks feared scarlet fever, which had become widespread. They also told Susanna that the boys had joked with Henry Price for having sent flowers to Susanna. "Henry has asked after thee several times, Sue—I fear it is getting to be serious."

I have my doubts that Susanna was serious about any boy. She did have friends who happened to be boys, however. In January, she received a letter from J. Byron D. inviting her to see *Twelfth Night* at the Broad Street Theater with Julia Marlowe, the actress.

A March 24, 1906, letter announced that Beulah had been elected to the Somerville Literary Society, so we know that Beulah was by then a student at Swarthmore.

Susanna's mother, Lizzie, received a letter dated April 27, 1906, from her husband's cousin in California—Lettie (Laetitia) Haines Cook—who had written from their ranch in 1898. I have included it in this chapter about loss because it describes the Great Earthquake in fascinating detail, which occurred in California on April 18, 1906. Lettie began the letter by assuring her cousin that they were all safe, but their apartment in San Francisco had been completely burned in the fire. The Great Earthquake and resulting fires destroyed over 80% of San Francisco and killed more than 3,000 people. Luckily, Lettie and the children were vacationing away from the city on their ranch, so they didn't have to witness the catastrophe; her husband, Evans, was in Alaska, so he was safe as well. They lost everything in the apartment—their bank books, important papers, mahogany furniture, oil portraits of the children, photographs, and clothes. "We had no insurance, it had run out & I felt the building was fire proof—steel frame & stone, and under most circumstances could they have had water, it would have stood it—the water mains being broken by earthquake they had no water. . . . many of our friends lost their all." There are lessons here: be sure not to let your insurance lapse; know that everything material can be taken away from you at any moment, so be careful where you set your heart. Lettie's Quaker faith kept her centered and away from depression; her family had suffered great material loss "But we are alive & well & are determined not to allow it to make us unhappy." Another lesson: in all circumstances, be grateful. Easier said than done.

At the end of the school year, in June 1906, Susanna had another house party for her Swarthmore friends at her home in Riverton. Girlfriend Tommy writes "Squzzy" that she could not attend because she'd be away in Maryland for a couple of weeks. A few days later, Tommy wrote to all the girls at the party that she wished she could have been with them. They sound like a fun group: "I know I would be cackling all the time at Gibby's monstrous phrases, Helen's squishiness, E.'s mooniness, and Sue's giggle." She told a funny story of how, as a Quaker, she was uneasy at a traditional church service: "Last Sunday night we went to church, and I acted like a fool. Of course, having gone to meeting all my long life, I didn't know how to act, so prayed when I ought to have sung, stood when the rest sat down, etc. I had two cents for collection in my glove, and in the midst of a prayer, the two pennies dropped one by one, and I know everybody could tell how much it was."

Several letters were forwarded to Susanna in East Fryeburg, Maine, where she and others from Swarthmore were vacationing with E. at her family's camp in mid-July. At the end of July, Susanna got a very testy letter from her mother, who was upset about miscommunications regarding timetables and was impatiently waiting for Susanna's written response. Sounds like a controlling mother wanted her daughter to come home. Luckily for Susanna, there were no telephones or e-mails, allowing her a few extra days of freedom and fun.

On August 3, Helen Price (sister of Henry who sent Susanna flowers when she was sick) sent a letter to "Sue" letting her know she had heard some talk about the goings-on at E.'s camp in Maine. "Thee must have had a lovely time up with E. It must be lovely up there from all I have heard (and I've heard a good deal, too)." What exactly had she heard, I wonder? Sounds like gossip abounded regarding the gathering in Maine. Susanna had left East Fryeburg to go with her family to visit her Auntie Sue in Linwood, Maryland, so she apparently had missed some buzz-worthy scenes.

On August 6, the gathering in East Fryeburg sent Susanna a package of witty and lighthearted letters recounting their escapades and saying how much they missed her. E.'s letter was full of surprises: "We do miss thee sorely, but are glad to have had thee even for the wee time we did. Everyone has been saying lovely things about thee, but I wouldn't think of telling thee, would I?" E. then described a lively barn dance they all went to the previous night and wrote that all the locals were talking about why she wasn't dancing with "H.", who must have been Herbert from their group: "Of course H. & I didn't dance together & so the whole hill is wild with curiosity as to the why & wherefore thereof." It was, by this time, no surprise that E. wasn't inclined to dance with anyone other than her "Wifie," especially a boy.

The plot thickened. In the following scene, E. seemed to describe some sort of dalliance with the girl she slept with—"Miss J.", and Herbert in the next room was so upset that he threw his shoes against the wall: "Miss J. slept with me, & we had a fine long talk and feel much better acquainted. Of course, we had the excitement of having numerous shoes, etc. thrown at our wall, because we had done some slamming, & the somewherementioned [sic] thought that if he couldn't slam us personally, he would make it up otherwise, I suppose." The important word here, of course, is "slamming." I don't know what the "slamming" was, but it certainly sounds physical and must have been loud enough for Herbert to have thrown his shoes at the wall in protest. Martha Vicinus's exploration of boarding school girl crushes at the turn of the last century sheds some light on a possible explanation of "slamming": "The adolescent crush was so common in the late nineteenth and early twentieth centuries that it was known by many different slang words besides 'crush': 'rave,' 'spoon,' 'pash' (for passion), 'smash,' 'gonage' (for gone on), or 'flame.'" E.'s "slamming" looks right at home among all these terms.[1]

E. closed the letter by telling Susanna of an apparent crush she had on Miss "L": "I have the worst case on Miss 'L'. She dances beautifully & is a perfect dear, isn't she?" Although E. closed the letter "Most lovingly," I wouldn't be surprised if the letter made Susanna jealous. Apparently, Susanna and E. had a very open relationship—how modern of these New Women. However, trouble loomed on the horizon: Susanna was serious about E., while E. seemed to be casually sowing adolescent Quaker oats.

In an envelope from summer's end in 1906, there was no letter but three small photographs or negatives, so faded that all that was left was a silver background. On one, I could see there used to be an image—perhaps of a house and a tree, but I couldn't tell for sure. Just the whisper of a ghost on the silver paper. They must have been pictures from the vacation at E.'s camp in Maine. The pictures were faded beyond recognition—dead, really—but how alive the words in the letters have remained. How powerful and lasting are printed words. How valuable are books. How precious a letter. If you want to give a friend an unusual, lasting gift, write her a letter in your own handwriting about what she means to you and send it via snail mail. Far more meaningful and lasting than a dashed-off tweet or a heart emoji. If you want future generations to remember you and the world you live in, keep a journal of your daily life, and save some postcards of where you've been and some newspaper clippings of world and local events that have touched you. Maybe a grandchild will find them in a dusty box while cleaning out your attic when preparing your home for sale. People fade away like century-old photographs. Their words, written and saved, remain.

The carefree, youthful antics of the summer of 1906 soon faded away. All vacations were over by September 1, and the mood had changed. E. sent Susanna—"My own dear Wifie"—a letter from her home in Mt.

Lake Park, Maryland. The letter dealt with loss and illness; the first time we learn of the death of Susanna's Uncle Joe, Auntie Sue's husband, the uncle who wrote Susanna such a tender letter on her eighteenth birthday. His death was caused by severe asthma, often a topic in Auntie Sue's previous letters. (There was no effective treatment for asthma at the time; epinephrine/adrenaline would not be introduced until the 1940s.) E. sent Susanna her touching condolences: "It is hard for me to realize that I won't see thy Uncle Joe again. He seemed so jolly and full of life that it is almost impossible for me to believe it. I am so sorry."

E. told Susanna she had heard of the serious illness of Helen Price's brother Henry, the one who had something of a crush on Susanna at the beginning of the year. "Thee has heard, I suppose that Henry Price has typhoid . . . Isn't that dreadful?" She signed the letter "Perfect love, E." Typhoid fever, the bacterial disease caused by poor sanitation which killed my great-grandfather Oliver Parry in 1894, has never been fully eradicated. The vaccination developed in 1896 was never widely available. Before antibiotics, the mortality rate was 10-30%; antibiotics reduced the mortality rate to 1-4%. In 1908, a significant advance would be made in the fight against typhoid by chlorinating public drinking water in Jersey City, New Jersey.

On September 2, 1906, Susanna's mother, Lizzie, received a letter from recently-widowed Auntie Sue (Sue Haines). The previously materialistic busybody, whose letters spoke interminably of clothes, social events, and home decorations, had been broken open by grief. With newfound clarity of vision, she realized that she had lost what truly mattered in life. "This beautiful home means nothing to me now, it is merely an empty shell & the care & worry of servants & housekeeping (since the object of my love and care is gone) weigh uncomfortably upon me . . . if you take me in, I will try not to be a care, but to make some recompense for this loving welcome extended."

Auntie Sue accepted Lizzie's invitation to come live with them at 809 Main Street in Riverton. She was lonely and miserable in her husband's home in Maryland, where she felt little or no connection to her grown stepchildren. I learned that the house and land at Forest Home in Linwood, Maryland, went to Joe's eldest son, so Auntie Sue really had no place to call home after Joe's death. She was grateful to have been invited to move into a familiar place. "I feel I will be more at home & happier there in my old quarters, than anywhere else." Given Auntie Sue's past meddling and critical nature, Lizzie must have been a saint to open her home to her widowed sister. It was indeed a beautiful gesture. In addition, she might have felt obliged to do so since 809 Main Street had been the sisters' childhood home, and the house was in part Sue's, as it had been passed on to the two sisters by their parents. At any rate, Sue hoped to move in with the Parry family around December 1, and our Susanna would have yet another pair of observing, critical eyes watching her every move.

On October 22, 1906, Susanna at Swarthmore received a note from J. Byron D. in Riverton honoring her recent birthday. He said that at twenty-one, he had become a "man" last December and that at twenty-one, she was now a "New Woman." He probably had no idea how much of a "New Woman" Susanna really was.

The collection contains no letters between October 22, 1906, and May 1907. The only item of note is a January 18, 1907, program for a reception at Swarthmore, which included a poetry reading by E. In May 1907, Susanna received another letter from J. Byron D., who was now in England studying at Woodbrooke, a Quaker school for social activism near Birmingham, founded in 1903 by the Cadburys, the wealthy family still famous for its chocolate. (Woodbrooke is still alive today as a Quaker study and conference center.) He wrote of his studies, Norwegians he had met, and the joys of afternoon tea. He praised the quality of education at Woodbrooke: "Beyond doubt, there isn't another place like it in the world . . . no place so ideal from the standpoint of the student of the most vital things that touch our lives: our relation to God—religion, and our relation to our fellows—sociology." He sounded quite full of himself in the letter, pontificating at length, and signed the letter "Sincerely thine,/J. Byron D."

On September 16, 1907, Susanna received a letter from her cousin in Kinderhook, New York—Alice Parry, daughter of yet another Parry brother: Charles, who married Anna Sill and had children Anna, William, and Alice. This cousin Alice was trying hard to lift Susanna's spirits.

Apparently, Susanna had been in a severe depression. "Will write thee a letter now so thee will get it shortly after thee reaches college. Perhaps it will cheer thee up a bit." She mentioned the engagement of a mutual friend to a Philadelphia doctor then told Susanna she too should find herself a mate: "It is high time thee was setten up Susie." Finding a husband was the last thing on Susanna's mind, but nice of this Alice to try to make her cousin feel better. "Wish thee was here, and I would make thee smile all afternoon." What had depressed Susanna, who used to be so lighthearted and in love?

In a September 18, 1907, letter from Swarthmore friend Jeannette Curtis in Berlin, we learn that Alice Paul was now in Germany. In Hamburg, "Alice Paul and Alice Merriman met me at the station, and we had a jolly Swarthmore reunion. The girls are both well and having a good time." A September 16 letter from J. Byron D. in Woodbrooke said that Alice, now in Germany, would soon be arriving at Woodbrooke, increasing the number of Americans there to seven. "Until thy letter came, I had not known that Alice Paul is in Germany. I suppose there is much to be learned of her service in Berlin, and it is fortunate that she can be there. She will also be in luck here, as beginning with this term, we are to have a special lecture in economics." He had no idea just how bright and educated Alice already was, already with a master's degree under her belt.

Alice had been incredibly busy since her letter from the settlement house in New York City. When she finished her scholarship year in 1906, she wanted to stay in New York and pursue a Master's in Political Science. Her mother was willing to finance Alice's advanced studies, but she wanted her daughter closer to home. Because Princeton didn't accept women at that time, Alice attended the University of Pennsylvania in Philadelphia, pursuing a Master's in Sociology with a minor in political science and economics. Alice was a trailblazer as a female graduate student at the University of Pennsylvania, where there were only one or two other female graduate students in political science. "Graduate women felt the need to carve out their own literal and symbolic space and turned to each other for support. As Alice Paul later remarked, 'We got to know each other very well.'"[2] Alice finished her master's in June 1907. She spent the summer in Germany, hoping to improve her German in case she decided to teach as a profession, then headed to Woodbrooke on yet another scholarship in case she decided to choose social work as a career.

Meanwhile, Alice's cousin Susanna was beginning her last year at Swarthmore. On October 7, her mother sent a letter to Susanna and Beulah on Susanna's twenty-second birthday. "My dear Girls—I just would love to step in your room & have a little chat with you." Susanna's roommate was no longer her beloved E. but her chubby younger sister, Beulah. Apparently, Susanna's and E.'s parents thought it in everyone's best interest to separate the young wives. Mother wanted to know all about the surprise birthday party for Susanna and, in a controlling tone, asked for all the details: "who went as chaperone and what time did you come back."

This explains Susanna's depression. I can't imagine the scene when Susanna was told she could no longer room with E. There must have been angry words, many tears, and afterward stony silence. Even though Susanna was now twenty-two, she was totally under the control of her parents. Unlike her cousin Alice, whose father died years before, Susanna's strict Quaker father was still alive, as was E.'s. If Susanna and E. ran off together, they surely would have been disowned by their families, read out of their Quaker meeting, and cut off from their fortunes and friends, with little opportunity to earn a decent living. They had no practical choice but to obey their parents.

This situation calls to mind the scene in my grandfather's biography of Betsy Ross—*Betsy Ross Quaker Rebel*—in which twenty-year-old Betsy Griscom announced to her Quaker parents, Samuel and Rebecca Griscom, that she was engaged to John Ross, an Episcopalian:

> There followed then a stormy scene the like of which had never taken place in that placid household before. The Father's face blazed with anger.
>
> Did she understand the full meaning of her conduct, he demanded. Did she realize that she would be in disgrace among Friends, that she would be an outcast from the Meeting?
>
> To which Betsy calmly replied that she had carefully considered these things, and while she deeply regretted them, her mind was fully made up.

Did she realize she was about to bring shame and humiliation upon her family?

She understood that, too, but she could not help it . . . "I love John Ross, and I will marry him whatever happens," was her simple rejoinder.³

Betsy Griscom and John Ross slipped out of Philadelphia quietly and got married. Betsy was excommunicated from the Society of Friends in a formal ceremony by the "elders" and alienated from her family for years. She would eventually be reconciled with her parents before they died in the Great Yellow Fever epidemic of 1793. Unlike Susanna, who would have been penniless as a single woman disowned by her family, Betsy had a source of income in marrying John Ross, the owner of a successful upholstery business. She was also a gifted seamstress and was already earning a living. Because Betsy could support herself, she could afford to stand on her rebellion. Susanna couldn't.

Betsy rebelled against her Quaker faith in marrying a man who was not a Quaker. In fact, none of her three husbands were Quakers. (Her first two husbands, John Ross and Joe Ashburn, died in the Revolution; her third husband, John Claypoole, my fourth-great grandfather, survived the war.) Betsy also rebelled against her Quaker faith in supporting the rebellion and war against the tyrannical mother country. The Quakers did not support war or rebellion, so Quaker patriots who joined the rebellion against British rule were excommunicated from the Society of Friends. There were hundreds of these so-called "Fighting Quakers" in Philadelphia, who in 1781 formed a separate religious society of which Betsy was a member: the "Free Quakers," whose religious practices were traditionally Quaker but did not embrace the old constraining precepts against war or marrying out of the faith. The Free Quakers stopped their religious practice in 1834 but continue to this day as a charitable organization helping Philadelphia's poor.

Back to our Susanna, who carried on in her last year at college with Beulah as her roommate. However, the old Susanna was gone without her beloved E. Her mother's letter expressed great concern for Susanna's health: apparently, her periods had stopped, and she looked sickly.

Mother was glad that chubby Beulah was doing exercises before bed and told Beulah to get Susanna to do the same: "You do it together [*sic*] it might bring her more regular and in this may get more color in her cheeks, make her prettier and brighter eyed. both [*sic*] of you try to keep it up, it is a thousand times better than medicine." Evidently, Susanna was clinically depressed.

On October 29, 1907, Susanna received another letter from New York cousin Alice Parry, who tried to be a matchmaker for Susanna and Beulah. "How is thee Susie dear [*sic*] Settin up any yet? It is about time thee was taking notice! Does thee know Lesley Hallocks [*sic*] brother? Is a good looking chap isn't he? He would be about right for Beulah. I think [*sic*] will have to see if I can't arrange things a little for you 'little monkeys'." How annoying it must have been for Susanna to have her cousin try to "settin" her and Beulah up with husbands; this cousin Alice was wasting her time.

Susanna received a Christmas card on December 16, 1907, from the cousin Alice she did enjoy hearing from—Alice Paul, who was at Woodbrooke in Birmingham, England. The card, at first glance, seems to depict two little girls kissing each other under the mistletoe. At second glance, however, the child in the shorter dress is probably a boy with a toy boat or wagon.

This was Alice's first time away from home and family at Christmas, and her note expressed great homesickness: "I do wish that I could be with you all at Christmas time. It is the first I've ever missed. I suppose all of us Americans will spend the day dissolved in tears." She then said that the rather full-of-himself J. Byron D. had made an appearance at Woodbrooke; it's clear just what Alice thinks of him by the nickname she gives him: "An old Swarthmore boy of '03 (Byron Beans) was out here to-day." A very funny name for someone who was, at least in his inflated letters, full of beans. I imagine that Susanna agreed with Alice, for the letters from "Byron Beans" soon ended.

Susanna was at least getting out a bit now. The collection contains her dance card from a December 28, 1907, dance at Phi Sigma Kappa. Of the twenty dances, Susanna didn't dance five of them, including the last waltz. There are two other undated dance cards in the collection. The

Christmas card from Alice Paul to Susanna Parry, 1907.

first is for the Junior Prom, which must have been the previous June; she sat out four of the twenty dances, including the last dance. She danced three waltzes with the same boy in another dance card, including the first and last waltz, but she sat out the ladies' choice dance. Susanna would never choose a partner.

On January 27, 1908, Alice wrote Susanna a nice long letter from Woodbrooke describing her activities over Christmas at the Canning Town Women's Settlement in London. She enjoyed the girls from many countries that she was boarding with, but she sounded more occupied than fulfilled, certainly less enthusiastic than she had been at the settlement house in New York. She spent a week of her Christmas vacation "visiting the Canning Town Settlement in London. It is one of the most famous in England. It is a women's settlement. Next door is Mansfield House, a men's settlement. . . . Christmas day was so strenuous that I had no time to be homesick. First I went with one of the residents to St. Paul's Cathedral . . . then we had our Christmas dinner—then went to a hospital nearby where they had a party for the patients—then to a neighborhood party at Mansfield House where we danced with men & women of almost 87 yrs until eleven o'clock. There are five Americans here this term. I am rooming with a Dutch girl whom I like tremendously. In the chalet where I room, there are three Dutch, two Norwegians, two Irish, one English, and myself. Isn't that Cosmopolitan! . . . May the New Year bring thee all possible happiness. Lovingly, Alice".

Wishing Susanna all possible happiness was a tall order. However, she did have international travel on the horizon, which would provide helpful distraction. "Sue and Beulah" received a February 6, 1908, letter from Auntie Sue about her intention to give them a very generous graduation gift. "My dear Girls, You have always been such a pleasure to me—your sweet babyhood, girlhood, & lovely womanhood! & last, before merging finally upon the latter stage, I want to say it has been such a satisfaction that you could, & were willing to avail yourselves of a college

Susanna Parry's Swarthmore College graduation photograph, 1908.

experience . . . I want to show my love & appreciation of you by giving to each to commemorate close of school life a remembrance—First I want for each an appropriate gown—suitable for all occasions." The girls would go with their aunt and mother to a well-known dressmaker, select the material and style and trimmings, and have a fitting. They would also be sent "a gift from one who loves to add her mite toward making you happy . . . on the day of leaving behind your 'school days,' I will have for each a cheque for five hundred dollars toward a trip to Europe to be taken when & as you wish." This was quite a gift: $500 in 1909 is worth over $12,000 in today's money. Auntie Sue was loaded, and because she had no children of her own, Susanna and Beulah were very lucky indeed.

Beulah wrote her mother about Auntie Sue's generous gifts of a gown and European vacation because she felt unworthy of them: Although Susanna was graduating with a degree, she was not, having attended Swarthmore only three years. Apparently, Beulah had painful problems with her eyes which slowed her progress at school and prevented her from continuing. On February 12, Auntie Sue wrote "Dear Little Beulah" that she wouldn't hear of her refusing the gifts. "Thee has had the suffering beside—but with it all thee has had . . . three years of college life which means much of development & of pleasure—therefore no more such talk!"

And so, the European trip was booked. Susanna and Beulah would be accompanied and chaperoned by none other than Auntie Sue. Mother Lizzie received a letter on March 5, 1908, from Swarthmore's Benjamin Battin saying how glad he was that the three of them would be joining the Swarthmore European tour group in the summer, which would be following the same itinerary as the previous year. The program giving the itinerary and members of the party was impressive. Susanna, Beulah, and Auntie Sue were three of fourteen attending, not including tour guides Dr. and Mrs. Battin. They were to sail from New York on June 18 (a week after Susanna's graduation) on the Cunard Line's *Slavonia* and would visit Gibraltar, Naples, Rome, Pisa, Florence, Venice, Milan, Bellagio, Lucerne, Interlaken, Munich, Nuremberg, Heidelberg, Frankfurt, Cologne, Amsterdam, The Hague, Brussels, Paris, London, Oxford, Warwick, Chester, and Glasgow, then sail back to New York on Anchor

Line's *California* on August 29, arriving in New York on September 6. Sounds exhausting to me, but knowing Auntie Sue, I'm sure they would be traveling first class all the way.

Susanna's school days were ending, as were her close ties with E. She was about to put on fancy clothes and see something of the world in high style. When she sailed from New York harbor, she would leave her old life behind in many ways.

Alice, too, was leaving her old life behind. While attending Woodbrooke, she also took an economics course at the University of Birmingham. One day she happened to attend a lecture by suffragette Christabel Pankhurst at the University of Birmingham, a pivotal moment when her old life passed away. Emmeline Pankhurst and her daughter Christabel had formed the Women's Social and Political Union (WSPU) the previous year, in 1907. The group's efforts to obtain the vote were notably more militant than those used by previous generations of suffragists; these more radical suffragists became known as suffragettes. At Christabel's lecture, the men in the audience jeered at the speaker's calls for women's suffrage and tried to silence her. Alice's outrage at their behavior inspired her to join the Pankhursts' fight. In a moment of clarity, she saw that her calling was not teaching or settlement house work but the struggle for the vote and, more broadly, equal rights for women. She would never stray from this path. She would join the WSPU and learn much from the Pankhursts about organizing large, news-worthy parades and disrupting political rallies, which would often land the suffragettes—and her—in jail. She would then take her organizational skills back to the States to orchestrate the long and difficult fight for a constitutional amendment guaranteeing all American women the right to vote.

As Alice was about to embark on a new career of political activism, our Susanna was literally about to set sail. In mid-June 1908, Susanna read several letters from Swarthmore friends as she installed herself in her stateroom aboard the *Slavonia*, waiting to set sail for Europe. The most heart-wrenching letter was from E., which began with a poem she addressed to Susanna, her erstwhile "Wifie" from whom she had been separated first by the parents and soon by an ocean: "When you are past New York's gay noise/and out upon the sea/then you may meet new girls and boys/all full of fun & glee./We ask—we pray—we beg—implore/ that you'll not forget me." E. was, of course, aware of Susanna's depression and its cause, but she tried to cheer her up and told her to have a good time: "We miss you terribly, of course, but know that you are going to have a glorious time, so try to be satisfied."

It was apparently too painful for Susanna to hear from E., so she hadn't sent her an itinerary of her travels with addresses to send letters to: "Thee didn't give me an address list, so suppose thee doesn't care for my foolishness—but in case thee should—let me know." She closed the letter with a declaration of love: "With oceans of love—(thee will realize how much that is soon)."

Heartbroken Susanna received many letters from family and friends during her three months of travels in Europe, but none from E., who intentionally hadn't been sent an itinerary with mailing addresses. Susanna understood that her life as E.'s "Wifie" had ended and that she must now start over and face the future as a single woman. She was about to embark on a three-month, first-class tour of Europe, which should help distract and hopefully heal her.

CHAPTER 7

SETTING SAIL IN HER VOICE

In reading the Susanna Collection in sequence, I learned about Susanna's life from the day she was born through her graduation from Swarthmore, a life like most others—full of joy and sorrow, romance and heartbreak, companionship and solitude. I also got to know the people in her life and hear their voices spoken in the letters. I was frustrated, however, not to have heard Susanna's voice. I wanted so badly to read a letter from Susanna, especially a letter to her beloved E. That would not happen: any letters from Susanna to E. had probably long been destroyed. But the collection surprised me, nonetheless, with letters Susanna wrote to her family when she traveled and studied abroad in 1908 and 1914.

What a wonderful surprise to open a letter posted from Gibraltar to Mrs. Howard Parry, the envelope addressed in a somewhat quirky hand. At last—a letter from Susanna. Susanna's first letter to her mother, written mid-ocean aboard the *Slavonia*, is a delightful, long (twelve-page) epistle, which she called her "letter diary," the beginning entries of a travel journal narrating scenes from her first European voyage. Given the intelligence and wit of the letters I had read from her friends, I was not surprised to find an entertaining, well-written account of life on board a luxury ocean liner written by an intelligent, well-to-do young Quaker woman traveling with her aunt, sister, and friends from college.

In the first entry, dated June 19, 1908, the ocean voyage on the *Slavonia* came to life, like scenes from Cameron's *Titanic*: staterooms, salt-water baths before breakfast, stewards bringing cups of bouillon and crackers, long walks on the deck, and shuffleboard. Susanna's perspective was that of privilege, as she looked down on the more common travelers in steerage. She was amused by the life on the deck below hers, a world from which she was separated by her station in life, although she and her fellow travelers took their walks on the steerage deck because the upper deck was crowded with steamer chairs for lounging. "At both ends we can look down upon steerage people, who seem to be having a thoroughly good time. Most of them are on their way home, singing, laughing, playing games or dancing jigs. . . . Last evening one of the steerage men had a violin down there & was playing & singing until quite late. It certainly is funny to see them run when the dinner bell rings. They go swarming down the hatchways like flies after sugar."

From these first entries in her "letter diary," it appears that Susanna was, at last, moving away from her depression and regaining her appetite for life:

> JUNE 20: This morning we are in the Gulf Stream and the water is the most beautiful blue anyone would care to see. There is a slight wind, just enough to make little white caps and vary the appearance of the water. . . . They have swung all the life boats over the railing and put up large awnings, so that you can walk from one end of the hurricane deck to the other as on a delightful shaded porch. It reminds me so much of a porch of a summer hotel. . . . The sunsets, too, are perfectly gorgeous. Last evening the atmosphere was so clear that we were able to see Venus until she went below the horizon in a beautiful red glow like a miniature sun. About that time last evening, Dr. B. came up with his mandolin and played while the girls sang.
>
> JUNE 22: I am getting to love it out here better every day. The sky & ocean are ever changing, and although the days are all more or less alike, still something new and funny is happening. . . . Captain Dunning came down from the bridge and talked to us a good while during the evening. He says our last chance of seeing an iceberg is gone at midnight for our course changes and goes in a more southerly direction. . . . The Capt. says they look like a sail in the

distance in the day time, and at night like a great ball of fire due to phosphorescence.

One can't help but think of the *Titanic* at the mention of icebergs; the *Titanic* would sink about four years after Susanna's crossing, on April 15, 1912. The *Slavonia* herself would be wrecked in the Azores in 1909, just a year after Susanna's voyage, and would transmit the first S.O.S. message; all passengers would be rescued.

June 24: After a day of rough seas, the weather calmed, and passengers played shuffleboard and other games on the upper deck. Susanna and her partner Mr. Watt won at shuffleboard.

June 25: Susanna and Mr. Watt won once again at shuffleboard during the day. The Swarthmore party enjoyed the Captain's Ball in the evening, with a buffet supper and dancing to piano music on the lower deck. Susanna enjoyed dancing with the girls for want of male partners and, with a good jab of rebellion, made a point to let her parents know that the girls had a "fine time" enjoying each other's company:

> There were not half enough boys to go around so we S'more girls mostly danced together, and had a fine time, too. Nome & Mary J. are so funny when they get started. During the Virginia Reel I thought one poor boy would go into hysterics laughing at the latter. . . . We finished with a Paul Jones which was simply great. . . . You run around in a circle until a whistle blows then a grand chain and end by two-stepping around with the person you happen to meet. This is repeated over and over again until you are about ready to drop. Nome had lots of fun with one of the little English officers (Mr. Marshal) who was rather unsteady on his feet (in fact none of the officers could dance at all). She would swing him around corners and into the gutter, or "scupper" as he called it, time & time again. And he just smiled and took it all for a joke. He being English could not see that she would do such a thing on purpose. She's a little imp when she gets started. But we all had a grand good time.

It's heartening to see Susanna at play, having a "grand good time." She seemed to have left depression behind her on American shores.

June 26: Susanna was delighted to win the shuffleboard tournament with her talented partner Mr. Watt: "At 3 pm Mr. Watt and I are victorious in the final game of shuffleboard tournament. I never was champion in anything before, but it certainly is not due to my own playing. In one shot Mr. Watt knocked two of our opponents' white men off of the 10 spot and left his own. He certainly is a wonder."

June 28: Reminiscent of the dove's letting ark-bound Noah know of land nearby, the passengers saw signs that the *Slavonia* was approaching land: "Things begin to happen. Yesterday Dr. B. saw a dove and two of those dragon flies." Then everyone saw land: "About six o'clock . . . Dr. Battin and some other men declared they saw land, especially the light house at Cape St. Vincent . . . as we gradually came nearer, we could see the mountain line and the whole line of a very steep precipice. . . . much farther back in the country we could see the peaks of the mountains and the little group of white buildings, mostly built in the very plain Moorish fashion." Susanna realized, like Dorothy in Oz, that she was no longer at home: "And it was hard to realize that we are so far from home and the whole Atlantic Ocean between us. The point of land we saw today was Portugal. Now we turn southward and go around Spain and into the Mediterranean Sea before we see Gibraltar." So ended the first installment of Susanna's "travel diary" with "lots & lots of love to you both, from Susanna."

An envelope mailed July 6 from Amalfi, Italy, to Susanna's mother contained letters from Beulah and Auntie Sue. Sue's letter enclosed pressed dried flowers from Amalfi. She wrote the letter while all the others were out walking. She had thoroughly enjoyed yesterday's beautiful hotel in Sorrento but was barely tolerating this one, the Hotel Cappuccini, because having once been a monastery, its guest rooms, once the monks' cells, did not appeal to her extravagant taste. She thought she was the oldest and most unattractive member of the traveling party, and probably was: "Mrs. Dickey too is delightful. We are the two extremes— she so dainty & little, very active, & I so big unwieldy & awkward—I never [*sic*] have felt so conspicuously ugly [*sic*] as I am compared with all these young lovely girls." Auntie Sue certainly must have been very out of shape because she wrote that she couldn't climb the steep steps to the hotel with the others but had to be carried up on a chair by four men.

Beulah's letter to her mother revealed her grammatical errors and more simplistic descriptions showing that she was not as bright or imaginative as her older sister Susanna. Beulah and Auntie Sue were quite an amusing pair. We know from previous letters that the Swarthmore girls had nicknamed her "Chubbs," so she was plump like Auntie Sue and just as complaining. She was so accustomed to an easy, privileged life that she tended literally to turn her nose up in the less fortunate quarters. In describing Amalfi, she didn't enjoy her walk "through narrow streets, where only two could pass, almost pitchy dark, with rooms and balconies over the street, and always steps, never a flat straight street, and besides being so dark and dingy, you see dirty Italians, old, crippled people, dirty begging children in dark doorways, and everything is so smelly we can scarcely breathe. . . . then we walked up a street where the people were selling fruit some of which were overripe, and that odor mixed with the garlic and other things was most too much. . . . The drive we took this morning was called the Amalfi drive from Sorrento to Amalfi, it was beautiful but so hot and dusty. . . . the mosquitoes are dreadful." Not exactly descriptions one would find in a travel brochure. Although the rooms in the Hotel Cappuccini were mostly monks' cells, the Parry girls had the best quarters: "S. and I have a bishop's room with a little balcony overlooking the water." Like Auntie Sue, Beulah much preferred the grand hotel in Sorrento: ". . . it was a perfect place, a part of it used to be a palace and has been added to until now it is perfectly beautiful, we had the rooms they always give to the royalty when they come." Although America didn't have royalty, it surely had upper classes to which Auntie Sue, Susanna, and Beulah clearly belonged.

On July 8, 1908, Susanna mailed her mother the second installment of her travel diary from the Grand Continental Hotel in Rome. The first pages were written on board the *Slavonia*:

June 28: Susanna and Auntie Sue walked on deck at night, gazing at the stars, which were unusually clear out on the ocean. Always intellectually curious, Susanna wished she had brought her star chart.

June 29: Swarthmore friends Alice and Nome and sisters Beulah and Susanna got up at 4 a.m. to see the sunrise. "It was perfectly beautiful coming up in back of a tiny little island." They then enjoyed the scenery of southern Spain, including Trafalgar Bay, "the scene of the great naval battle." (The Battle of Trafalgar was fought in 1805, with the Royal Navy led by Admiral Lord Nelson defeating the combined Spanish and French fleets. However, Nelson was shot during the battle and died soon after; he is memorialized in the iconic statue in London's Trafalgar Square.) The *Slavonia* then passed "the town of Tarifa, from which we get our English word tariff . . . about 10 miles to the south we could see indistinctly the great Rock of Gibraltar projecting into the Mediterranean. On our right hand about 7 miles away were the mountains of Africa."

A July 8 letter from Beulah contains a fascinating description of the complex transatlantic communications before satellites. When the ocean liner arrived at Gibraltar and passed the wireless station, "the Captain signaled to them by sending up four flags and they answered by one flag meaning 'alright,' and that is the station that telegraphs to London, and they cable to New York that the boat has passed that point. Dr. Battin says the rate of insurance [*sic*] on the boat changes the minute they pass that point."

Susanna's travel diary continued with the group's stop in Gibraltar. The travelers jumped into small boats, went ashore, and boarded yellow carriages with white curtains drawn by white horses. Their first stop was at the post office to buy stamps and mail the correspondence written on board.

> Everywhere you went there were soldiers on guard, in companies marching through the streets. The whole town shows the influence of military discipline. The rock of Gibraltar itself is covered with stone walls and barricades. Dr. Battin told us that the interior of the rock is honey combed, with passageways and store rooms of ammunition and food supplies. They keep enough provisions on hand to last through a three years siege. Just north of the rock is a strip of neutral land between the English & Spanish possessions. Soldiers of the two countries are stationed on their respective sides. . . . The people were

dressed in the Spanish costumes, nearly every girl & woman had some bright pink or red flower in her coal black hair.

After their tour of Gibraltar, the group boarded the *Slavonia* once again for their Mediterranean voyage toward Naples.

June 30: The party was informed about Italian money and the Naples sites they would visit. After dinner, the stewards performed a minstrel show, which in 1908 was entertaining instead of offensive.

> We had an early dinner as the stewards would have time to decorate the dining room. And we luckily had time to see the beautiful sunset glow. It was the purest pink I ever saw in the sky. The clouds & mere thread of the new moon were exquisite. . . . at 8:30 the dining room had been transformed entirely. A little stage with footlights had been put up at one end, the piano moved in, and the whole place decorated with flags. This Minstrel Show by the stewards was quite a success. Of course, they were funny, all blackened up, and it was lots of fun to guess who was who.

It would take decades for black-faced minstrel shows to become politically incorrect. Al Jolson belonged to the distant future in 1908. He would appear in the wildly popular *The Jazz Singer* in 1927.

July 1: The group had a morning tour of the engine room and boiler room "where the stokeys are kept constantly at work shoveling the coal." In the evening they enjoyed a farewell concert and dance.

July 2: The women had their hair shampooed by the barber, preparing for their upcoming travel, and they prepared their baggage to go ashore. Susanna wrote of the beautiful sunset approach into the Bay of Naples at the end of the day.

> The sunset between the islands and the glow afterwards was perfectly magnificent. . . . Ischia was the first island we saw and then there was the long chain of these great rocky cliffs rising from the water. Quite a while afterward we were able to see a great white cloud which later developed into the peak of Vesuvius. Then as the day light faded, we

could see the lights from Naples come out one by one like the stars. At first they seemed like a long string of diamonds floating on the water. I don't think I ever saw anything as much like fairy land.

Surely our Susanna must have thought of E.'s letter to her about the beauty of the Bay of Naples, where she said they must go together on their honeymoon. However, Susanna was now much too busy to dwell on her sad memories. Her ocean voyage had carried her away on a voyage filled with new experiences and changes of scenery. A busy tour of the Continent awaited her, with stops in beautiful places and stays in luxury hotels, some of which are still hotels today. I would love to retrace Susanna's steps by traveling to her favorite places: a "Susanna Tour."

CHAPTER 8

THE SUSANNA TOUR BEGINS: ITALY

Susanna, Beulah, Auntie Sue, and the rest of the Swarthmore tour group disembarked from the *Slavonia* on July 2, 1908, and checked into the luxurious Hôtel Royal in Naples right on the Bay. This was the very hotel E. wrote to Susanna about three years earlier, where she wanted them to spend their honeymoon. Undoubtedly Susanna thought about E.'s promise: "When thee & I take our long-deferred wedding trip we must spend two weeks in the Hotel Royal, which overlooks that Bay of Azure hue." The hotel was indeed splendid, and unrealized dreams didn't keep Susanna from enjoying her stay, even though her companion was Beulah and not the beloved E. Susanna pasted a picture of the hotel in her travel diary. "The Hotel was immense. Thee should have seen B's and my room. To begin with the floors in all houses in Italy are tiled, then we each had a little bed and all the rest of the furniture was the most beautiful mahogany thee ever saw, wardrobe, tables etc."

July 3: The group walked to the famous aquarium after breakfast. "It is considered about the finest at present and professors come from all over the world to study here. They had lots & lots of different kinds of fish, crabs, coral, star fish and indeed everything which comes from the bottom of the Mediterranean. Even some little sea horses strutting around & prancing as lively as you please."

After the aquarium, they visited all the local tourist attractions:

The Susanna Tour Begins: Italy | 83

> 19.) But by 10.20 we were all packed in a cab and bound for the Hotel Royal. As we passed through the streets we had a very good idea of the way the Italians live. The tables at their restaurants were set out on the pavements & men were sitting around drinking & talking. Some of the streets were very narrow, but every where you looked there were flowers or plants on the high stone walls or the balconies which came out from every window. We have gotten several postals which give a very good idea of the peculiar buildings, step-streets etc. The Hotel was immense. The should have seen B— my room. To begin with the floors in all houses in Italy are tiled, then we each had a little bed and all the rest of the furniture was the most beautiful mahogany I ever saw, Wardrobe, tables etc. Here is a little picture which will give you a fairly good idea of its position. Immediately after breakfast the next morning July 3rd we came out on this street which runs parallel with the bay and walked a short distance to Aquarium. It is considered about the finest at present and professors come from all over the world to study here. They had lots & lots of different kinds of fish, crabs, coral, star fish and indeed everything which comes from the bottom of the Mediterranean. Even some little sea horses strutting around & prancing as lively as you please. It was so interesting to see all these things really alive. The man fed an octopus for us.

Susanna Parry's travel journal from Hôtel Royal, Naples, Italy, 1908.

We took the tramway as it is called and went as far as the museum, where we walked through a funny covered street & looked in the shops . . . took a funny little bus drawn by horses down the main street of the city, the Toledo, by many places of interest. . . . After lunch we were all tired enough to take a nice rest before starting out for a 3 hour drive through the crooked streets of Naples to the old fort and monastery (San Elmo & San Martino) where we had a most beautiful view of the city and the peaks of Vesuvius in the background. When looking down on the red tile roofs and the white houses you can hardly imagine what they look like at close range. Large families live in one room . . . and naturally they use the part of the street around the door for all sorts of domestic duties. Some are working at their trades of wood work, dress making, shoe making, others are combing their hair. But in the midst of all this dirt, the beggar children & donkeys flourish as well as the flowers which are planted in every nook & cranny. Sometimes the little iron balconies which are seen at every window are perfect bowers.

That evening they packed their suitcases for the next day's journey to Sorrento.

July 4: In the morning, the Quaker travelers took rowboats out to the steam launch, crossed the Bay of Naples, and picked up more passengers at Sorrento & Amalfi. At the Blue Grotto, they took rowboats once more to visit the cave, then lunched at the Hotel Grotte Bleue in Capri "out on the terrace under a canopy of a beautiful wisteria vine. The Italian musicians came off the boat and played while we ate. We hear so much Italian music that we are becoming quite familiar with it. Coral was forced upon us at almost every turn."

After lunch, the group proceeded to Sorrento, where the boats landed at the bottom terrace of the Imperial Hotel Tramontano, whose regal accommodations Susanna gushed over as much as Aunt Sue and Beulah:

> It is the most palatial place I ever saw . . . the immense building situated about 125 ft. above sea level was right on the edge of a very steep precipice and on the other side we had a view of the most beautiful Italian garden all laid out with little cement walks, which came out upon little surprises every once in a while, now a little tunnel, bridge, view of the street or sea. . . . Our last dinner ended with a grand strawberry ice & delicious chocolate cake & we all agreed that everyone should see Sorrento, eat that dessert and die happy. Our rooms were all arranged as a suite with a private sitting room & balcony. It is the very same the royalty always use when visiting there. . . . My, it was thrilling! We felt very important.

Susanna pasted a picture of the luxurious hotel in the diary, marking their rooms with private balconies overlooking the sea and garden. After dinner, they watched tarantella dancers in the courtyard. Based on Susanna's account, I would choose Sorrento as the first stop in Italy on the "Susanna Tour."

July 5: Susanna and the girls went for a morning swim "in the Mediterranean before breakfast in the funniest bathing suits thee ever saw, kind of kilt arrangements." After breakfast, they went shopping then

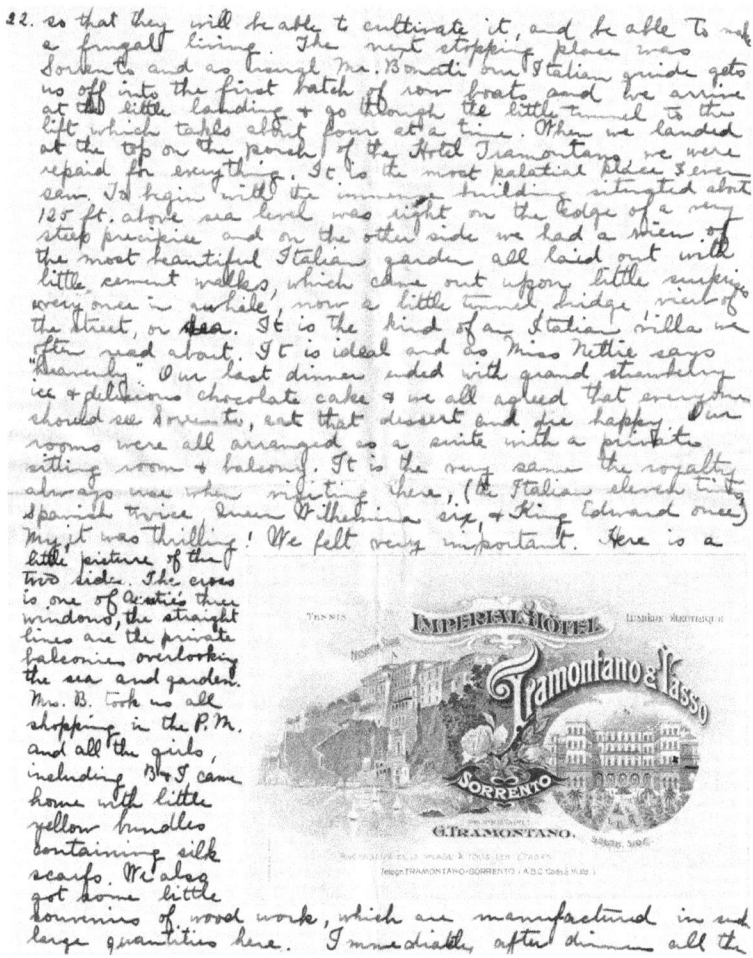

Susanna Parry's travel journal from Imperial Hotel Tramontano, Sorrento, Italy, 1908.

took a trolley ride along the coast to Castellammare, with "a fine view of the bay and Vesuvius all the way."

July 6: The group left Sorrento after an early breakfast, and a five-hour drive to Amalfi via the coastline of the Bay of Salerno took them to Amalfi. Like Beulah's and Auntie Sue's accounts of Amalfi, Susanna's description of the place wasn't at all flattering. Apparently, Beulah wasn't exaggerating. I hope it has improved from what it was 100 years ago, but even so I certainly wouldn't include it on the "Susanna Tour."

> (The Hotel Cappuccini) was once the monastery of the Capuchin monks and is reached by a series of about 160 steps. Auntie & Mrs. Dickey did not attempt them at all but had men carry them up in little chairs. B & I had a room which once belonged to the Abbot but all the rest had just the plain cells of the other monks. It was a very funny old place. . . . But don't talk about the dirt of Naples. It is mild compared to this place. The streets, children & people were filthy. Our narrow street led down a dark, damp, smelly staircase under houses & around corners which were simply terrible. We all willingly consented to come back the long way so as to avoid it all.

Despite the disappointing stop in Amalfi, Susanna, her sister, and her aunt were having a splendid time. "We are all well and I think thee can see from the above that we are enjoying ourselves and having a fine time. Auntie got us each a dear coral necklace on a gold chain in Naples. Lovingly thine, Susanna." Susanna's parents must have been relieved to read that their daughter was healing after her forced separation from E., thoroughly enjoying every day of her European tour.

On July 8, Beulah mailed a letter to her mother from Rome. Beulah's grammatical and spelling errors and lack of poetic vision make her letters far less enjoyable to read than Susanna's. Although she was globally enjoying her travels, Beulah described the unpleasant aspects of each place in greatest detail. Instead of the beauties of the scenery and architecture or the historical interest of the various sites, she mostly seemed to enjoy the regal accommodations and the food. Their hotels "are always the best wherever we go, and we have such grand things to eat, we are getting so fat." She particularly loved the fruits in Italy, especially the cherries. What impressed her the most in Rome was not the Colosseum but the flies: "The flies here are worse than in Naples. We have all changed our mottoes to 'scratch em'—amonia [*sic*] don't [*sic*] seem to have any effect, all the floors are tiled, and are just full of flies, especially in the cathedrals where the poorer people kneel all the time. Nome and I stand on one foot all the time and scratch with the other. I counted 60 on my left leg yesterday morning and had lots more by noon, that is just one leg, they are all over me all down my back where I can't reach them."

Susanna's July 12 letter containing several more days of her travel diary gives an account of Pompeii and Rome far more detailed and interesting than Beulah's.

July 7: This entry begins with an amusing account of Beulah ("Chubbs") apparently suffering from diarrhea after eating too much of the fruit she loved, consequently having to be carried down the 160 steps by porters from the hotel to the carriage in Amalfi, just as Auntie Sue and Mrs. Dickey had been carried up the stairs the day before. "Tuesday morning Beulah did not feel very well on account of having eaten too much fruit, but we started off as usual. Mrs. Battin had the men come up with the funny little chair and carry her down the 160 steps to the carriage."

The group was driven along the bay to Vietri, where they boarded the train to Pompeii. Apparently, Beulah hadn't exaggerated about all the flies: "At the Hotel Diomede we had a lunch, but things did not taste very good because flies were thick over everything on the table. Every once in so often one of the waiters would come around with a little pink or green paper duster and shew them away." Then follows an amazingly detailed description of what everyday life was like in ancient Pompeii before the eruption of Vesuvius destroyed the city and its inhabitants.

> Auntie says that more than half has been excavated since she was here, but in the cork model which we saw the next day in the Naples Museum, there still remains covered almost 2/3 of the entire city. Beulah again rode in state in one of the arm chairs, until we were nearly through, then Auntie slipped on the rough pavement and had a very hard fall, so she rode back to the hotel. . . . There are many

wonderful things in Pompeii. Some of the houses, which have been buried for so many hundreds of years, still have the walls decorated with the most wonderful paintings and mosaic pieces. In the house which has just been excavated . . . we saw a beautiful little medallion in the wall made of gold inlaid, we also saw the remains of a looking glass made with mercury, not of polished brass as they used to use. . . . They even had boilers to cook things by steam. We think we are very advanced, but everything made now is copied from the instruments & utensils of those days. They even had those extensible candle sticks like Auntie's lamp which canse [sic] be raised or lowered at will. But the greatest surprise was to see the traces of lead pipes which had been laid through the streets to carry water from the mountain to the different houses. There were large stepping stones in the middle of the streets so that you can walk dry shod from one pavement to another, but at the same time they do not prevent the chariots from passing. In some places the wheels have worn the stones away, in great ruts. At one of the public fountains, the stones had been worn away where the hands rested as the people leaned over to drink as the water spouted out the mouth of a marble statue. Many of the houses now have the gardens filled with flowers and the fountains going as they used to before the terrible eruption of Vesuvius.

July 8: The group visited the Museum of Art and Sculpture. When Susanna saw statues she had studied in school, "it seemed quite like seeing old friends." Auntie bought both her nieces yet another coral and gold necklace on an afternoon coral shopping tour. After an early dinner, the group boarded a train for Rome, and they arrived at Hotel Continental at midnight.

July 9: The group enjoyed a driven tour of Rome, hosted by the guide, Mr. Gallo, vice president of the Archeological Society of Rome. They visited all the major tourist attractions, including the Trevi Fountain, the Baths of Diocletian, and the Pantheon. "We crossed the Tiber, which is not as beautiful as one would imagine. It's even muddier than the Schulkill [sic], if that could be possible." Then they visited St. Peter's Cathedral and the Sacred Stairs, which according to Catholic legend, were the white marble steps leading to Pilate's praetorium in Jerusalem. From the Quaker point of view, the ritualistic gestures of the Catholics approached idol worship:

> The sacred staircase was the next point of interest. Here is the place where the people come to worship and climb all the way up a long flight of steps on their knees because they suppose that these were the steps that Jesus climbed when he went to see Pilot [sic]. They stop on every step to say their prayers and often stoop to kiss the spots where his blood is supposed to have stained the marble. So many of the people here, rich & poor alike seem to have this blind faith, but it seems more like worship of idols to us. Mr. Gallo says that the latest interpretation is that this flight of steps was that which led up to the Palace of the Lateran where the old, old popes used to live, and that they were not brought here from Jerusalem.

Susanna stopped her travel diary here and prepared it for mailing, even though it was not yet updated. She needed to prepare her bags for the trip to Pisa and Florence.

Susanna's July 20 letter posted from Venice continued the diary with more events from Rome:

July 10: The group visited the Vatican. They first saw the souvenir shops, then St. Peter's "guarded constantly by Swiss guards in gaudy red & yellow suits originally designed by Michael Angelo [sic]" and the Sistine Chapel painted by Michelangelo with "many scenes from the Creation, the prophets, sybils and ancestors of Christ that Beulah has often copied." While Susanna was gifted at wordcraft, Beulah was very artistic, giving much of her time to painting and needlework.

Susanna wasn't impressed by the Colosseum: "The one word 'massive' explains it better than anything else." On the other hand, she waxed poetic about the Cathedral of St. Paul:

> It is the most beautiful cathedral we have yet visited. So simple and refined, yet magnificent . . . the long columns of white marble, the gold mosaics, the frieze of medallions of the popes from the

beginning to the present time, 264 in all and costing $600 each makes the interior very beautiful, but it is not more so than the outside. At one end there is an immense mosaic representing the River of Life. The background is entirely of gold, and as we saw it in the late afternoon sunlight shone most beautifully.

Factoring in the time value of money, each of the 264 medallions costing $600 in 1908 would cost about $15,000 today.

July 11: The group made stops "at the Rospigliose [sic] Palace where we nearly broke our necks looking at Guido Reni's ceiling painting of the aurora"; at the Vatican Museum, its statuary, and library; and at the Council Chamber at Palazzo Spada "to see the statue of Pompey, at the foot of which Caesar was stabbed." Susanna's account of the group's next church visit expressed the Quaker criticism of Catholic ritual:

> The little church of St. Augustine is famous for its image of the Madonna and the Child, which is kept decorated from head to foot with jewels and presents of all kinds made by women who have been cured of sickness through the influence of the Virgin. During our five minute stay many people during their worship came up and kissed the feet of the Virgin and then anointed their heads with oil. There seems to be nothing but form in their religion, especially with the poorer classes . . . it looks as if they were going through with a lot of gymnastic exercises, as the priests jumped up and sat down while they were performing a kind of mass, chanting the service.

The group's long day of tourism in Rome continued with visits to the Appian Way, the Circus Maximus, and then the catacombs of the Church of St. Sebastian. "Here a priest gave us each a little taper to light us in the dark underground passages and vaults where the people had been buried for so many years. Spooky was hardly the term." Far less "spooky" was the group's evening tour of the Colosseum and Forum by moonlight.

July 12: A day much more relaxed than the previous. The group attended a mass at St. Peter's, saw masterpieces of sculpture at the

Capitoline Museum, then visited the Trevi Fountain again, this time everyone throwing coins "so that we all would be sure to come again."

July 13: The group's very busy day began with shopping for silk pictures and jewelry, followed by visits of the mosaics of the American church and the Capuchin Church "where they have the cemetery in five rooms and the walls covered with different designs made of human bones." They then drove over two of the seven hills. By the time they visited the Forum after sunset, the group was suffering from tourist fatigue: ". . . after the sun had gone down in the west, we arrived at the Forum, for the most tiresome part of our sightseeing. We were so tired with looking that we could hardly appreciate it as we should have. To really know anything about it would take months and years of study."

July 14: After an early breakfast, the group took a train to Pisa, where they saw "the Cathedral in which hangs the swinging lamp used by Galileo in his experiments in connection with the laws of gravitation . . . The Campanile or leaning tower is always associated with Pisa, and it was here that Galileo continued his experiments but with a longer pendulum." In Beulah's July 19 letter, which contained an account of the group's trip to Pisa, "Chubbs" complained about having to climb the leaning tower: "We went to the very top, but it made me very dizzy, there were so many steps, and the spiral ones leaning made it very queer to climb."

After Pisa, the group headed to beautiful Florence, which charmed Susanna and is my second stop on the "Susanna Tour": "Then we started on a most beautiful ride to Florence. . . . especially the latter part along the Arno. At the Hotel Grande Bretagne we had beautiful rooms overlooking the Arno. The moonlight and other lights made an exquisite picture. The situation of the hotel could not have been better; it was very near the Ponte Vecchio and central to both places of interest and shopping districts. I like it better than any place we have yet visited except Sorrento." Glued to this page of the diary is a letterhead picture of the hotel right next to the Ponte Vecchio.

July 15: Another busy day: "After breakfast a short walk brought us to the Palazzo Vecchio or old town hall. The great hall on the second floor was where Savonarola was condemned. He was imprisoned in the tower and burned to death in the square." Typical tourists, the group

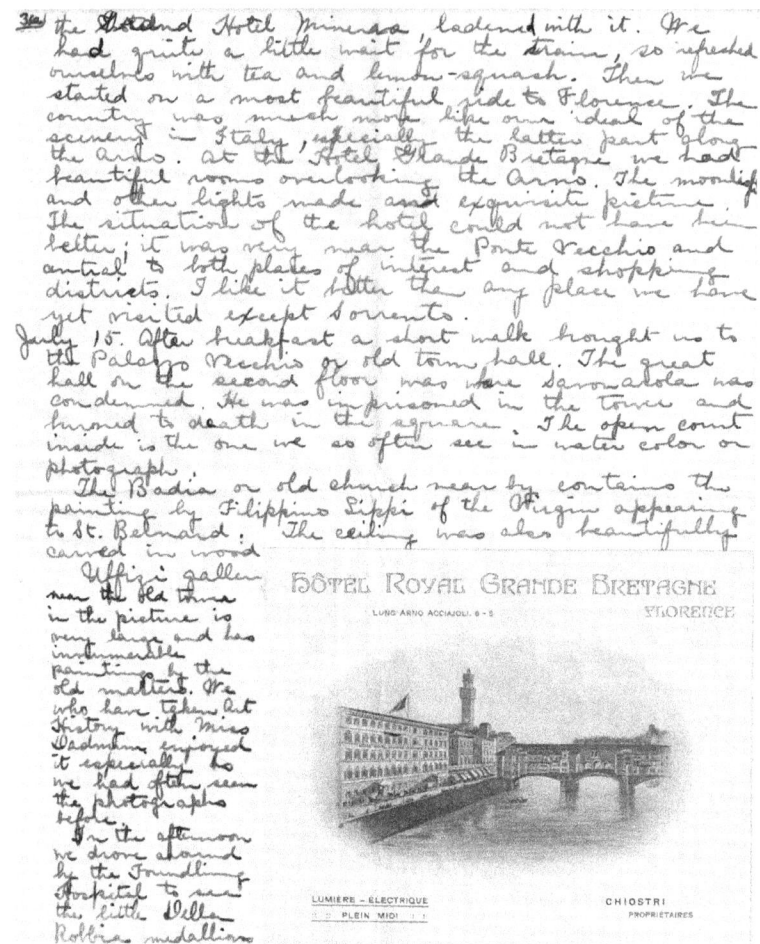

Susanna Parry's travel journal from Hotel Royal Grande Bretagne, Florence, Italy, 1908.

then visited the Badia or old church with its painting by Filippino Lippi of the Virgin appearing to St. Bernard, then to the Uffizi Gallery with its "innumerable paintings by the old masters" which Susanna recognized from her studies. Next, they toured the Florentine mosaic factory, followed by a stop at the Protestant Cemetery where Elizabeth Barrett Browning was buried. "Our road homeward wound down the hillside through the most beautiful arch of trees like a long avenue. The large estates belonging to the villas lined both sides and every once in a while we could see through the iron gates in the high stone wall into some beautiful private garden. The only thing that marred the pleasure was the constant sight of beggars holding out their hands for money. It seems second nature even to the little children."

July 16: The Florentine tourist marathon continued with the "Baptistery which contains the beautiful bronze doors by Ghiberti and Pisano; Giotto's tower with its bas-reliefs; the cathedral with the dome by Brunelleschi considered by some the finest because of its simplicity . . . We are all getting so tired of cathedrals and it is an impossibility to keep them straightened out when we see so many in a day." Susanna's favorite attraction of the day had nothing to do with cathedrals: "Mother, thee would have enjoyed the next place. We got out of the carriages and walked all around in the Boboli gardens of the Pitti Palace. This is the King's home when he comes to Florence and it certainly is beautiful. . . . there are numerous walks laid out. Most of them are covered with ivies or the trees are trimmed to form perfect bowers. These arbors lead down to beautiful fountains filled with fish and surrounded by potted plants . . . pieces of white statuary are tucked around in little niches cut out of the hedges."

July 17: A far more relaxing day, with Pitti Palace shopping then a trolley trip to Fiesole, the Etruscan town on a hillside overlooking Florence.

July 18: In the morning, the group visited the Dominican monastery at San Marco, where they saw Savonarola's cell with his desk and chair, as well as Fra Angelico's frescoes in the cloisters. At the Academy, they saw Michelangelo's David. In the afternoon, they boarded a train for Venice under pouring rain, which traversed forty-nine tunnels. Beulah's July 20 letter describing the trip to Venice is a masterpiece of complaint: "It started to rain before we left Florence, we did not mind it on the train, as it kept the dust away and made it cooler, we passed through 49 tunnels, the first half were awful, as we had to have the windows closed and going up hill all the time their [*sic*] was a great deal of smoke, but the second half was not as bad as we just coasted down the other side of the Appenines." The group couldn't take gondolas from the train station to the hotel by moonlight as originally planned because of the rain; they had to take a steamer which Beulah didn't like at all: "(We) had to take a steamboat that had a top and kept us partly dry. That boat was worse than a ferry boat, dark, with only a small light in the middle, dirty old Italiens [sic] sitting all around with their black shawls, it was enough to scare us, but it only struck us the more funny."

Susanna and her sister once again had luxury accommodations in Venice: the Grand Hotel Danieli "which faces the Lagoon just a little below the place where the Grand Canal & Guidecca meet, and almost next to the Palace of the Doges. Beulah & I had a fine room overlooking the Lagoon, and even in the rain the reflection of the lights in the water was beautiful." Venice is the third destination on the "Susanna Tour." I went online and found the Grand Hotel Danieli, which is still a hotel and still luxurious, even palatial—supposedly once the home of Desdemona and was home to Robert Browning.

July 19: As luck would have it, the group arrived in Venice just in time to witness a sumptuous spectacle: "This is one of the greatest feast days of the year in Venice. . . . About 9 o'clock the celebration in honor of the Feast of the Redeemer began: a long procession of priests, carrying their banners & candlesticks, and arrayed in all their rich golden robes with red, green, and blue trimmings came out of the church of San Marco singing as they walked over through the winding, crooked streets over two pontune [sic] bridges built temporarily of boats to the church of Santa Maria della Salute."

The group then visited one of Venice's most famous churches, the Frari—the Basilica di Santa Maria Gloriosa dei Frari "which contains a most beautiful tomb designed by Canova for Titian, but carried out by the former's pupils for their master after his death." At St. Thomas, they saw paintings by Bellini and Titian. The group traveled in gondolas through the little Venetian canals during the rest of the morning.

"In the evening we again took the gondolas and went out to watch the fireworks & floats and listen to the beautiful music. It all seemed exactly like the 4th of July. The little gondolas crowded around the beautifully decorated band floats by the hundreds. They were just jammed together. But it gave us a good chance to see the Italian customs, etc."

July 20: The group returned to the Academy to admire its masterpieces:

> (Titian's) *Assumption & Presentation of the Virgin* . . . also the dear little lute player by Carpaccio. We also saw many paintings & frescoes in the Palace of the Doges or rulers of Venice. There are some holes in the walls which were once in the form of lions' mouths and it was here that the people dropped their grievances. The doges considered these complaints and people were often imprisoned or killed very unjustly. We went out onto the Bridge of sighs across which so many people went never to return. Then they took us down through the miserable dark dungeons, where no sunlight ever penetrates, and where all food and air came through a hole in the wall. They also used to kill so many people with the guillotine and we saw the place where it formerly stood.

Gondolas then took the group to the island of Murano, where they were fascinated by the craft of the Venetian glassblowers. They were even more thrilled back at their hotel, where the Dowager Queen Marguerite was having lunch.

July 21: Our Quaker tourists began their day with a trip to St. Marks, then to a lace factory: "The girls work for about 5 hours a day for only 16 cents. But as the woman said they are mostly daughters of fishermen and their living is naturally gotten very cheaply." After a shopping excursion in the square of St. Mark's, the travelers took their suitcases in gondolas to the train station and took a train to Milan, whose urbanity Susanna seemed to appreciate: "This city is large, the streets are wide and beautifully clean. Such a relief after Southern Italy. . . . The Hotel Continental is fine."

July 22: After climbing up the 480 stairs to the top of the Milan cathedral and back down again, the group visited yet another cathedral where "there was a mass going on, the organ was playing, the choir singing, the sunlight through the beautiful rich stained glass windows made us want to stay there for the rest of the morning." The group had lunch and anticipated their departure from Milan. "We are now eating lunch and will soon start on our ride to Lake Como, then take a little steamer to Bellagio." So ended this installment of Susanna's travel diary.

The diary continues in the next letter mailed from Munich. The first entry describes the three-hour steamboat ride up Lake Como to Bellagio:

> We were especially interested in the way the women come down to the water's edge to do the washing, they just dip the clothes in the water and then rub them on a board. . . . The Lake is quite large and is surrounded by mountains on all sides. The mountains are terraced sometimes to the very top. At Bellagio the view was even more beautiful. The city or rather town was situated on the point where the two arms of the lake separate. The mountains some of which were snow capped peeped out at times, and everywhere the most beautiful gardens of flowers.
>
> After dinner the younger members of the party went out for about two hours. The sunset was perfectly gorgeous. The pink glow over the clouds & mountains was perfect, as well as the reflection in the water. The old man who rowed our boat was very kind and let B. help him part of the time & told her how well she did it. When we got around to the far side of the peninsula, he made all sorts of queer noises so that we might hear the fine echo. As it began to grow darker the search light began its night work of travelling along the shores of the lake looking for smugglers. We had quite a time trying to guess what the bells were; some thought they were cow bells on the mountain side, and others a little bell buoy, but the next morning Dr. B. laughed at us very much and said that it was a series of little bells the fishermen put on their nets so that they can be found in time of fog.

July 23: The group took a steamer across Lake Como, where the gardens enchanted Susanna at the Villa Carlotta:

> Villa Carlotta, the spring home of one of the Grand Dukes. . . . The main attraction of the place was the immense Italian garden with its winding paths, arbors of lemon and wisteria, and flowers of all kinds everywhere. . . . whole groves of bamboo, Japanese varieties of

grasses, different kinds of cacti. The beds were not arranged in any set way but put together so beautifully that they seemed to grow there naturally. . . . The precipice which led down from the palace was terraced & covered with roses, the little fountains half way down were nearly hidden with maiden hair fern growing in profusion; while the large one at the base was filled with beautiful water lilies and water hyacinths.

Add Bellagio and Lake Como to the "Susanna Tour." The next day the group would say *arrivederci* to Italy and head to Switzerland.

CHAPTER 9

TRAVELS CONTINUE: SWITZERLAND, GERMANY, THE NETHERLANDS, BELGIUM

July 24: The group left Bellagio, Italy, and traveled to Lucerne, Switzerland, which required three boat trips and two train rides through mountain tunnels. "At Fluelin we took the steam boat up the beautiful Lake Lucerne through the Wilhelm Tell country, past his chapel & the place where he had his meeting with the representatives of the cantons. Farther up the lake was the famous Schiller stone, and the place where Wagner lived while he was writing Tannhauser and other of his great operas." Susanna pasted a picture of their hotel in her diary—Grand Hôtel du Lac Lucerne with its view of Mt. Pilatus and the old tower bridge built in the thirteenth century.

After resting at the hotel for several hours, the group went to the cathedral for a concert of organ, voice, and violoncello. After dinner, they went to see the lion of Lucerne, then slept under the novel feather beds: "They were so light and airy that we hardly felt the weight of them at all."

July 25: In the morning, the group went shopping at the marketplace, a feast for the eyes with "vegetables, fruits, flowers (potted and cut), meats, cheese & butter, etc. Even a kind of daisy that they use for tea." This daisy was probably chamomile, which wasn't widely used in the U.S.

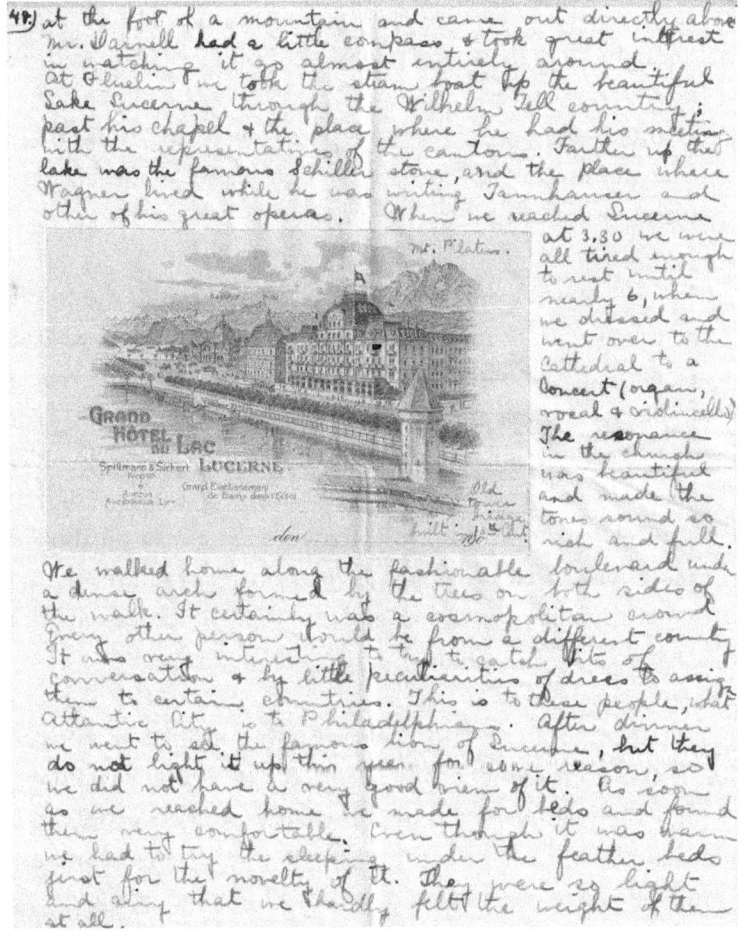

Susanna Parry's travel journal from Grand Hotel du Lac Lucerne, Lucerne, Switzerland, 1908.

After the marketplace, the group went shopping for embroidery, which they thoroughly enjoyed because one hundred years ago, girls were taught needlework as part of their education at home. "At the embroidery shop that Mary Lippincott told us about, we had a fine time. Everything was done exquisitely. It was a good thing the checks we just had cashed weren't any larger. B. says to tell thee she has laid in a supply of handkerchiefs for the next 3 yrs. We got several little things that would be nice for Christmas presents. B. & Nome were just in their element and rushed around like mad from one place to another getting bargains. It is just as it always is at home. B. always beats me in that." Typical sibling rivalry: Susanna thought Beulah was better at shopping; Beulah said Susanna was the better letter-writer.

In the afternoon, the group took a trolley to the funicular, which went up the mountainside for a panoramic view of the city and lake below and the sound of the Alpine yodel.

> The evening was spent on our own balcony out from Auntie's room and the two just below it. From these points of vantage, we had a magnificent view of the fireworks on the lake. The hotels were all illuminated, as well as the bridges. Ships were decorated with different colored lanterns and towed around in a regular procession. Then they anchored and began bombarding a little fort-like float with fireworks. We think ours in Riverton are pretty, but these went off about six times as fast, often as many as ten or more rockets in the sky at once. About the last piece was a magnificent thing which looked like a sheaf of wheat.

Susanna's next long, descriptive letter to her mother was postmarked July 30, 1908, containing pages 51 to 62 of her travel diary. I am impressed by the volume of this ongoing correspondence and am certain that such lengthy epistolary expression is a rare if not extinct art form today. I miss the days when I would sit down for an hour to write a chatty letter to a friend or be delighted to recognize a friend's handwriting on an envelope. Nowadays, standard correspondence between people is quickly accomplished by sitting down in front of the computer or phone to shoot off a short e-mail or even shorter text. I have conceded to e-mail communication but still refuse to initiate texts. And I shall never tweet.

July 27: The Swarthmore group left Lucerne and traveled toward Munich, taking a train through the Brünig Pass to Lake Brienz, then a boat ride to Interlaken, where they stopped for the night. "The cog and pinion roads used so much in these mountains, with their funny little open cars and the powerful engines which pulled five of the cars up a very steep grade, took us through the Lauterbrunnen to Kleine Scheidigg. The ride up was wonderful. We had a fine view of that famous waterfall, a sheer leap of 980 feet. It is quite a stream at the top but falls on the rocks below as a fine mist. The other smaller ones were just as fine and in a way more beautiful because they were more irregular."

Their hotel in Interlaken was near the little train station, about five miles from the massive Jungfrau glacier. The young and fit in the group took a walk toward the Jungfrau before dinner, but "Miss Nettie, B. and I could not keep up the pace, so after resting at the top of the second hill walked back slowly to the hotel and gathered flowers on our way. It seemed so funny to have all these lovely Alpine plants blooming almost in a snowdrift. We threw some snowballs and washed each other's faces just for the fun of it." Lovely to see Susanna at play in the snow at the end of July.

Susanna continued to be touched and awed by the Swiss countryside:

> After dinner we put on our sweaters and went out to see the sunset glow on the mountains. At times we could see all four peaks . . . The Jungfrau is the highest in this part of the Alps. Just to the right is the peak of Silberhorn which is always covered with snow. To the left is Monch and Eiger. We thought we were very fortunate in having such a beautiful view of the mountains, especially as we were only there overnight.
>
> July 28: I don't think I shall ever forget the view I had from our window about 3 o'clock in the morning. The air was perfectly clear and it was still early enough for the stars to be shining brightly. Around the edge of the eastern mountains was a faint red glow of the rising sun, which far down in the valley below were the lights of the peasants' little chalets, and on all sides we could hear the sound of the cow bells as they grazed on the hillside. It certainly was very different from anything I had ever experienced before, and made me think of the Christmas pictures of the shepherds on the hills around Bethlehem. I do wish you all could have seen it.

At this moment, Susanna was perfectly at peace.

After breakfast, they descended the other side of the mountain to Grindelwald, then changed cars at Interlaken, Bern—the Swiss capital, and Zurich to arrive finally at St. Gallen. At Hotel Hecht, the very tired travelers went to bed right after dinner.

July 29: The group woke up to a rainy day and visited two old churches of St. Gallen "with their superabundance of decoration... many old manuscripts of the Nibelungenlied and German bibles. The two greatest curiosities were the inlaid wooden floor and the pictures of Christ's head written in the passion of Christ."

Then more travel: train, boat, and another train to Munich, "where the women seem to be doing most of the work; in the fields they average about 3 or 4 to 1 man, they do all the street cleaning, oiling the car tracks, and turning of the switches. Dr. Battin says that it is almost a life position, so they are very glad to do it." Susanna was intrigued by the German women doing full-time, paid railroad work, jobs unavailable to women in the U.S. The weary Quaker travelers settled in at the Hotel Bellevue in Munich.

July 30: A busy day of tourism: "We visited first the art gallery of the old masters of the Italian and Flemish schools, and recognized as old friends many of the pictures we had learned... Murillo's little Italian beggar boys, a fine interior by Pieter de Hooch as well as many by Holbein and Velasquez."

After lunch, the tourists took a long car ride through the English park and saw the "Royal Brewery, which is a beer garden and lunch counter combined, very much like the automats in Philadelphia where you wait on yourself." They then visited Shock's Gallery and monuments of victory and finally stopped "on the other side of the town before the Bavaria which is much like our own Statue of Liberty."

Susanna and the Quaker girls had quite an adventure after dinner and drank beer, surely for the first time:

> In the evening all except Auntie, Mrs. Dicky and Mrs. B. went to the Lowenbrau, or Lion beer garden to see it at night. It is just exactly like the pictures, people sitting around at the small round tables under the trees, the band of music on a raised platform near the center of the garden, the fountain where the maids go to wash the beer steins, and the counter where the barrels of various kinds of beers are found. We

of course had to do as the Germans do; so we had beer and pretzels. The latter both large and small were grand, but the former—oh my! Mr. Thatcher presented each of the seven girls with little souvenir beer steins with the lion prancing around on its hind feet.

July 31: The group visited the modern art gallery and sculpture gallery in the morning. Susanna liked Munich and was particularly impressed by the working women, this time the street cleaners: "Munich is a beautiful city, such wide streets, fine trees and large houses. There are a great many autos, tooting around at all hours of the day and night. And it is such a relief not to see beggars around as in Italy. But the streets are kept beautifully clean by women instead of men as at home." In the evening, the group enjoyed a vaudeville dinner theater.

August 1: The travelers hit the road again, leaving Munich for Nuremberg. "Now we begin to see the large fields of hops growing on the poles or strings; also the planted pine forests; the neat little villages always with the church spire in the center looming above the red tile roofs of the whitewashed houses." They checked into their hotel, the Wurttemberger Hof. Susanna delighted in the quirky nature of Nuremberg, except for the instruments of torture in the old tower.

> This is the quaintest old town we have been in yet, perhaps with the exception of Gibraltar. The houses are very peculiar with the steep slanting roofs and windows peeping out like eyes at different heights. Every window in a straight wall contains a box just filled with the most beautiful deep geraniums, and consequently the glimpses down the crooked streets are very fascinating. In the old tower we saw the old instruments of torture which were used up to the beginning of the 19th cent. when Nürnberg [the German name of Nuremberg] ceased to be a free city. They nearly made us sick to look at them. But the buildings nearby with the plastered walls and dark brown wooden beams fastened on the outside, and the brilliant window boxes, were all perfect.

In the afternoon, they visited the old museum of local culture with peasant costumes and interiors, Albrecht Dürer's home, the Gooseman fountain, "and the Ring in the market place which we all turned in order to insure our getting a husband sometime in the future." I guess Susanna and Beulah didn't turn the ring in the right direction, as neither of them would marry.

August 2: A rare and much appreciated day of rest. The girls stayed at the hotel to gather for a sewing bee and write letters and postcards.

August 3: In the morning, the group traveled from Nuremberg to Würzburg, where they toured the Royal Palace of the Prince Regent, whose opulence didn't impress the Quaker girls who preferred their own homes. "The Palace of course was an immense affair, with any number of rooms built around seven courts. But everything had that stiff, cold air, just as if you had to stand off in awe and not touch anything. One room was built almost entirely of painted looking glass and cost nearly 2 million dollars. They were all decorated very much in what is called the rococo style, but there is no real beauty to it. We all preferred our own homes, many times over, to such a place."

In the afternoon, they boarded a train for Heidelberg and the Hotel de L'Europe. At night they took in the illumination of the old Castle on the Hill followed by fireworks.

On August 8, 1908, Susanna mailed the next installment of her travel diary from the Bible Hotel in Amsterdam. The entries detailed the group's tour of Heidelberg and Frankfurt. Susanna found the name of the hotel amusing: "How is this for a name of a hotel? But it doesn't seem to phase us in the least, we just keep on in our same way without feeling at all religious. Tomorrow we are going to leave entirely and spend the day at the Island of Marken that Tommy is so crazy about. We are going to take our Kodaks and expect we will snap everything in sight. But this was to be a diary and not a prophecy, so I will have to turn backward a few days to the stay in Heidelberg." (It might seem surprising that the girls were using Kodak cameras, but George Eastman introduced the first Kodak camera in 1888.)

August 4: Their first day in Heidelberg, the girls witnessed a sickening mock fencing duel or *mensur*, a chilling rite of passage for university students in Germany at the end of the nineteenth and beginning of the twentieth centuries; the victor was not the student who scored the hit but the one who took the hit and forever after carried a visible scar, usually on the face, as a sign of courage. This sadomasochism of the *mensur* was a dark whisper of the cruelty to come from the Germans in the two world wars on the horizon.

> The morning after we arrived in H., . . . we drove around to see a mensur, or duel that is not in earnest. It is just about time for the large University of 750 students to close for a short vacation, so they are trying to settle up all the petty quarrels in short order. They therefore hold the duels every morning . . . They certainly were awful and none of us felt like watching them very long and went into the student prison gladly to forget the other. Whenever the boys cut classes too often or commit some other similar offense they are put in this prison for a proportionate number of days. Dr. B. says that they all do something early in the year, so that they may have the experience. The walls, floors, ceiling, stoves & chairs were all decorated with silhouette pictures of the offenders, in some cases even photos were plastered to the wall.

The group then visited the old castle, which they had seen illuminated with "Greek Fire" the night before. Although its walls were seventeen feet thick, the castle was in ruins for the most part. Its wine cellar, however, was impressive: "The large old wine cellar still contains the large barrels or tanks that held the wine, the most wonderful one was large enough to have a dance platform on top . . . Just above this was the banquet hall and in the adjoining room was a pump used to draw the wine right up for the feasts and big dinners."

In the afternoon, they headed to Frankfurt. They loved the luxurious Palast-Hotel Frustenhof, where Auntie had a private bathroom. She let all the girls treat themselves to hot baths: "The girls engaged the tub for hours ahead. It was fine to have all the hot water we wanted, and we did all the family washing for a week or so." After dinner, they saw the *Flying Dutchman* at the Grand Opera House, which was "much more beautiful on the outside than anything we have in Phila." They were surprised by the intermission they had never experienced in America. "After the second act nearly everybody got up and went out, so we wanted to see what was doing [*sic*] too. Outside they promenaded up and down, made social calls on their friends, ate all kinds of refreshments, etc. for about ten minutes until a little bell rang for them to return to their seats. It is entirely different from anything we have in America, but it seems like a fine custom."

August 5: "We walked to Goethe's house and the little adjoining museum, where are still kept many things connected with his childhood. We saw the little theatre given to him by his grandmother when he was about seven years old. He used to write plays, and then give them with little figures on strings, for the amusement of his little friends." In the evening, they went to the impressive Palm Garden. "They have hot houses galore, of all sorts of rare plants. Thee would have gone wild over the begonias, fuschias, palms, cacti, orchids, and many others whose names we did not know. Outside were beautiful rose gardens, summer houses covered with blue clematis near the tennis courts, and around in front of the large building magnificent beds in set designs. It seemed that every flower in the bed was at the same stage of development."

August 6: The group left Frankfurt, taking a train to Biebrich, then a longboat down the Rhine through the mountains to Cologne, reading *Legends of the Rhine* as they sailed by the ruins of castles. They visited the cathedral in Cologne, then settled in at the Hotel Disch.

August 7: A heavily charged day for our tourists. In the morning, they visited the Walhaf-Richarts art gallery, the market square, and the "Church of St. Ursula, where we saw the caskets, gold busts, bones, etc., of the 11,000 virgins who were massacred over 500 years ago." After dinner, they boarded a train for Amsterdam and stayed at the Bible Hotel, "which derives its name through the possession of a very old Dutch bible."

August 8: The day began with a rather disappointing visit to the Royal Palace of Queen Wilhelmina: "everything was so covered up for the summer that we did not get a very good idea." However, the subsequent visit of the Rijksmuseum was far more interesting: "Upstairs in the art gallery we saw many of Rembrandt's masterpieces, lots of the Dutch School, such as Pieter de Hooch's interiors, Gerard Don's candle lights and Ruysdael's landscapes. We could not get out of there without buying little copies on post cards." My heart skipped a beat when I read this account of the trip to the Rijksmuseum, at the end of which the Parry sisters bought copies of the paintings they had seen. The framed print which my mother brought back from Susanna's estate sale and which was passed down to me was *Dutch Interior* by Pieter de Hooch, signed on the back of the frame by Beulah Parry and dated 1908: she must have bought it then and had it framed upon her return to the States. Now I know the story behind this inherited treasure. Another puzzle piece in place.

The visit to the Rijksmuseum continued with a look at what must have been Impressionist paintings: "Down on the lower floors were the fine modern pieces that are so soft in coloring and in some cases appeal to us so much more."

After lunch, they enjoyed a carriage ride around Amsterdam, the "Venice of the North . . . Although like the Italian Venice in its canals, it is very different. There are horses everywhere, the streets are wider and cleaner, many of them are lined with trees; here the dogs pull around the brass kettles of milk in little wagons, there it was delivered in gondolas. But here especially we notice the effect of unstable foundations for the houses many of them look very tipsy, either leaning over the street or away from each other."

The day ended with a trip to the Delft store. Susanna chose to stay in that evening and write her travel diary instead of going out for more shopping with the others: "In the evening I started this while some never-tired-of-walking people went out for another stroll through the shopping district."

August 9: The group enjoyed a canal tour on a private launch, including a stop on the Island of Marken. They were amused at the children in native costume and the little Dutch houses:

> The girls in their full skirts, aprons, and little close fitting caps just showing their curls and bangs; the boys and men in the full knee trousers looked almost as if they might have borrowed a pair of our gym bloomers. . . . These were all fishing villages and the houses were very small two or three room affairs, but beautifully clean. One room

that we saw through an open door had such a high polish on the floor that the reflection of the brass kettle stretched half way to the door. . . . I forgot to tell thee about the rows and rows of dishes in the Marken houses that lined the walls almost up to the ceiling and made the rooms look like showrooms of a store. Another thing the people did that amused us was the way they stepped out of their wooden shoes just outside of their doors and then walked around inside in their stocking feet. It was a good way to tell how many of the family were at home.

Susanna ended her letter to her mother here because she had to pack her trunk for tomorrow's trip to The Hague.

I am adding Amsterdam to my list of cities on the Susanna Tour, but none of the others before in this chapter. I visited Lucerne when I was a college student; although the panoramic view from the top of Mt. Pilatus was exhilarating, I wasn't overly impressed by the town and would probably not return to give it a second chance. I have similar feelings about Munich: the Rathaus-Glockenspiel mechanical clock and the beer halls were fun, but I wouldn't return there. I would, however, go back to Amsterdam in a heartbeat. I was disappointed that the Rijksmuseum was closed for renovations when I was there, but I loved the "tipsy" houses along the canals and was pleasantly surprised by the very good restaurants. Susanna and the others arrived too late for all the spring tulips and other flowers around Amsterdam; my favorite day in Holland was visiting the must-see Keukenhof Garden, which Susanna couldn't have seen because it wasn't open to the public until 1950. Our Quaker girls, of course, didn't visit Amsterdam's smoking cafes: theirs was a world before popularized marijuana. And Susanna, of course, didn't see the Anne Frank House: hers was a world before Hitler. Hers was also a world that had not experienced a world war—hers a world that would not remain innocent for long.

August 10: The group's train from Amsterdam arrived at The Hague, and the girls took a carriage ride "to the Royal Palace of Queen Wilhelmina. It seemed much more homelike and nice than the others we had seen. We went through her private dining room (sat in her chair), her drawing room, the East India Room given by some of her subjects for a wedding present." They then "drive through lovely streets and beautiful woods to the 'House in the Woods' where the first Peace Conference was held. The Orange Room was of course the most important, but it now is entirely empty, the frescoes on the walls were hard to look at because the floor was so terribly slippery we were afraid of taking a header any minute. . . . In a vacant field nearer the center of the city, Andrew Carnegie has started the building in which the Peace Conference will meet in the near future."

This mention of the Peace Conferences and Andrew Carnegie's building fascinated me, so I researched. There were indeed Peace Conferences at The Hague in 1899 and 1907, also known as The Hague Conventions. The first Conference of 1899 was initiated by Tsar Nicholas II and gathered in the Orange Room of what Susanna called the "House in the Woods," the Huis ten Bosch Palace; the twenty-six nations in attendance extended the 1864 Geneva Conventions to the seas, and the rules were in large part based on the Lieber Code of conduct established by President Abraham Lincoln in 1863 to instruct Union soldiers on how to conduct themselves in war. The second convention, which President Theodore Roosevelt initially called for in 1904, was delayed until 1907 because of the war between Russia and Japan; the forty-four nations in attendance expanded the focus of the rules at sea and established a Permanent Court of Arbitration. The third convention was scheduled to take place in 1915, and Andrew Carnegie donated the money to finance the construction of the Peace Palace. The Carnegie Foundation was established for this project and owns and operates the building to this day. Construction was started in 1907—this is the building site that Susanna referenced. The Peace Palace would be finished in 1913. Sadly, the third conference scheduled for 1915 would never take place due to the outbreak of World War I. Germany would violate many of the conventions established by the first two Peace Conferences by invading Belgium without warning and using the horrific poison gas. After World War II, the Nuremberg Trials would use the rules established by the 1907 Hague Convention as the basis for judgment, claiming that all nations needed to abide by these rules whether or not they were signatories. Today, the Peace Palace is the home of the United Nations' International Court of Justice and is open to the public. For this reason and the lovely surroundings, I am adding The Hague to the Susanna Tour.

Back to Susanna's travel journal: After lunch at the Hotel Paulez, the girls visited a small art gallery where they saw Rembrandt's self-portrait and *The Anatomy Lesson*. They then took a trolley to the seaside resort of Scheveningen.

August 11: The travelers left The Hague and took a morning train to Delft, Rotterdam, and Antwerp, and another train to Brussels where they visited a lace shop and settled down for the night at the Hotel Metropole.

August 12: After a rather lackluster day of sightseeing in Brussels on a cold and rainy day, they boarded a train for Paris.

CHAPTER 10

PARIS

On the Susanna Tour, I must include Paris, by far my favorite city, even though Susanna's first impression of the City of Lights was less than welcoming. The Swarthmore group arrived in Paris at 11 p.m. On the way to their hotel, "one of the first sights was a drunken man making up with the lamp post." The weary travelers found the enormous Palais d'Orsay Grand Hotel quite overwhelming: "we almost get lost in the immense hall as we search for our rooms. It is a good five-minute walk from the elevator."

The next installment of the travel diary arrived in an August 16, 1908, letter on stationery from the Palais d'Orsay Grand Hotel. When I saw the etching of the hotel on the letterhead and envelope, the sprawling building on the banks of the Seine looked very familiar. I know Paris quite well, having lived there as a junior-year-abroad student and having visited many times when I first lived in France. The palatial building certainly looked like the Musée d'Orsay, the art museum which used to be the train station—La Gare d'Orsay. I knew the building as an abandoned train station in my student days, but I didn't know there was once a hotel there. After some research online, I discovered that, indeed, the museum had once been a train station and a hotel. The hotel where Susanna and Beulah stayed in 1908 was built on the site of the Palais d'Orsay, which was completely burned by the communards in 1871. A new beaux-arts train station and an attached hotel were built on the site of the ruined palace in time for the 1900 world's fair. The main lines of the train station were closed in 1939, but the hotel remained open until around 1970 when I was a student. The government transformed the abandoned yet architecturally significant station and hotel into the enormous Musée d'Orsay, which opened in 1989 and houses French art from 1848 to 1914, including the world's largest collection of Impressionism and Post-Impressionism—my favorites. When I visited the Impressionist collection of the museum, it is quite possible that I walked through

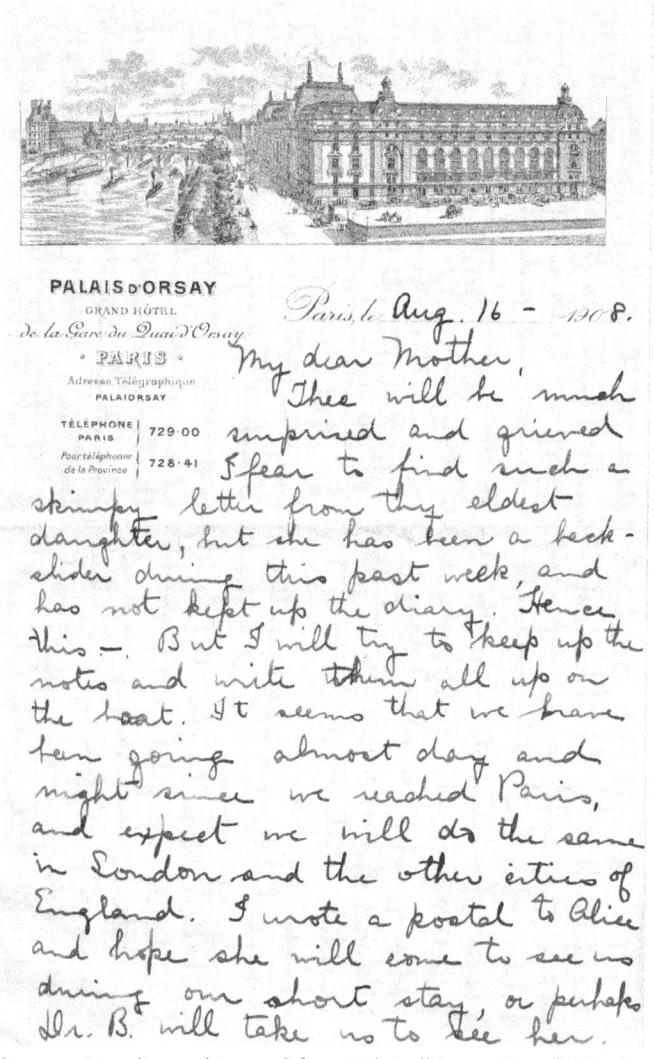

Susanna Parry's travel journal from Palais d'Orsay Grand Hotel, Paris, France, 1908.

what was previously Room 310 of the hotel—where my distant cousin Susanna stayed in 1908. Yet another goosebumpy coincidence in my genealogical adventure with the Susanna Collection.

Susanna's letter joked about the enormity of the Hotel Palais d'Orsay: "This is about the largest hotel I have ever been in. It is really quite an effort to go to the room. Beulah timed herself one day, just for fun to see how long it took to go from the elevator to Room 310 at her usual rate of speed and found it exactly three minutes. How is that for a walk when you have forgotten something." The next time I'm in the Musée d'Orsay, I shall certainly try to find Susanna's room—a three-minute walk from the elevator on the third floor.

Susanna appeared to be suffering from traveler's burnout, as she was no longer numbering the pages of her travel diary and hadn't kept up with the accounts of her travels. She and the girls had been "going almost day and night since we reached Paris, and expect we will do the same in London and the other cities in England."

The group did the usual tourist excursions while in Paris. They first visited Montmartre and the Church of the Sacred Heart—*Sacré Cœur*—with its panoramic view of Paris. Then the Louvre, about which museum-weary Susanna didn't give any details. She did, however, go into great critical detail about their evening in the old opera house—the beautiful edifice of *Phantom of the Opera* fame: "Then in the evening the twelve of us . . . went to the Grand Opera to hear *Samson and Delila*. But we were somewhat disappointed. The one at Frankfurt had been so very good that I expect our hopes were pitched too high. The opera was short, so they had a regular ballet afterwards, which kept us there until nearly twelve o'clock. The dancing was all right but the pantomime between was so long drawn out that we all got extremely sleepy. The building itself though is perfectly beautiful, especially the staircase and foyer in front. Between the acts we went out and walked around these places to see the people. Some were eating in the buffet but most were walking up and down to show off their pretty clothes. This is the off season though and the dressing was nothing wonderful."

Susanna sounded a bit like her Auntie Sue here, not at all impressed by the clothes of the Parisian off-season opera crowd.

The next day Susanna was impressed by the beautiful stained glass at Ste. Chapelle, which is one of my favorite places in Paris on a sunny day. The tourists next visited the Sèvres porcelain factory and then took automobiles to Versailles: "We went through the two palaces. The larger one can accommodate at least 10,000 people for any length of time. It has about 17,000 rooms. Then we walked through the carriage house with its golden chariots of state. They were very beautiful to look at but such a waste of money."

With the group's Parisian visit at an end, they planned to take an early train the next day and stop at Canterbury on their way to London. Susanna told her mother that she had written her cousin Alice—our Alice Paul—who was currently working at a settlement house in London. After she completed her studies at Woodbrooke, Alice had been offered a full-time paid position at a settlement house in Dalston, a poor neighborhood of London. By the time Susanna arrived in England, Alice had switched to part-time work at the Peel Institute settlement house and attended classes at the London School of Economics. Susanna, who hadn't seen Alice for a very long time, hoped to see her busy cousin when the touring group arrived in England: "I wrote a postal to Alice and hope she will come to see us during our short stay, or perhaps Dr. B. will take us to see her."

Alice had realized that social work was not her calling by that time. Frustrated by wasting her time babysitting women and children enslaved by poverty, she preferred taking action to attack the causes of their poverty. When she heard Christabel Pankhurst speak in Birmingham in December 1907 about suffrage for women, she found her glorious obsession—getting the vote for women so they could effect change for themselves—and soon began to work with Christabel and her mother, Emmeline, the leaders of the militant group of suffragettes—the Women's Social and Political Union. By the time Susanna arrived in England in 1908, Alice had already marched in two suffrage parades, joined the WSPU, attended weekly meetings, and learned the art of organizing and publicizing demonstrations. Having reduced her full-time social work to part-time had freed her schedule for the work she really wanted to do: help women by working with the WSPU.

Research shows that Susanna, Beulah, and Auntie Sue did, in fact, meet up with Alice in London in August 1908, as Beulah wrote to Alice's mother about the visit, saying that Alice seemed "very happy and well, but does not know when she is coming home!"[1] As we shall see, Alice had no intention of coming home just yet.

CHAPTER 11

COMING HOME

The Quaker travelers left Paris and headed to England to finish their tour. After stops in Canterbury, London, and Melrose in Scotland, they returned to London, their last stop. They stayed at the St. Ermin's Hotel in St. James Park; in the last letter of her travel diary, Susanna included a postcard of the impressive hotel, marking which room was Auntie's and which was Susanna and Beulah's. St. Ermin's is still a luxury hotel today. If I were to travel to London, I would certainly love to stay there if I could afford it. However, I'm not a big fan of London. Although I enjoyed visiting the Dickens House, Westminster Abbey, and the lovely parks during my stays in London, first in 1970 and again in 1984, I didn't find much architectural beauty in the city. In World War II, much of London was destroyed by the German blitzkrieg, and many of the replacement buildings stood as witnesses of efficient but unattractive postwar construction. Perhaps the look of the city has evolved since then, or perhaps as a tourist, I didn't see the best neighborhoods, but that's the London I remember. For this reason, I'm not including London on the Susanna Tour. I would, however, love to have seen the London that Susanna saw.

The group sailed home as planned on August 29 on Anchor Line's *California*, arriving in New York on September 6, 1908.

The next letter in the collection is dated September 4, 1908, written to Beulah and Susanna in Riverton from their mother at the Dufferin Hotel in New Brunswick. Their parents were heading north to Nova Scotia in hopes of alleviating Howard Parry's recurring problem of hay fever. (At the turn of the last century, the only available option for allergy

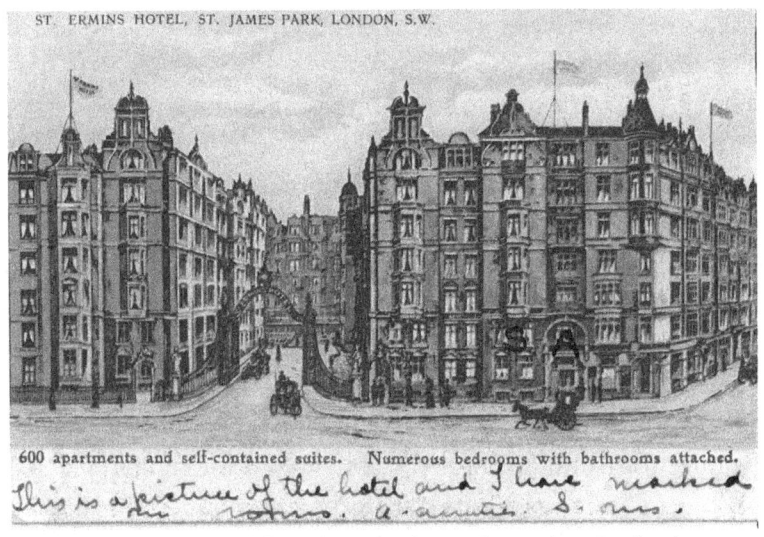

Susanna Parry's postcard from St. Ermin's Hotel, London, England, 1908.

sufferers was to take in the salt air; the first antihistamines were discovered in the 1930s and weren't widely used until the 1940s.) Mother Lizzie seemed most taken by the shopping in New Brunswick: "The furs here are just beautiful and so much more reasonable than with us. Such beautiful sables, beavers, & white fox."

Susanna and Beulah must have been suffering a terrible let-down after their transatlantic vacation, having to keep watch over the homestead in Riverton with Auntie Sue while their parents were away. In her next letter, Lizzie wrote that she didn't want to leave her girls so soon after their return from Europe, but Howard's health had not been good: "it was necessary for Father to do something, not allow the cough to settle. . . . Father not so well now we are off of the salt water." They planned to stay away from Riverton for another month until after the first frosts. She told her girls not to feel burdened by the housekeeping: the household help could do most of the work—Alice, Martha, and Arthur, who were probably live-in. She told them: "Try to keep well & have a good time in your own experience of housekeeping." For Susanna, it must have been like going from the sublime to the ridiculous to keep house in Riverton with her aunt and sister after her graduation from Swarthmore, two transatlantic crossings, and a first-class European tour.

Lizzie's next letter was dated September 12 from Ellis House in Port Maitland, Nova Scotia. She said there were many people with hay fever at the hotel. "Father is feeling better he has turns yet but eyes are stronger but lips covered with fever blisters. He is sitting on porch in the sun it feels good, he says." Obviously, Lizzie didn't have Susanna's mastery of grammar: her letters were full of run-on sentences and punctuation errors. Nor did she have Susanna's eye, which always noted the beauty of the natural world around her.

Lizzie gave her girls detailed instructions about running the household: where to buy more canning jars, getting rose cuttings ("slips") from Aunt Lydia (my great-grandmother Lydia Satterthwaite Parry, the Betsy Ross connection), and putting vegetables in salt for making pickles later. "Don't forget to put lids on those jellies of crab apple or the mice will eat the parafine [sic]." What, I wonder, did our Susanna feel about her future of domesticity? Talk about being in a pickle.

Lizzie seemed concerned about her girls' social skills. Perhaps Auntie Sue had written her sister that Susanna was acting depressed again. (Who could have blamed her?) Lizzie advised her daughters to be pleasant: "I expect you will have lots of company and make every one enjoy being with you."

Lizzie's next few letters continued along the same lines. Howard's hay fever was better, but he still had fever blisters on his lips, which were slowly drying. It was very cold in Nova Scotia by that time; they had had two frosts already and fires in the hotel every morning and evening. She thought Howard "took some cold yesterday driving but he is taking camphor." Lizzie asked the girls to hire a painter to varnish the floors and paint the woodwork while they were away so that Howard didn't have to breathe the fumes upon their return.

One letter began with an unusual account of the shoeing of oxen up in Nova Scotia, ox carts being the sole method of transportation in Port Maitland at that time. "They put the head between poles then strap a great thing like sacking under them and raise them entirely from the floor & raise each foot by ropes. The shoe is in two pieces."

Lizzie said she was "very sorry not to hear better accounts of Mary Turner." This was Susanna's and Alice's cousin Mary, my grandfather's sister, who, as a child, wrote to Susanna and drew the little sketch of a witch and cat. She was now married but continued to be very sickly. She would die at the early age of thirty-one.

Lizzie let her girls know they were expected to continue running the house: "Hope you will keep on having a good time until we get home then we will try to help you keep it up and you will enjoy your home life as you have enjoyed your study." I don't know about Beulah, but I am sure Susanna was depressed at the thought of a restricted life of keeping house with her sister. Lizzie was doing her job as she saw it, instructing her daughters in women's work, preparing them for marriage and keeping houses of their own. Neither would marry, however, and neither was trained or educated for pursuing the few careers available to women at that time. Consequently, their life now was maintaining the household and taking care of their aging parents and aunt.

On September 21, Lizzie wrote that they had delayed their return home because Howard was recovering so well. They'd return after the frost arrived in Riverton. She asked Susanna and Beulah to sell their spare eggs, a common practice. The note on a September 25 postcard portraying an "oxomobile" in Nova Scotia let the sisters know that the parents were now in Maine and heading to Boston. The postcard's dominant

Lizzie Parry's postcard of an Oxomobile in Nova Scotia, Canada, 1908.

image was not the "oxomobile" cart but the poor beast of burden yoked to it; I wonder if Susanna felt empathy with this animal, which, like her, was bound and constrained.

An October 8 letter from Boston announced that they would sail for New York the next day.

There are no more letters of note in the collection for the rest of 1908 and nothing of interest in 1909. It is very unusual for Susanna not to have saved letters and keepsakes. What had happened? Susanna's long "silence" is explained by the invitation addressed on March 18, 1910, to Susanna in E.'s handwriting: an invitation to attend the marriage of E. to W.J. on April 7, 1910, at the Friends Meeting House in Baltimore. What a terrible blow to Susanna: Her beloved E., her "Wifey," was marrying some man, not marrying her as she had hoped. Had E. really fallen in love with a man, or had she been married off by her parents? Was E.'s professed love for Susanna merely an adolescent infatuation? Given Susanna's summer-long depression as a student when she was told she would no longer be rooming with E. but with her sister Beulah, it is probable that Susanna suffered another prolonged depression, a mourning, when E. first courted, then got engaged to, then married, another.

Susanna didn't attend E.'s wedding or the reception because the calling card "Present this card at the door" was still with the invitation. Another card in the invitation announced that the couple would be "at Home Thursdays after the fifteenth of May," giving their address in Media, Pennsylvania. E. had moved on and left our Susanna behind, with a new husband and home of her own, while Susanna was still in her childhood home and, although surrounded by a loving family, must have felt quite alone.

There are no more letters in the collection for the rest of 1910.

Alice had been on fire in England all the time that Susanna had been pining away in Riverton after her return from Europe. Soon after her reunion in London with cousins Susanna and Beulah in August 1908, Alice dropped her social work altogether and concentrated full-time on her studies at the "left-leaning"[1] London School of Economics, which her mother enabled her to do with continued financial support. She was also intensifying her work for the Pankhursts' Women's Social and Political

Union and came clean to her mother about her involvement with the WSPU in a January 1909 letter: "I have joined the 'Suffragettes'—the militant party . . . the ones who have really brought their question to the fore (amid) much comment and criticism."[2]

However, Alice hadn't told her mother just how involved with the WSPU she had actually become. She was now selling the WSPU's newspaper, *Votes for Women*, on street corners, courageously enduring jeers, insults, and the occasional barrage of rotten produce[3] thrown by men who did not take kindly to female political activists. The once retiring Quaker girl was becoming increasingly emboldened by her cause.

Alice was soon asked to take on a more challenging task for the WSPU—public speaking, at first simply introducing the main speaker at rallies, then becoming the principal speaker. The Pankhursts themselves asked Alice to join a deputation presenting a petition to Prime Minister Asquith on June 29, 1909, warning that she might be arrested or imprisoned. Undeterred, Alice accepted. At the June 29 demonstration, Alice met red-haired Lucy Burns, the only other American at the WSPU. Their mutual attraction went well beyond nationality: Lucy was also college-educated (Vassar 1902) and a banker's daughter.[4] Alice and Lucy would become partners in suffrage work in America. Besides meeting Lucy at the June 29 demonstration, Alice also had her first run-in with police brutality and being in the public eye. To protect herself, Alice wrapped wool around her body under her clothes. When the police roughed her up, her buttons burst and the stuffing spilled out from her clothes, delighting the crowd. Over 100 suffragettes were arrested at the demonstration, including Alice and Lucy.

Alice wrote home about the arrest and had no choice but to confess the extent of her involvement. After all, she was awaiting trial. To her Quaker friends and family, her arrest was a terrible disgrace. When Alice crossed the line of respectability, Tacie ordered her daughter to come home.

At the trial on July 9, the judge ruled that it was legal for the suffragettes to have presented a petition to the prime minister but illegal to have insisted that he receive the deputation. The arrestees were released after the Pankhursts accepted the right to appeal. Alice was not thrown into jail—this time.

Emmeline told Alice and Lucy that they didn't have to wait for the appeal, that they could return home to the States, and she would explain their case to the judge and pay any fines imposed. Alice booked her passage home. However, she agreed to help the WSPU one last time before she sailed by disrupting a meeting in Norwich at which the young cabinet minister Winston Churchill was giving an address. Alice and two others forced their way past the police to heckle Churchill. They were taken away by the police but weren't prosecuted. However, Alice had missed her ship home. She told her mother she would book another passage home, but she didn't. She continued her suffrage work, and her mother continued to send funds to enable her to do so. After all, Tacie had taken young Alice to her first suffrage meetings, sowing the first seeds of rebellion.

Alice didn't avoid jail time for long. She was one of thirteen suffragettes arrested for disrupting a speech by David Lloyd George, Chancellor of the Exchequer. She was ordered either to pay a fine or to serve fourteen days in Holloway Gaol, a women's prison. Alice refused to pay the fine and was imprisoned. She protested not being granted political prisoner status by going on a hunger strike. When she and the other women refused to wear prison uniforms, they were stripped of their street clothes. To protest the unfair treatment, Alice broke every pane of glass in her cell, and the others followed their leader and did the same. Alice was released after serving five of the fourteen days.

Emmeline asked Alice and Lucy Burns to accompany her on a speaking tour. They accepted and rode in the WSPU car with Emmeline. She and Lucy were arrested in Scotland trying to enter a men-only audience attending a speech by Lord Crewe. They were sentenced to ten days in jail—the first suffragettes ever sentenced in Scotland. They went on another hunger strike and were released after four days. In appreciation of their brave sacrifice, the WSPU presented each with a silver brooch shaped like a grated prison door.

Alice and Lucy then organized a large demonstration in Edinburgh on October 9.[5] Alice was arrested for disrupting a MP's speech in Berwick, just south of the Scottish border, about a week later.

Alice was arrested once again in London on November 9 when disrupting the Lord Mayor's banquet featuring the prime minister as the principal speaker. Alice and another suffragette dressed up like cleaning women to gain access, broke a window, and shouted "Votes for women!" before being arrested. Once again, the suffragettes refused to pay a fine, choosing a month of hard labor at Holloway Gaol instead. Both went on a hunger strike. After three days, Alice was force-fed, a painful and dangerous procedure of running a tube through her nose and down her throat to her stomach. Alice endured this torture twice daily for a total of fifty-five forced feedings. Emmeline Pankhurst asked American suffragists to send letters to President Taft protesting the treatment of Alice Paul in Holloway Gaol, but the U.S. government refused to intervene on her behalf.

Alice's mother received letters of support from family and friends while Alice was imprisoned. On November 20, 1909, Edwin S. Parry wrote to Tacie, his aunt, that "suffragettes all over regard her as a <u>heroine</u> [sic] ... I myself being a <u>man</u> [sic] do not agree with their views on the voting question, but I rather admire Alice's pluck and determination than otherwise."⁶ I was disappointed by my grandfather's attitude toward Alice and the suffragettes—paternalistic at best, if not misogynistic. Apparently, Quaker men at that time believed that women, although spiritual equals of men, were not their social or political equals.

Alice was released on December 9, 1909. She remained bedridden for weeks after the torture of relentless forced feedings, cared for by WSPU workers. Christabel Pankhurst offered both Alice and Lucy full-time work as WSPU organizers. Lucy accepted and remained in England for another year or so. Alice, however, chose to return home to begin suffrage work in America. In her farewell address to her fellow suffragettes on January 3, 1910, reported in *Votes for Women*, Alice said she "had often longed to be one of those who fought in the Revolution instead of being merely a descendant" and likened the fight for women's suffrage as a new great rebellion—and this time she found herself in the thick of the fight.⁷ Alice had truly become a Quaker rebel.

On January 6, 1910, Alice sailed for home on *The Haverford* and arrived in Philadelphia on January 20. Reporters and photographers met her arrival. Our Quaker rebel was already newsworthy, having endured seven arrests, three imprisonments, and fifty-five forced feedings.⁸

However, she was also quite ill. All her jail time, hunger strikes, and forced feedings had destroyed the blush of her youth, and she now looked sickly and frail, shocking her family and friends. She recuperated at home in Moorestown, but she would never fully recover her former health. However, she had lost none of her zeal for the cause of women's rights and never would.

CHAPTER 12

A NEW CHAPTER

*U*ndoubtedly, Tacie Paul was relieved to have her daughter Alice back in Moorestown, convalescing under her protective wing. News of Alice's notoriety in England had reached home—her militant protests, disorderly conduct, jail time, hunger strikes, and window smashing. Such unseemly public displays of aggression were frowned upon by the Hicksite Quakers. However, while Betsy Ross was read out of Quaker meeting for marrying out of the faith during the Revolutionary War and the Quaker patriots in Philadelphia read out of meeting for taking up arms against the mother country, the more "modern" Quakers in 1910 did not expel Alice from the Moorestown meeting. Although the Quakers supported the cause of suffrage for women, they did not approve of the unbecoming actions of the radical suffragettes. They frowned upon our Alice, perhaps, but they tolerated her.

Alice had become something of a celebrity. She was asked to take public speaking engagements as soon as she was back on her feet, and the National American Woman Suffrage Association (NAWSA) asked her to serve on its Executive Committee. Although her plan to obtain suffrage differed radically from NAWSA's, Alice accepted. While NAWSA aimed for state-granted suffrage, Alice's goal was universal suffrage guaranteed by an amendment to the U.S. Constitution. In 1910, only four western states had granted the vote to women. Alice wanted the vote given to all women at once, guaranteed under federal law.

On February 9, 1910, Alice was one of the speakers at the Philadelphia Symposium on the Woman Suffrage Movement at the University of

Pennsylvania. She showed herself to be a rising leader of progressive reform in America, an unabashed feminist rallying support for social change, speaking of a "great spirit of rebellion" at work in the world. "This old idea of women as created solely in order to minister to man is akin to the idea that the working man's whole purpose in the world is to contribute to the happiness of the upper classes . . . Both ideas have been hard to kill."[1]

In the summer of 1910, Alice gave a lecture at Haverford for a Woodbrooke Symposium on Social Reform. Woodbrooke was the Quaker school for social activism near Birmingham, England, where Alice had recently studied and where Susanna would soon study. Alice called upon the Quaker activists to remember the revolutionary courage of their Quaker ancestors and not let the Quaker desire for peace and propriety stifle the fighting spirit needed to effect political and social change. She asked her Quaker audience, "Why should we be so impotent compared to the early friends" and called upon them to be "worthy of the great traditions we have inherited" as "more valiant soldiers in humanity's cause than ever before."[2]

Alice could well have been talking about the original Quaker Rebel, her cousin Edwin's great-great-grandmother Betsy Ross. Marla R. Miller's impressive research of the iconic Quaker flag maker reveals that Betsy Griscom Ross Ashburn (later Claypoole) was deeply involved in the Revolution, far beyond making flags. She was a Rosie the Riveter of her day: "With her husband, friends and family deeply engaged in the rebellion, Betsy Ashburn joined as well. She and thousands of women like her contributed to the war effort by producing cannon cartridges, fuses, musket cartridges and other munitions."[3] Family lore claims that British officers in occupied Philadelphia called Betsy Ashburn the "Little Rebel."[4]

In early 1911, Alice began doctoral studies at the University of Pennsylvania, where she received her Master's in Sociology and Political Science in 1907. This time, she uniquely combined the disciplines of sociology, political science, and economics. Always a brilliant student, she was awarded a doctoral fellowship that would pay her final year's expenses.

In the summer of 1911, Alice and Lucy Burns, who had returned from working with the Pankhursts in England, organized very successful open-air suffrage meetings in Philadelphia for the Pennsylvania NAWSA, culminating in a rally at Independence Square. Alice and Lucy had been well trained for this task by working for the Pankhursts' WSPU. Alice was particularly brilliant at organizing speakers and volunteers, fundraising, and generating publicity. Their primary strategy was to hold the political party currently in power in Washington responsible for the lack of universal suffrage. In this, they were at odds with NAWSA's less confrontational strategy of seeking state-granted suffrage. Alice and Lucy agreed that their tactics in the States would be less militant than those of the WSPU in England. Completely non-violent, they would be suffragists, not suffragettes.

After her successful suffrage campaign in Philadelphia, Alice returned to her doctoral work and dissertation: *The Legal Position of Women in Pennsylvania in 1911*. Women at that time had few legal rights: A third of the states denied women full ownership of their wages and inheritances,

Alice Paul in doctoral robes wearing grated prison door brooch, University of Pennsylvania, 1912.
(Library of Congress Prints & Photographs Division)

nor were they allowed to serve on juries. In most states, they were discriminated against in divorce and custody of their children. Alice had good reason to fight for the right to vote. She received her doctorate in 1912, one of two women among thirty-two men. The doctoral process had exhausted Alice, whose health had been weakened by the prolonged incarcerations, hunger strikes, and forced feedings in England. She recovered at her Moorestown home for a while, then carried on for the cause.

Alice proposed that NAWSA allow her and Lucy to resurrect its Congressional Committee and organize a suffrage parade and demonstration in Washington to coincide with the newly elected President Woodrow Wilson's inauguration on March 4, 1913. (Presidential inaugurations would be changed to January 20 in the 1930s.) Thanks to the support of Quaker board member Jane Addams, NAWSA reluctantly agreed on the condition that Alice and Lucy raise all their funding. NAWSA was reluctant to support a Congressional Committee seeking federally mandated suffrage because they continued to seek suffrage at the state level, which hadn't been very successful: by 1912, only nine western states had full suffrage. To NAWSA, achieving a Constitutional amendment seemed impossible, requiring a two-thirds majority in both the House and the Senate and ratification by three-quarters of the states. They underestimated Alice's ability to do the impossible.

Alice was appointed the chair of the Congressional Committee, Lucy the vice-chair. The two activists moved to Washington, DC, in December 1912, settling in at a Quaker boarding house for women and beginning to organize the grand suffrage pageant. They chose a small team, including Dora Lewis from the NAWSA board. They also enlisted Crystal Eastman, Lucy's classmate from Vassar and a lawyer with lobbying experience at the state level[5]; she was also the sister of Max Eastman, editor of *The Masses*. Emma Gillette, a Washington lawyer, became the treasurer and set up the Committee's headquarters in an office next to hers at 1420 F Street NW, across from the White House. Journalist Helen Gardener became the press chair. The Committee's leadership team was now in place, and plans for the extravaganza rapidly materialized.

With all of Alice's organizational skills learned from the Pankhursts in England, it is no wonder that her suffrage spectacle was enormously successful despite logistical problems with permitting and security. On March 3, 1913, the day before Wilson's inauguration, a huge crowd estimated at a quarter of a million to half a million people watched the colorful procession down Pennsylvania Avenue. The 8,000 marchers were led by the new symbol of women's suffrage—the beautiful Inez Milholland riding her white horse named Grey Dawn. The lead banner demanded a constitutional amendment for the enfranchisement of American women. The Committee's new colors of suffrage were purple, white, and green, the colors used by the Pankhursts' WSPU, replacing the yellow and blue of NAWSA. With its colorful marchers, dozens of floats, chariots, and bands, the event was described by *The New York Times* as "one of the most impressively beautiful spectacles ever staged in this country."[6]

As often happened with WSPU demonstrations in England, men in the crowd who opposed suffrage and equal rights for women became raucous and violent, and up to 100 of the demonstrators were injured. Initially, the police did nothing to protect the women; they stood by and enjoyed the show. Finally, the cavalry arrived to break up the fray. The riot made Alice's suffrage demonstration a resounding publicity success with interesting news coverage sympathetic toward the women. Suffrage was now at the center of national attention. Donations to the Congressional Committee increased, including a $1,000 contribution from the editor of the *Washington Post*[7], which in today's money is worth $25,000.

In March, after two weeks of Senate hearings about the violence against women at the parade, the report concluded that the suffragists indeed had had the right to gather and that the parade had not been adequately protected. Another victory for the suffragists.

After the parade, southern-born President Wilson received a suffrage delegation consisting of Alice Paul and four others. In her first meeting with the new president, Alice boldly told Wilson that a suffrage amendment was the most important issue facing the nation and asked him to call for a suffrage amendment in his first message to Congress. He responded that he had many issues on his agenda other than suffrage. Alice countered that he didn't have the right to pass any legislation without the approval of voting women.[8] Wilson quickly dismissed the group. A suffrage amendment to the Constitution did not have pride of place on

Wilson's political agenda. Instead, he wanted to enact financial reforms. To his credit, he managed to pass tariff and currency reforms, establish the Federal Reserve, and levy an income tax on the wealthy to reduce dependence on tariffs. As a southerner, Wilson was not particularly inspired by women's issues, and he didn't want to jeopardize the southern votes he needed to pass his reforms. Wilson would be Alice's principal adversary for the next seven years by ignoring the suffrage issue. She, in turn, would be a very bothersome thorn in his side.

On April 7, 1913, the Congressional Committee made its first appeal to Congress. Over 500 suffragists marched down Pennsylvania Avenue, bringing petitions to Congress. Alice was at the front of the parade, helping to carry the banner demanding "Nationwide Suffrage By A Constitutional Amendment."[9]

Later in April, Alice's recent successes in Washington compelled NAWSA to allow Alice to transform the ad hoc Congressional Committee into an official standing committee of NAWSA whose goal was a federal suffrage amendment to the Constitution. The new committee was called the Congressional Union for Woman Suffrage (CU), soliciting paying membership. NAWSA must have felt threatened by our Quaker rising star, and the NAWSA leadership certainly disapproved of the aggressive tone our Quaker rebel had taken with the president at her recent meeting.

In late spring, Alice contacted her Swarthmore friend Mable Vernon, her public speaking coach when she gave her commencement address as "Ivy Poet." Alice convinced Mabel to leave her teaching job in Philadelphia and come to Washington to help her at the CU. Mabel would be by Alice's side as a valuable suffrage organizer for five years.

On June 13, 1913, the Senate's Committee on Women Suffrage issued an encouraging report, and on July 31, another delegation delivered petitions with 80,000 signatures and attended the first suffrage debate in the Senate since 1887.[10]

Riding the momentum of her recent success, in November 1913, Alice started publishing a weekly CU newspaper, *The Suffragist*, edited by Rheta Childe Dorr, a journalist for the rights of working women and children who, like Alice, became a militant suffragist after meeting the

Pankhursts in England. Dorr held press conferences and suggested questions about suffrage that reporters should ask the president and congressmen. Alice wrote most of the articles published, with Lucy contributing from time to time.

Also, in the fall of 1913, Alice helped Emmeline Pankhurst organize her American tour and presided over the Washington meeting featuring Pankhurst as the principal speaker. Rheta Childe Dorr, the editor of *The Suffragist*, accompanied Pankhurst on tour. NAWSA disapproved of the strong ties between the CU and the notorious militant suffragette from England.

Organizing a successful suffrage campaign cost a lot of money. Luckily for Alice, her mother, Tacie, who had financial control of the substantial family estate, continued to support her daughter by sending regular checks to pay for her living expenses. Lucy Burns' father did the same for his daughter. Alice also established a program of monthly pledges to help support the Congressional Union, although it was difficult for married women to contribute even a small amount to the cause since husbands alone could sign checks and most of them tightly controlled their wives' expenditures and activities. Since many husbands didn't support suffrage or equal rights for women, many suffragists had to resort to subterfuge to contribute to the CU. But they managed to do so.

Women found in the Congressional Union a source of hope, the possibility of release from their restricted, controlled lives. The CU membership rapidly increased as growing numbers of women were inspired by the CU's dedication to feminism, which Alice defined as "gender equality in all respects."[11] To Alice, obtaining the vote was only the first step toward equality for women. Her goal was and always would be full equal rights for women under the law. Alice was the iconic New Woman and one of the twentieth century's first feminist activists.

The increasing membership and bank account of the Congressional Union and Alice's growing fame as its charismatic leader became too much for NAWSA to bear. At the NAWSA convention in the fall of 1913, Alice was cheered and lauded by some, including well-respected social activist and Quaker Jane Addams. However, NAWSA leader Carrie Chapman Catt vehemently criticized Alice and Lucy because their CU was too much at odds with NAWSA's goal of state-granted suffrage. The rebuff by the NAWSA leadership distressed fragile Alice, who retreated to the family home in Moorestown to regain her balance and strength.

The inevitable breakup happened at the end of 1913 at NAWSA's summit: Alice, Lucy, and their Congressional Union were expelled from NAWSA, much in the same way that Betsy Ross was read out of Quaker meeting for marrying outside of the faith. Although painful to Alice, this expulsion helped propel her toward victory. Alice Paul was an innovator, not a follower, and her Congressional Union could never achieve its goal of a suffrage amendment while under the control of narrow-thinking, slow-moving NAWSA.

Alice would soon discover that she and her CU had a great deal of ideological support and financial backing from like-minded and very influential women. In January 1914, soon after her break from NAWSA, Alice received a jaw-dropping gift of $5,000—almost $125,000 in today's money—from Alva Belmont, who left NAWSA to join the CU. Belmont was a fascinating figure in the Progressive Era—a socialite turned socialist. Formerly Alva Vanderbilt, a Gilded Age social climber famous for her extravagant spending during her successful effort to become one of New York's social elite, she divorced Vanderbilt in 1895 then married his wealthy friend Oliver Belmont. When Oliver died in 1908, Alva went to England and became a suffragette after meeting the Pankhursts, at the same time that Alice fell under the spell of the Pankhursts and decided to give her life to the cause. It is an amazing coincidence that the two American suffragettes in England would join their powerful forces six years later to help procure the vote for women in America.

Alva augmented her support of Alice and the CU by raising another $1,000 from her wealthy friends.[12] She would continue her support of and relationship with Alice until her death in the 1930s, co-founding the National Woman's Party with Alice and occasionally hosting suffrage meetings at her summer "cottage" in Newport, "Marble House." She also supported the financially struggling socialist magazine *The Masses*.

Louisine Havemeyer was another influential supporter of Alice and the CU. Wealthy widow of a sugar magnate and collector/patron of the arts, Louisine gave generously to the CU. The only public showing of her art collection benefited Alice's Congressional Union.[13]

Elizabeth Kent also generously supported the CU. Elizabeth Thacher Kent, environmentalist, women's rights activist, and wife of California Congressman William Kent, became involved in the suffrage movement in 1911 when the Kents moved to Washington for the congressman's first term. Elizabeth raised $10,000 for the CU—almost $250,000 today. She would be one of Alice's Silent Sentinels arrested for picketing in front of the White House in 1917.

While Alice was busy establishing herself as a leader in the American suffrage movement after her return from Europe in 1910, at first working with NAWSA then being on her own as head of the CU in 1914, her cousin Susanna was, by comparison, almost lifeless. After Susanna's return home from her trip to Europe in 1908, there are almost no letters in the Susanna Collection until the heartbreaking invitation to E.'s April 1910 wedding. There is no correspondence of note for the rest of 1910 and the first half of 1911, only occasional graduation and wedding invitations, among these the 1909 marriage of Mary Bond, my grandmother, to Edwin S. Parry—Susanna's and Alice's cousin—and in 1910 the birth of their daughter, Charlotte Parry, my mother.

In July 1911, Susanna received an announcement of the birth of E.'s son on July 14, 1911, signed by E.'s husband. Also forwarded was a note from a friend Cassie about the birth: "E. was taken sick about 10:30 last night, she had a hard time but bore it very bravely. He is a splendid boy, weighs 10 lbs, has fine lungs, we love to hear him cry. . . . With much love to thee from E. as well as myself." This was the only correspondence saved from 1911. I can only imagine the abandonment sensitive Susanna felt. Having long since turned away from her "Wifie," E. had left Susanna far behind on her traditional path as a busy wife and a mother with a home of her own. Susanna was still in her childhood home; although surrounded by family, she must have felt quite alone and was not doing much of anything apart from household chores. Susanna needed to snap out of her doldrums, shake off her disappointment in love, and find a new passion inspiring her to live again.

Susanna received a long letter from her Auntie Sue dated January 27, 1912, written from Haddon Hall in Atlantic City, one of her favorite vacation spots. (It's difficult for anyone today to think of Atlantic City as fashionable, but it was indeed an upscale gathering place of the Northeast's well-to-do set.) The purpose of this letter from Auntie Sue, who had never hesitated to meddle in Susanna's life, seemed to be to give her niece a pep-talk to coax her out of her reclusion. When she addressed Susanna as "My dear Little Girl," herein lay the problem: Susanna was no little girl; she was a twenty-seven-year-old woman. Auntie began the letter by talking about the great "humiliation & sorrow" an acquaintance of theirs had suffered at the hands of her "devilish" and "insane" husband who had died and her subsequent new courtship with another man, her second chance at a caring relationship. Then she talked of a period when she and her late husband had been separated. She implied the separation had been her fault and an unfortunate waste of years. This was perhaps Auntie's way of letting Susanna know that everyone had romantic troubles and disappointments in their lives that they had to rise above to be ultimately happy.

Auntie then not very subtly encouraged her niece to socialize with the right kind of people. Since it had been snowing in Atlantic City, she suggested that Susanna organize a sleigh ride:

> I have been wondering & if I may be allowed to say so, hoping—you have invited some of the young people of Philadelphia to help you enjoy it this afternoon & evening as I presume there is much more snow at Riverton. If Laurence would loan his sleigh & team wouldn't it be lovely? . . . To be entertained, you must, & I should think you would feel it a great pleasure, <u>entertain</u>. Now is your season to <u>widen</u>, enjoy & strengthen <u>suitable</u> friendships, the time for which, to those who have had their day, seems very short realizing—oh! So much— how I dwarfed myself by being satisfied within small limits—makes me more desirous that you may have a broader field from which to select the thing, the good, & the people <u>worthwhile</u>.

In her ramblings, Auntie made it very clear that she didn't think Susanna's current friendships were "suitable" or "worthwhile." This piqued my interest: whom, I wonder, had our Susanna been frequenting?

Auntie finished the letter by asking Susanna if she had enjoyed herself at a recent reception and if she had made an effort to look nice for the event, then encouraging Susanna to entertain some worthy and suitable people, offering to pay for the expense of a gathering. "When you write tell me your impressions of the reception, whether you enjoyed it or not—who you met etc . . . also did you look nice & how were your pretty dresses. . . . I would <u>love</u> to do something toward your entertaining this winter, which shall it be, a weekend house party at Haddon Hall or a dance in Porch Club, Hall or Golf Club?" Perhaps Susanna was not at all interested in throwing a party. Perhaps Susanna just wanted to be left alone. However, she must have known that Auntie was trying, in her meddling way, to help her beloved niece.

On February 19, 1912, Susanna and Beulah received a letter from the husband of their Swarthmore friend Naomi. The letter was addressed to "Sue and Chub." (I imagine that twenty-five-year-old Beulah was by now sick of being called "Chub" and "Chubbs.") The letter announced the birth of Naomi's first child, a son. "She and the baby are doing fine . . . We are as happy as two people can be. Come out and see us soon." Happy as two people could be. What joy for Susanna and Beulah—another friend married with a baby.

There are no other letters of significance in the collection for 1912 until a letter from Birmingham, England, from Helen Paul, Alice's sister, who was studying at Woodbrooke. Her letter revealed what Susanna had been doing to make a life for herself without E.: devoting a lot of her time to Quaker activities, recently organizing a conference at the Whittier Fellowship Guest House, a Quaker retreat in Hampton Falls, New Hampshire. Were some of Susanna's new Quaker acquaintances the ones whom Auntie found so unworthy and unsuitable? Or did Auntie disapprove in general of the Hicksite Quaker way of living the simple life because she had higher material and social aspirations for her niece?

Helen complimented Susanna's hard work on the Quaker conference. "I want to tell thee what a 'ripping' thing it is that you are planning it. Heartiest best wishes for all success . . . God bless thee Susanna for thy beautiful character. Thee little knows what an inspiration thee has been to many of us. It made my heart warm with pride to hear the English

Friends talking about thee." Helen ended on a familial note in looking forward to going for a drive with Susanna in their luxury automobiles and hoping Susanna's father was feeling better. "How splendid it will be when we go out in our Cadillacs together. Three cheers for Uncle Howard's good judgment. . . . I hope thy Father found relief from the Hay Fever."

That was in the fall of 1912. Just when it looked as if Susanna had found a distraction from her former heartbreak in her new Quaker activities, Susanna received a probably unwelcome envelope at Christmastime—an announcement of the birth of E.'s second child, another boy. Merry Christmas, Susanna: another wound to lick.

The collection has almost no correspondence after the announcement of the birth of E.'s second child in December 1912—until a May 23, 1913, thank you letter addressed to "Sukey" from Lillie in Philadelphia, thanking Susanna for the "shad party . . . a joyful success." (Shad parties were common 100 years ago; shad, a large cousin of the herring, still around today, spends most of its time in the Atlantic but swims upstream in coastal rivers to spawn in May and June; the shad at Susanna's party surely came from the Delaware; shad roe has remained a delicacy across the generations.) Lillie must have enjoyed visiting the Parry family in Riverton and mentioned Beulah in the "Cad"—apparently, Beulah and Susanna both liked to drive about in the Cadillac. Lillie closed the letter, "Thank thee Sukey dear for such a happy time." Maybe Susanna was getting on with her life and having some fun with friends.

A few days after this letter from Lillie, Susanna received a letter to "Dear Miss Parry" from a Dwight C. It appears from the letter that the two of them had already exchanged a few letters. He sounded very prissy, but the letter is of great interest because he asked Susanna about her reference to E. in a recent letter. He tried to disguise this query by writing in French. "Et je ne vous comprends pas quand vous dites, 'a second E., n'est-pas?' . . . What's very likely I'm too dense to catch your meaning. I hope you'll explain." It sounds like Susanna had met another woman—"a second E."—or perhaps she had simply expressed the hope of one day meeting another E. No wonder that dense Dwight didn't understand what Susanna was talking about. It mattered not if the "second E." were real or only dreamed of: clearly, Susanna had no romantic interest in Dwight C. or any man, and never would.

In June 1913, Susanna received a polite, somewhat dry letter from Will B. in Tyner, North Carolina, thanking her for her letter. They apparently had met at the Whittier Guest Conference Susanna organized. He told "Dear Miss Parry" that he was going to teach history and political science at Whittier College in California after helping to organize a Bible school conference at Guilford College in North Carolina, which would begin right after the North Carolina Yearly Meeting. He asked if she were going to the Yearly Meeting and invited her to attend at least a few days of the Bible school. "There are lots of young people in N.C. and lots of good fun at the School." Not exactly an impassioned or enticing invitation. We learn from a future letter from Will that Susanna would not go to North Carolina to see Will at the Bible school. No surprise.

Susanna received a far more interesting letter dated July 23 from Beatrice H. in Germantown, Pennsylvania, who seemed to have something of a girl crush on Susanna, whom she had met at a meeting at the George School. "Thee has often been in mind & I should like very much to see thee oftener." She invited Susanna to spend the afternoon and evening with her soon and gave information about the train from Philadelphia. "Bring some needlework & we will have a cosy little time. If cool we might take a little walk for there are some pretty spots near my 'wigwam'." Susanna apparently went to see Beatrice, for on the envelope Susanna wrote a note about a July 31 afternoon train. Could Beatrice be Susanna's "second E."?

On August 18, Susanna received a rather gushy letter from another special girlfriend—Lillie in Buck Hill Falls, who had so enjoyed Susanna's shad party in the spring. "It is so nice to hear from thee. I take very special pleasure in letters signed lovingly mine Susanna. . . . Love to thee Sukey dear from Lillie." Could Lillie be Susanna's "second E."?

On August 28, Susanna received another letter from Will B. in Tyner, North Carolina, responding to her letter. "Dear Miss Susanna . . . I am glad to be able to count thee as one of my friends. Thee was so nice to me during those few days I was at the Guest House. I have always wanted to see more of thee. . . . Last spring . . . I planned to have a day with thee when passing through Philadelphia, but then I was asked by a dear friend . . . to take charge of a summer Bible School at Guilford." He said he would like to see Susanna again, but he must head west to start teaching at Whittier College. "Whittier is a Friends' School located in the little town of Whittier about twelve or fourteen miles from Los Angeles . . . It is one of the youngest of the Friends' Colleges but it has had a splendid growth and has a bright future, I am told. There are a great many Friends in these parts. The Whittier Meeting has a membership of five or six hundred. . . . I look forward to my work there with a good deal of pleasure. I shall have the department of History and Political Science."

Will was a young, educated, articulate Quaker man with something of a spirit of adventure who showed some interest in developing a relationship with Susanna. However, he was not in too much of a rush to make it happen, as he was willing to wait over a year to see her again at the World's Fair of 1915—the Panama-Pacific International Exposition in San Francisco. "When you come West to the Exposition in 1915 we must make some plans to be together for a while./With the most sincere regards./Yours very sincerely,/William B." Not exactly an offer Susanna couldn't refuse, although she probably wanted to see the World's Fair. We don't know from the collection if Susanna went to the 1915 Exposition in San Francisco, but we know that Alice did and was prominently featured as a suffragist. More later.

A letter to Susanna dated October 4, 1913, is, to me, the most heartbreaking letter in the collection. This is the last we hear from E. Apparently, Susanna hoped to see E. at two social gatherings—one in Trenton and one in West Chester. Although E. had accepted the invitations, she did not attend either event. She wrote that her children were the reason she couldn't get away. Instead of Susanna being addressed as "Dearest Wifie" as she had been in their college years, she had become "Dear Old Pal." However, although she signed the letter "as ever fond", in between the lines of the last paragraph was perhaps a declaration of enduring, impossible love. Oddly, the envelope containing's E.'s letter appears never to have been opened—not the usual slit made by a letter opener, no evidence that the envelope's seal had ever been broken. It seems to me that Susanna saved the unopened letter for a distant cousin one day to find and tell her reader that Susanna didn't care what E. had to say. To show that she had moved on. To show that she had turned the page on this romance and was starting a new chapter.

I do wish Susanna had read E.'s letter. Although hope for a future together had long gone for the two friends, Susanna might well have found some comfort at the close:

> Dear Old Pal,
> Congratulations & best wishes for the best of birthdays.
> We were certainly disappointed that we could not arrange to go to Trenton, but it was a busy week—too busy, in fact, for comfort. I guess you all had ever so much fun at West Chester, too. My kiddies demanded my time. You see I can only partially accept invitations, for my real place is here, and I feel that I can only leave when everything is running very smoothly, and as thee may have noticed, they (things) do not run that way early in the morning. . . .
> Well, Sue dear—just one more word—I love thee, not only on thy birthday—but every day. I think thee knows this.
> As ever fond,
E.

October correspondence to Susanna from the University of Chicago Press indicated that Susanna was working for or volunteering at the Westfield Friends Meeting School. Enclosed were teaching materials for textbooks on the life of Jesus that she had recently ordered, a pamphlet marketing their similar materials, and an order form for "Textbooks for Graded Work in Religious Education."

In November 1913, Susanna received a letter from Isaac Braithwaite from Woodbrooke Settlement in Birmingham, England. He was looking forward to Susanna's coming to Woodbrooke, along with Anna Griscom, for the spring term beginning in January 1914. This was the same school that Alice had attended about five years before. A January 1914 letter from Dr. Braithwaite revealed that Susanna couldn't make the spring term at Woodbrooke because of the death of Anna Griscom's father. He hoped that Susanna and Anna would make the summer term starting on April 25.

Susanna's family apparently had decided it would do her some good to leave the country again, so they arranged to have her attend the Quaker school in England, as her cousins Alice and Helen Paul had done. Woodbrooke, in addition to teaching social reform, was also a good place for Quaker girls to meet suitable young Quaker men. I'm sure her family would have loved Susanna to come back with a prospect. Even if that didn't happen, at least sending "Sukey" to England would separate her from the company she was currently keeping, whom Auntie didn't judge to be "suitable" or "worthwhile."

The next letter is from Susanna to her mother, dated March 27, 1914, and written from the steamer SS *Haverford* on the Delaware River, about to take to the high seas. She and Anna were finally on their way to England. She thanked friends and family who had sent baskets of fruit, candy, and bunches of sweet peas, and Beulah, who had sent a diary and some maps. She had just dined at "the Dr.'s table." Susanna was carrying on, once again crossing the Atlantic, leaving E. and America behind her. She once again turned the page and started a new chapter.

CHAPTER 13

1914

In January 1914, Alice and her Congressional Union had been expelled from NAWSA, but Alva Belmont and other influential suffragists generously endorsed the CU and Alice. In its first year of independence, the CU raised over $37,000 for its cause of a suffrage amendment, about $925,000 in today's money. Alva Belmont gave more than $10,000 in 1914, the equivalent of $250,000 today.

Alice was admitted to the Quaker-run Woman's Hospital of Philadelphia in the spring of 1914 for a three-week rest cure; her sister Helen often visited her, bringing changes of clothes and such. When Alice left the hospital, she went to Dora Lewis's home for further recuperation. Dora Lewis had left NAWSA to support Alice and the CU; she first served on the executive committee of the CU then became one of the co-founders, with Alice and Alva, of the National Woman's Party, and one of its most successful fundraisers. She also became one of the NWP's Silent Sentinels, arrested multiple times for protesting in front of the White House.

Thanks to the care given by the suffragists, Alice was back in the fight for the May 2, 1914, nationwide Mayday demonstrations organized by the CU under the leadership of Mabel Vernon. Alice and Lucy spoke at the Carnegie Hall demonstration, and Alice's sister Helen helped with the Mayday event in Moorestown. On May 7, Mayday delegates from across the country met in Washington to march to the Capitol and demand a vote for suffrage. No vote was taken.

When the nationwide demonstrations failed to produce fruitful results, Alice decided to change tactics and turn up the political heat on the need for universal suffrage. In the late summer, Alice and the CU gathered at Marble House, Alva Belmont's Newport mansion.[1] Proposing a new plan of attack in the war for suffrage, Alice suggested using their four million votes—women in the nine western states with suffrage—to pressure their congressmen to support the amendment, threatening to vote the Democrats out of office if they didn't pass the amendment. Alice's proposal of mobilizing existing women voters to achieve the CU's goal was a stroke of political genius. *The New York Tribune* called the Marble House strategy "'the entrance of women into the arena of practical politics.'"[2]

In the fall of 1914, the CU rolled out its bold new campaign against the Democrats, the party in control. Imagine the reaction of men in Congress and at home, with women now on the political scene making a fuss and threatening to vote out Democratic officeholders in the upcoming midterm elections in the western states where women had the vote. Horribly unladylike behavior, especially for a Quaker. Alice's Uncle Mickle Paul sent her a harshly critical letter, but of course, Alice would not be deterred. The new campaign raised nationwide awareness of suffrage as a constitutional issue and had impressive success with 23 out of 43 Democratic losses in suffrage states.

While Alice and the CU planned their new strategy in the summer of 1914, the assassination of Austria's Archduke Franz Ferdinand ignited the First World War in Europe. Also that summer, President Wilson's wife Ellen died of kidney disease. For a very long time to come, Wilson would be so distracted by grief and the possibility of American involvement in the war that he would give little thought to the cause of suffrage. To Alice, however, suffrage was the only cause. The struggle for the vote was her only war, and she would make sure that suffrage was not forgotten during the war years.

While Alice was fighting the good fight for suffrage, her cousin Susanna sailed off to Europe in March of 1914, unaware that, during her stay, war would begin in Europe and might jeopardize her return home. The choppy voyage across the Atlantic foreboded the storm ahead. Susanna wrote her Auntie Sue that the SS *Haverford*'s crossing had been rough and had delayed their arrival in Queenstown a bit, but they would arrive the next day. "The waves look like young mountains, and we bob around at a great rate . . . We roll around in our chairs at the table but eat just the same." The weather, however, hadn't kept Susanna and Anna from making friends with the family whose deck chairs were near theirs, and the group had been taken under the wing of the captain, whose quarters were near their chairs. "Last night he took us all in to see his little tame bird. About six months ago it got lost in the fog and sought rest on the ship. They caught it and have made a pet of it. It flies all over his cabin, not caring much for the cage one of the sailors made for it, but best of all it loves the top of the clock where it is continually slipping off to fly down to a perch in front of the mirror. The Captain seems very fond of it and loves to feed it from his hands."

Susanna gave her family the details of her itinerary for her tour of the Continent with Anna before their work began at Woodbrooke: Paris, Bruges, Brussels, Amsterdam, The Hague, then a steamer back to Harwich, England. Anna had never been to Europe, so Susanna would have to be a tour guide since she had visited most of these places six years ago with Beulah and Auntie Sue.

Susanna's travel letters are, as always, a pleasure to read, with her powers of observation and detailed descriptions, especially about the beauties of nature. For example, she wrote as the SS *Haverford* neared land: "Yesterday again was an ideal day. About ten o'clock we began to see land and all day we skirted the high rocky southern cliffs of Ireland. About four we entered Queenstown harbour. It was perfectly beautiful. The ocean was a most brilliant green, spotted with many little whitecaps. In back of the hills, which were just beginning to look spring-like with the yellow gorse & budding trees, were the great banks of white clouds like still higher mountains before we came to the very blue sky."

Susanna wrote Beulah on April 14, 1914, from the Mont-Thabor Hotel in Paris, which was not as grand as the Palais d'Orsay Grand Hotel where Susanna, Beulah, and Auntie stayed in 1908, but was nicely located between the Tuileries and the Place Vendôme. Susanna, the tour guide, had been showing Paris to first-time European traveler Anna. The girls had taken a Cook's sightseeing automobile tour to see all the usual tourist attractions: "Notre Dame, Pantheon, Cluny, Luxembourg . . . Tuilleries [sic] . . . Champs Elysees . . . Bois du Boulogne, Trocadero, Hotel des Invalides, etc." They had plans to go to the Opera the next evening to hear *Tristan & Isolde*. "Anna sends lots of love & says she is trying to take good care of me."

Four days later, Susanna wrote to Beulah from Belgium. The letter began in Bruges, where Anna had a cold and was confined to bed. Susanna, however, had been out and about, as she hadn't gone to Bruges on her last trip and wanted to see the city. She told Beulah she would love Bruges:

> Thee would love it, I know. The canals are most fascinating, likewise the brass and other markets along the streets. . . . This is where we begin to see the wooden shoes, dogs hitched to the carts, women with the yoke for milk cans, etc. . . . This is the funniest little hotel I was ever in. It is packed to overcrowding with all kinds of furniture and pictures and dishes. I am sitting right next to a big stove but it seems to fail to give out any heat so until Anna is ready, I am going up stairs and get in bed with her to get warm for I don't want a cold, too.

In 1914, people were clueless about catching colds from germs; the last thing that Susanna should have been doing was cuddling up with someone sick in bed. Although Pasteur and Lister introduced germ theory, some vaccinations, and sterilization at the end of the 1800s, bacteriologist Alexander Fleming wouldn't discover penicillin until 1928, and the first successful treatment with penicillin in the U.S. wouldn't happen until 1942. It's hard for us today to imagine a world without antibiotics.

The second half of Susanna's April 18 letter was written in Brussels. "Well, here we are at last A's cold being much better. She stayed in bed all yesterday afternoon (I took a nice long nap with her) and until about one o'clock today." Independent Susanna didn't want to miss seeing Brussels because of Anna's cold, so she went out alone during the day, thoroughly enjoying herself. "All the older women wear most attractive little white caps and long black hooded capes. All around one side of the town are dyke [sic]-like ramparts now planted in trees & shrubs and made into a beautiful little park. I walked there and thought of Riverton as I did so. The fruit trees are out beautifully and it made our ride here from Bruges so very interesting. All the little farms were so very neat & spick & span."

Susanna and Anna traveled to Amsterdam and The Hague, staying at Hotel Paulez in The Hague, where Susanna and Beulah had stayed in 1908. They then took the steamer to England. Susanna's April 26, 1914, letter to her family described their arrival at Woodbrooke. "It all seems just like a dream to really be here at Woodbrooke, of which we have always heard so much." After their first communal teatime, they spent the rest of the day exploring their delightful surroundings and checking out the other students:

> The rest of the afternoon was spent in getting acquainted with the surroundings. The pool & the swan which chases us if we go near his nest, the barracks where some of the girls live, the Lecture Hall, the cinder path which leads to Bonneville, the tennis courts, and other various little walks around the grounds. I can readily agree with everyone who has raved about the location. Our room is in the very eastern end of the main building and overlooks the prettiest part of the garden. In the distance we can just see the tops of some of the Bonneville houses and hear the chimes and church bells. . . . There are a great many foreigners. Five Americans at present and three more coming in June, two Dutch; five Norwegians, one German and all the rest are English. I should judge about thirty or thirty-five . . .

Upon arriving at Woodbrooke, students needed to choose their course of study in their effort to find the calling which would guide their lives. "We have had two lectures this morning (Dr. Harris on the Spiritual Life, and Mr. Annison on Industrial Cooperation) but it is rather hard to know just what to decide upon. Lydia suggests that we attend all the lectures for the first week then at the end of that time consult our 'shepherd' or course advisor upon the best program. . . . Mr. Wood, otherwise known as H. G., is to be my advisor."

Not only did students attend all lectures the first week so they could choose their area of specialization for the rest of the term but also went on social service excursions. Susanna's April 29 letter recounted her visit with four other students "to Woodland, a home for crippled children. We were there for about an hour or so entertaining the little cripples who spend most of their time in bed. The two Norwegians sang to them while the rest of us went from cot to cot doing picture puzzles, showing some how to crochet, some to make bright worsted balls, etc. The most of them were very bright happy little youngsters, but they spoke with such a very cockney accent that it was quite hard to understand them."

The students looked forward to their daily break from their busy schedules: teatime. All the faculty made a point of inviting new students to tea, a relaxing, low-key form of English fellowship that Susanna and Anna have come to enjoy. "Yesterday Anna and I were invited down to have tea with Barry Brown and his wife. They are certainly a lovely couple and they made us have such a nice time. We didn't take much stock in having tea every afternoon, but it is really a very nice way to entertain and so much easier than a meal. It is most informal. You just drop in without having to get all fixed up." (This form of English entertaining is much like the French *quatre heures* or four o'clock break, which my husband, Laurent, and I enjoyed very much when we lived in Normandy and exchanged weekly *quatre heures* with our neighbors. The principal is the same as British teatime, but the beverage in France is coffee, of course. Everyone has an espresso machine, which is part of the ritual. It's entertaining without all the fuss: so much easier to make a dessert instead of a whole meal. After all, the point of a gathering isn't the food but the fellowship.)

Today's younger reader might never have thought about how their rooms are heated, but 100 years ago, keeping the fires going required constant attention. Susanna was interested in the English way of heating with coal instead of her family's way of using wood. "Mrs. Blomfield, the librarian, is putting more coal on, which will make another paradise here after a little time. The coal is funny. It is great large chunks of soft coal which they put on with a scissors like instrument, a little larger than Mother's large scissors. They answer for this purpose but would not do for our large pieces of wood."

Whether the chilly April air was the culprit or sharing a room—and bed—with Anna, who was sick in Bruges, Susanna was now sick and had a cough so bad that she had to skip the silent Quaker meetings. Her May 1 letter described the remedy of the time: "Lydia gave me some iodine to paint my throat with last night and so I have to be entirely well again before long." (I was surprised to discover that iodine is still used as a treatment for sore throats, either gargling with properly diluted iodine or rubbing iodine on the skin of the neck, throat, and wrists; there is now clear iodine to minimize staining. I might have to try that at the onset of my next sore throat before resorting to antibiotics.)

Susanna's May 4 letter explained why Auntie had not yet received the letters Susanna had written her. "You see we did not get to Liverpool until time to see the *Lusitania* steaming down the river on the 7th day the 11th. It may have been too rough weather for the steamers to call at Queenstown and thus no mail even started west until the 15th which was probably a slow boat. But you should have quite an avalanche by this time, for we have been writing comparatively often." It's hard for today's reader, used to instant worldwide internet communication, to imagine the frustration of being out of communication 100 years ago due to rough weather and slow steamer schedules. I got goosebumps when I read about Susanna's steamer arriving in time to see the *Lusitania* on April 11, 1914; the *Lusitania* would be torpedoed and sunk by German U-boats a year later in World War I.

Susanna's May 8 letter told the family that she had visited the doctor because of her continuing cough. So much for painting the throat with iodine: "He gave me a great big bottle of pink medicine to be taken 2 tbsp at a time. I told the girls it looked as though it ought to either kill or cure, and I am happy to say it did the latter." In addition to taking the cough syrup, Susanna stayed in bed for a day and a half to stay warm and get some rest, after which she was back to health. She was feeling well enough to plan a room party: "Anna and I have been to several little room parties and have determined that we must return the same so this p.m. we are going down to Selly Oak to purchase some little cakes and the where-with-all to make real American punch, so that we can invite a few for Seventh Day evening."

In the States in 1914, owning a car was a novelty and a status symbol, and those who had cars treated their friends and family members who didn't. The Parrys and the Pauls had cars—cousins Beulah Parry and Helen Paul both enjoyed driving their Cadillacs; however, Anna's family, the Griscoms, didn't own a car. Susanna wrote that she was glad to hear the Parrys and the Pauls were using their cars to bring some joy to the Griscoms, grieving after the death of Anna's father. "I was glad you have called on the Griscoms & hope you will take them autoing quite often for I know they enjoy it judging from one of Aunt C.'s letters. Helen Paul had promised to take them the first nice day and they were all looking forward to it."

In her May 10 letter to Beulah, Susanna confessed that she was not crazy about all the Americans at Woodbrooke, nor did she take to all the religious practices there. Susanna enjoyed being alone when Anna was "out autoing" and the other Americans were away. "I had one of the most enjoyable afternoons since I have been here. It was really lovely not to be on the lookout for Americans and trying to avoid them at every turn." She had company in avoiding some of the many prayer meetings and mocking the prim Woodbrooke ways: "All the good people soon adjourned to go to 'prayer meeting' but I could not see it my duty so soon after Lydia's description of her first and only experience. About five of us had a very nice, little cozy time around the fire in the Common Room. One played, two sang, and one danced (sh, sh, don't let the secret out) some sort of fancy dance."

Susanna didn't particularly like visits to the home for crippled children, so working with the handicapped was not her calling. She did, however, enjoy the parlor games she and the girls played, some reflecting the current fad of spiritualism with the reading of auras and palms. (Harry Houdini was all the rage at the time.) "This is my week to clear the tables after lunch and tea so while we were waiting for the late comers about five of us girls gathered around the little Norwegian who says she can see colors in nearly every person and that these colors mean certain characteristics. It was most interesting to hear what she saw in different people. From that we got on to palmistry . . . Most of the people went to the Common Room, where Mr. Aytown played the piano for us while the rest of us played musical chairs which is only another name for our 'Going to Jerusalem'."

Susanna wrote her family that she and others were to attend Yearly Meeting in London, and they had been invited to stay the weekend before at the home of Catharine Albright. Susanna found an inspiring role model in Miss Albright: a wealthy, unmarried woman living alone (except for the live-in servants), who nonetheless had a busy, interesting life and lots of friends. "We had a perfectly lovely time at Miss Albright's. Dorothy Rutter, Anna and I were the three from Woodbrooke, a Miss Satterthwaite, who has been to America and consequently they knew many people & places, having met a ___ Satterthwaite Parry, who I supposed to be Aunt Lydia at Yearly Meeting about seven years ago." (This was certainly her Aunt Lydia Satterthwaite Parry, my great-grandmother, widow of Oliver Parry and mother of Edwin and Mary.) She went on and on in her admiration of her self-reliant new friend:

> Miss Albright is so perfectly lovely in her own home. . . . She lives entirely alone with the exception of her servants, but has a house full every week-end. Seventh-day evening we sat around in her living room or study, talking or listening to her sing or play. First-day five of us went to meeting, read, & rested & did exactly as we pleased all the beautiful afternoon. And about 6:30 she had an evening meeting in her own home. She is so thoroughly all round. She is extremely intellectual, being a great writer & worker in all ways, beside being so spiritual. She speaks so beautifully, but with all this she makes you feel so much at home. Her garden is perfectly beautiful. Over here they all have lady gardeners. Wouldn't it be a nice position? In the evening Miss A. read us several stories.

Susanna was certainly smitten with the independent lifestyle, if not with the person as well.

Susanna addressed her May 25, 1914, letter to her Auntie, probably because a large part of it concerned her extensive summer travels in the British Isles after school let out, which Auntie was probably financing. Susanna would be touring with Anna, who had not yet seen the places

Susanna had already visited, which restricted the itinerary. Reading between the lines, it sounds like Susanna would much rather have toured by herself and seen new places she had wanted to see; however, such an unchaperoned excursion would never have been allowed. As in so many other ways, Susanna wasn't free to do what she really wanted to do. "In order for Anna to see the places she ought to see & that I have seen, we are going to waste so much time that we shall have to rush through the nice part. We have had to cut out all thought of Ireland and I see North Wales gradually disappearing from sight, much to my disappointment." Susanna and Anna were unable to book passage home on the September 2 sailing of the *Haverford*, so they would have to sail later. Hopefully, they would be able to reserve one of the few rooms still available on the *Merion*, which was scheduled to sail on September 23.

Susanna's May 28 letter to Beulah described her morning's outing to the juvenile court, which fascinated and troubled her; the case histories could be scenes from a Dickens novel. Susanna had great compassion for the children brought before the judge, children who were victims of the industrial revolution and its slums:

> Today Anna, Mrs. Trueblood & I have been in at the Juvenile Court all the morning, it was most interesting and at the same time very pathetic. About 13 boys were brought up before the judge for playing football in the streets. He told them they should go to some empty lot or out in the park but not on the streets and charged them a shilling each. I never before realized how badly the children's playgrounds are needed. It's boy nature to want to play football, throw stones or anything else they can get, and jostle & wrestle, and those poor little waifs probably had no other place without going squares away from home. . . . Another poor woman & her little girl were brought up for stealing a piece of mutton. It seems there are 7 children living (one or two having died or been sent away as epileptics). The father has to support that family on 25 shillings (about $6.25) a week, and the oldest boy is working for only $2.50 a week. There were other cases of stealing and one boy of 16 being found drunk and disorderly. The latter was a very nice little fellow, but had gotten into bad company

because his mother was dead and his father had left him. Nevertheless his employer seemed to be very good to him & wanted to help him. He was put on probation for two years. Then . . . the cases for the Children's Employment Act were tried. In 1903 the law was passed prohibiting the employment of children less than 14 years of age after 9 o'clock at night . . . Their inspectors in the last three months have brought in over 140 cases.

Susanna told Beulah that she was enjoying the diversity of the students at Woodbrooke, a refreshing change from the monotonous conformity of her Hicksite Quaker lifestyle in Riverton. She was delighted to have made new friends among these unusual students:

> I don't believe there are two people who could under any circumstance be classed as alike. From funny, little, joking, teasing Dr. Mingana from Syria down to the Americans, they are all so totally different and yet seem to get along very well. Their occupations seem to be mainly teachers and social workers, but we have one minister, one factory girl, Dr. Mingana a writer, an engineer who is here for a rest, and a man from New Zealand. They are of all nationalities and all religions. . . . We have been having a fad of giving flower names (a la Norwegians) to the various people. Margaret Edminson says A. is a peony and I am a dahlia. What do you think of the comparison? But the biggest joke is that the Norwegians say I am a twinkling star. It has certainly been the cause of many hearty laughs.

Heartening to see Susanna enjoying such playful camaraderie with new friends far away from her loneliness at home. Remember the Norwegians who called her a "twinkling star": that reference would come around again decades from now.

In her June 2 letter to her family, Susanna described her vacation plans to date. She and Anna had booked passage on the *Merion* which was to sail on September 23, but they hoped they might be able to get passage on the *Haverford* which would sail three weeks earlier on September 2. "Anna and I want to spend about two weeks in North Wales

& the Eng. Lake Country, meet the Lewis' and Jones' about the 28th of July in Glasgow, take a three weeks train, coaching and boat trip through Scotland to Edinburgh, leave the party there and go down through the cathedral towns to London spending about ten days there so that we shall be ready to sail on the 2nd of Sept. if there is room, but if not we will spend the two weeks before sailing in Devonshire & Cornwall."

Susanna's June 4 letter described Anna's and her visit to the Summer Lane settlement in Birmingham, with a tour of the facility given by one of the ladies she had recently met at Catharine Albright's:

> Miss Morrison was very cordial, took us into tea and then showed us all over the new building. It is wonderful what they have done down in that district, instead of one little house they have grown until now four houses are used. Old buildings have been torn down to make a nice large playground for the children, a new parish house has been built and as they say the neighborhood is getting almost too respectable for a settlement. . . . They have . . . a poor man's lawyer, and a Juvenile Employment Bureau which does much the same work as the After Care Com. in finding work for children just after they leave school and seeing that they are started in the right direction.

The Summer Lane settlement reflected the best of Progressive Era reforms; such settlement houses, at the heart of the Quaker reform movement, were truly trying to make a difference with bricks and mortar, volunteer work, and great compassion.

Dutiful young Quakers, Susanna and Beulah were searching for their calling to social service. Susanna was at Woodbrooke for that purpose, although her mother and aunt no doubt prayed that Susanna would also find a husband in the process. Beulah must have been having a difficult time finding inspiration, so Susanna's June 18, 1914, letter shared some of the things she had learned during her semester at Woodbrooke, offering her sister some suggestions about community service:

> Do kindly personal service but not in a benevolent way (condescending).

Tell stories, sing, or collect magazines for children's wards or convalescent hospitals (This is being done for our Cinnaminson Home.).

Help start gardens among children of orphanage in almshouses or homes for the aged.

In Blind Inst. read to adult blind, also in Almshouses or homes for the aged.

Sewing classes in deaf and dumb schools . . . Friendly visiting & big brother work.

Why don't you help Gertrude Roberts with her Camp Fire Girls or do something else for the public school children during vacation. . . . Mr. St. John says to look around and see what is lacking in the neighborhood & then set about bettering those conditions. . . . Are you going to get some good lecturers to come and talk of factory conditions in N.J. or some such subject which concerns everyone?

Susanna told Beulah that she would be staying an additional three weeks in September "following Auntie's suggestion." Auntie, who was financing Susanna's trip abroad, probably told Susanna not to worry about the cost of the additional weeks.

Susanna's June 28, 1914, letter to Beulah reports in fascinating detail a dinner party she attended at "Manor House," home of the Cadburys, Quaker founders of Woodbrooke. The stunning formality and opulence of prewar England evokes scenes from *Downton Abbey*:

A maid in her stiffly starched apron & cap opened the door for us and escorted us to the drawing room. Well! I have seen pictures, and empty palace rooms, but I only wished there hadn't been quite so many people around to be polite to, so that I could have had a chance to take everything in. As we entered, the picture we often see in magazines of the big organ in Sharpless House flashed across my mind. The drawing room or library was spacious to the extreme, an enormous fireplace, inset carved wood bookcases, beautiful thick carpets and hangings and cozy, comfortable chairs. . . . We were soon asked to dinner. The table was set on a lovely little terraced porch with lovely pink roses trailing carelessly around the big varnished oak posts.

> Three maids stood around until we were seated. Miss Kelman at Mr. C's right & I to his left. (My, my, I can't help straightening up every time I think of it.) Then the others made a table of fifteen, quite a party, I should say. But I believe it is just about what they have every week. Wouldn't you think they would want to be alone sometimes, but I am mighty glad the notion didn't strike them today. . . . Then after the meal of two meats, three vegetables, six desserts & cheese & biscuit, Mrs. took us for a walk through magnificent green houses. The temperature of the one where the tropical plants are kept being 108, we did not venture in, but the geraniums & lots & lots of things I didn't know were perfect. The roses on the trellis were lovely. From the terrace with its little fountain, stone benches, etc. you could get the most beautiful vistas . . . one was especially beautiful; the big stately trees made a beautiful oval green frame so that you could see beyond to the most adorable little waterfall. Then the garden proper in back of the house was one mass of bloom—rose gardens and arbors, lilies, foxgloves, iris, phlox, and all sorts of things. I was talking quite a while to Dorothy Cadbury, who is a dear girl. Her sister Mallie is coming down here tonight to play the violin during our music hour.

That was Susanna's happy June 28, 1914, in England. On the Continent, Archduke Franz Ferdinand was assassinated in Sarajevo by the Serbian student Gavrilo Princip, and war in Europe would be declared a month later. Luckily, Susanna had booked her passage home. Susanna was blissfully ignorant of the storm to come, enjoying a perfect summer day: "Life under an apple tree in a comfortable deck chair on a warm afternoon is most delightful. Ever since last Seventh day we have been trying to appreciate every moment for fear it might be the last. Yesterday about this time I got so sleepy here, the words of my book all ran together, the distant calls of the energetic tennis players and the nearer sounds of the birds and bees was too much, so I borrowed a corner of a girl's steamer rug and had a lovely nap."

Susanna's July 3, 1914, letter related yet another encounter with an alternative lifestyle during her Woodbrooke experience. Catharine Albright was the first, a financially independent woman living an active and happy life on her own. Then Susanna met two women friends—New Women—living happily together in a "Boston marriage." Susanna found everything about them delightful and felt right at home in the company of these independent women: "A few days ago Margaret Edminson took lunch with a Miss Barrow, who is going to America with two others in August, and she was asking about Americans here, from what part of the country they came, etc. In order to know a little bit more about the eastern cities etc. she invited A. & me to dinner with her last night. We had a perfectly lovely time. She and her friend live together in a lovely little home, with a beautiful garden . . . and they were both perfectly lovely. . . . Altogether we had a perfectly lovely little party."

As its summer term drew to a close, Woodbrooke, in the spirit of community service, organized a party for disadvantaged local children:

> About 120 children, between 5 & 12 yrs, came out from the slums to enjoy the Woodbrooke grounds for the afternoon. Some met them at Selly Oak, some entertained with games, Anna & others in Indian costumes entertained with various war dances, some of the boys rowed them about 16 at a time around the pool, and it was my job to tie pink & blue streamers on their arms as they came out which was a diplomatic way of our knowing who had been before. They had a lovely time playing in the hay field and throwing it on each other. . . . After running races and ball games, they went to the dining room and sat at long tables for their tea and bread, cakes and strawberries. My how they did enjoy it, and were then washed by another committee, given a box of sweets, and sent home.

Susanna's last letter from Woodbrooke is dated July 10, 1914. With the school term now ended, she and Anna would leave for their excursion through Wales & Scotland in two days. "Anna and I have been having a great time packing trunks for three different destinations (two for the ship's hold, one for our stateroom and one for London, besides our suit cases to last us all through Wales & Scotland)." She then gave an amusing account of one of the games—"the Dutch race"—played at the closing festivities. "We had sports yesterday afternoon, and great was the surprise for me to win in the Dutch race, but someone had to hold up the reputation of the Americans. The object was to walk a distance to a table, put on a cap, raise an umbrella, pick up a candlestick, light it, set it down, drink a glass of water, blow out candle, put down umbrella, take off cap & walk back, in this order." I've never heard of this Dutch race before, but it certainly would be a terrific drinking game. I am certain, however, there was no alcohol at the Woodbrooke party.

Susanna started her next letter to her sister Beulah from Galthlyfryd, Wales, on July 13, 1914. She sounded content and happy at her out-of-the-way little boarding house on a rocky cliff overlooking the wild Welsh sea:

> I have come down to take a few more nice little breaths of fresh sea air. Anna & I have had supper in our little private dining room, and now out on the porch at quarter of eight it is quite light. Our little boarding house is built right on the side of the cliff; the steps & zig zag path up makes you think much of the Angel Trail in Grand Canyon or the ascent to the Cappucini monastery at Amalfi. But once up here we have a grand view of the ocean, the breakers rolling in, and down on the broad stretch of sand at low tide the children are still playing and the people walking. It is the most ideal resort place I have most ever seen. . . . On First-day morning Anna, Ernest Montford and I spent the whole morning wandering . . . over the hillsides through ferns & gorse interspersed frequently with fox glove, heather, and other wild flowers of almost every color and variety . . . Then in the afternoon A & I had a nice nap & between tea and supper took our writing to the sands. I felt exactly as though I were at Atlantic City when I looked seawards, but when I saw the mountainous island to my right the long range stretching out to sea on my left and in back the sheer wall of rock with houses stuck on near the bottom at such an angle that you wonder what keeps them from sliding down on the others, I could not help but know we were not in Jersey. . . . Now A & I are on the train for Port Madoc, coach to Beddgelest and some unknown conveyance to Pen-y-Gwryd Inn where we stay for about 3 days near Snowdon.

Susanna's next letter was written to her mother several days later from the Pen-y-Gwryd Inn. Susanna continued to wax delighted about Wales:

> When I wrote to Beulah a few days ago I thought we were having a lovely time, but today has capped the climax. Never will I say anything about English people again! What would you say of entire strangers who took pity on two girls and took them for a 77 mile auto ride for no reason at all except that they would like to do it. . . . The first night here we were put with an entirely strange couple, yesterday we talked a little with them, and after dinner in the drawing room we were talking about the distance down to Betws-y-Coed. 10 miles did not sound far to walk if we could get a ride back, and Dr. Smith said if you would care to we would be glad to take you down in our car. . . . This morning at breakfast when the maid asked what kind of sandwiches they wanted put up for lunch they said 'We want enough for four, please.' So we started about 10:15, Dr. & Anna on the front seat and Mrs. & I on the back seat of a lovely new Darracq (French) car. My, luxurious wasn't the term, Anna & I both had grins from ear to ear. Instead of starting towards Betws-y, we made for the opposite direction at a good speed. First we went down to Carnarvon Castle & saw the room where the first Prince of Wales was born, and the place where all the Princes of Wales since have received their titles. . . . Then on to Conway Castle where we ate lunch up in one of the battlement towers. I was especially crazy about that; it was such a nice grass & ivy overgrown ruin and yet well enough preserved to see where the old stair cases & fire places had been. You would have thought that would have been enough wouldn't you. But no, we went on around the coast, clear out to Llandudno where we are going on Seventh day . . . stopped at a very sporty hotel for tea, back to a very pretty falls and home by quarter of six. . . . We cannot get over how very kind it was of them to just happen to take us.

I was excited to read Susanna's accounts of the same Welsh tourist attractions that I had visited, first while traveling with my family in the British Isles and then when staying with friends in North Wales decades later. My mother told me that Susanna and Beulah had visited Wales because the Parry clan originated in Carnarvon. The Parry name was everywhere in Wales, on storefronts and in newspaper advertisements and such; the name was so common in Wales that there were jokes about "Harry Parry." I felt a strong connection with Wales—the strange, melodic Gaelic language, the singing of hymns, the ever-present wild wind, the rugged landscape with its scruffy hills, rolling waterfalls, and rocky cliffs overlooking stormy seas. Susanna seemed to feel the same connection and, for some reason, wanted to climb Snowdon:

> Well, of course, the thing to do here is to climb Snowden, 3,560 above sea level, 2,653 ft from here, so at 10 o'clock A & I clothed in the oldest garments we could find (and no more restrictions than were necessary, sweater pockets stuffed full & pinned & the sleeves tied around our waists) started off for a 5 ½ mile journey. . . . We thought in past years that the Bright Angel Trail was quite an achievement but this was the real thing. The black clouds hung low over Snowdon & it looked as though it would pour any moment but on we struggled over fixed stones & slippery stones around boulders and across miniature waterfalls, but at last the apparent summit was reached and we discovered the bleak, cold wind from the sea side as well as a very dense mist. . . . The wind began to disperse the clouds and such a glorious view as we did have from the sea coast on the south, west & north to the far valleys of the east.

Unfortunately, Anna twisted a muscle in her leg, but they bought a walking stick and came down slowly, Anna leaning on Susanna in the rough places.

Susanna had found a new favorite place: "Anna thinks I am very unpatriotic when I wonder why our ancestors ever left Wales." Because Susanna and I were both captivated by the wild beauty of North Wales, I am adding it to the Second Susanna Tour: Carnarvon, Conway Castle, Llandudno, Betws-y-Coed. I would highly recommend staying at a place Susanna couldn't have seen because it didn't yet exist when she was there—Portmeirion, a fanciful, quirky Italianesque tourist village built by the eccentric Sir Clough Williams-Ellis between 1925-1975, which served as the location of the cult classic TV show *The Prisoner*. In addition, I would recommend nearby Llangollen, where the famous "Ladies of Llangollen" lived blissfully together at the turn of the nineteenth century.

Our Quaker voyagers next traveled south through Chester to the Lake District. Susanna's July 21, 1914, letter to her Auntie was written from the home of Woodbrooke administrator Dr. Braithwaite in Ghyll Close, Kendal, where they spent three luxurious days. Susanna and Anna were impressed by the home and all the servants, a bit out of their league but they seemed to hold their own: "This is a lovely place. . . . The house itself is a large stone (almost a mansion) house. The rooms are quite large and furnished in such beautiful taste. The maids (four in all at the morning bible reading) rush around so, it keeps you jumping to live up to the reputation of America."

The next letter to Beulah was written from the Keswick Hotel in the Lake District. It looks like a lovely, grand place from the picture on the letterhead. The luxurious Keswick Hotel is still in operation today, now known as the Keswick Country House Hotel; built in the 1860s, it became the leading hotel of the Lake District, visited by dignitaries including Queen Elizabeth II.

Susanna continued the account of her visit with the Braithwaites, who hired a seven-passenger Studebaker for escorting the American tourists. "The first day we came north through the Kirkstone Pass to Ullswater where we had lunch at a sporty hotel, then north & around by a new road on Thirlmere, & back to Grassmere to tea, stopping to see Wordsworth's home (Dove Cottage). Then the next day we took a south-easterly direction visiting the old Carinel Priory, George Foxe's meeting, Swarthmore Hall (passing through Ulnesstone), then Furness Abbey and home by way of Coniston where we saw Ruskin's home & his grave in the little church yard."

Susanna began her July 25 letter to her mother from Buttermere, Keswick. She asked for a bit more money to be sent to London in case of emergency. (Money transactions were slow and complicated in the days before wire transfers and ATMs.) The letter continued from Glasgow,

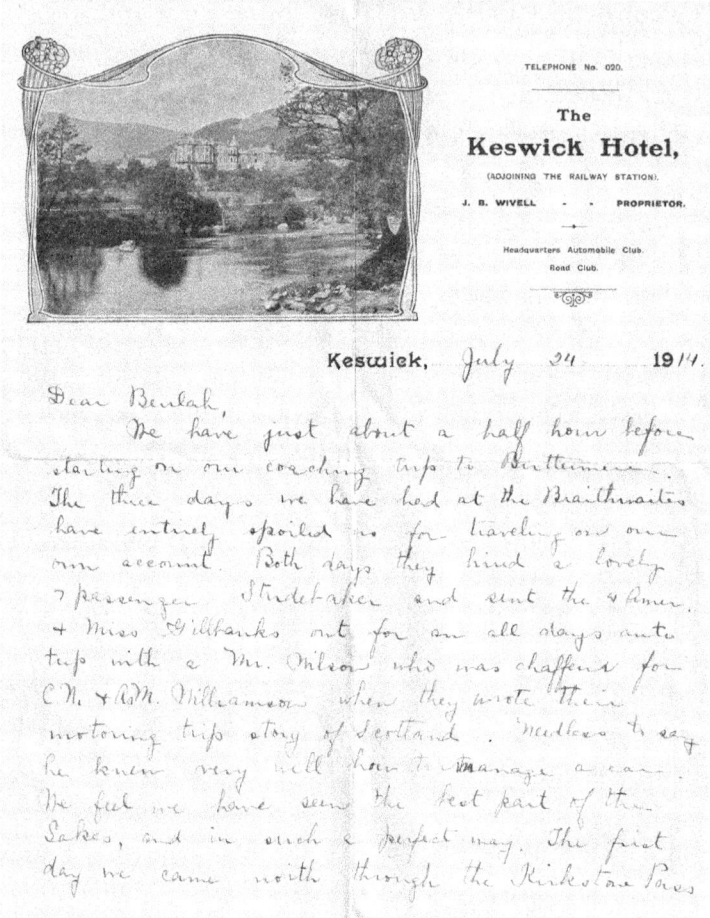

Susanna Parry's letter from Keswick Hotel in England's Lake District, 1914.

where the girls went to the Ruskin Pottery store and bought two wedding presents each, which they sent directly to their return steamer. The Ruskin Pottery studio was established in 1898 by Edward R. Taylor, whose art pottery became famous for its innovative glazes. When the pottery closed in 1935, the studio destroyed the formulae for all the glazes so they couldn't be duplicated. Some Ruskin pieces now sell for thousands.

Susanna ended the letter with her usual comments about how much weight she and Anna had gained on their travels. She mentioned the Susanna Crocroft Diet that everyone was talking about. Women's obsession with their weight has been around for generations, as has weight loss quackery.

Susanna, in her next letter written to Auntie from Oban, Scotland, on July 30, 1914, didn't mention that war in Europe was declared two days earlier. News was slow to travel in those days; apparently Susanna was unaware that World War I had begun and the age of innocence had ended. Luckily, she and Anna had booked their passage home in September. Susanna's ignorance of the war allowed her to enjoy Scotland's natural beauty: "The hills are all so beautiful, and that first night the sunset was gorgeous. The light made all the nearer hills a most gorgeous golden mist, and the more distant ones a lavender. Our window on the top floor of our tenement, as we call it, looks out over the bay, and we sat there and raved until about ten o'clock. The sun did not set until about nine and then the new moon was perfectly beautiful as the silver light followed the gold. Really I was tempted to say that it is as beautiful here as at Sorrento."

The previous day they had taken a day trip via steamer through the Sound of Mull to the Atlantic and Staffa, where they took a rowboat to Fingal's Cave:

> That was very interesting. The huge mostly 6-sided columns of basalt rock, from about a foot to two feet in diameter and twenty or forty feet high, formed this large cave in the side of the island and when we got up on the rocks on the side it looked like a beautiful little chapel with black columned walls, tinged with pink near the water at the end, and a floor of lovely clear green water below. The rocks were very slippery, but there was a rope railing and we all got along nicely, except Mrs. Jones whose knees got very wobbly. Under the water, we could see lovely little pink sea anemones and green sea weed. Then we walked or rather climbed on these broken columns to the other side of the island to a great formation which looked like a clam shell. At Ione we were taken ashore again to see the ruins of some old, old abbeys, nunneries, etc. which are supposed to have been founded by St. Columba when he landed there from Ireland in 563 and began the Christianization and civilization of Scotland. The old crosses and the

graves of old Scottish, Irish & Norwegian Kings with these beautiful carved stones were most interesting.

The next morning, they headed to Mallaig.

Susanna wrote her next letter to Beulah on August 1, 1914, from the RMS *Gael* steamer. They had traveled from Mallaig to Portree on the Isle of Skye. Still no mention of the unimaginable: war. That came in her August 4 letter to her father: "We have been going along from day to day having a very good time in this beautiful country, and have not seen the papers from one's week's end to the next. Once in a great while we would hear a war rumor but thought it all a farce until this morning's paper came and we really began to understand the seriousness of the situation . . . the banks are to be closed until Friday."

Because of the war, the girls changed their itinerary and headed earlier than planned to Edinburgh, where they would be more in touch with the news:

> We do not even know yet whether Great Britain has declared war or not, but suppose you are reading your papers about it now. In this little fishing village of course everyone is talking. . . . Even up here it affects them very closely for so many have volunteered for service. The rumor from Stournaway says that all the fishermen left last night to go on duty, and Miss Cameron says that business is really their only means of subsistence and wonders how they who are left behind will get along. We four are together and everything so far seems to be working smoothly for us, so don't you worry about us. We are going to the American Consul as soon as we reach Edinburgh and get his advice upon the best plan to pursue. If things get too hot here you may see us at home yet before we planned. We hope this is nothing but a scare and will soon pass over.

Given the threat of war, the girls wanted to come home as soon as possible and hoped the American Consul could get them passage on an earlier steamer. Susanna told her father not to send the money previously requested until they had definite plans. She would cable if their plans changed.

Susanna and Anna arrived in Edinburgh, closer to the news of the war. Susanna's August 10 letter sent birthday wishes to Auntie. She wished she had been able to send a gift to her, but she was being frugal with her expenditures so that she'd have enough money to last until she was back on American shores. Luckily, it appeared their ship home would sail as planned. "We are somewhat relieved to hear that the American Line is the only one which has continued with unaltered sailings. Some poor people are taking even third class to get home quickly. Even battleships from America have been suggested as a possible means of transportation. But one thing is certain: we won't worry until we have to and hope you will do the same."

Susanna's August 13 letter expressed her compassion for the many people they knew, of all nationalities, whose lives had been disrupted or ruined by the war, particularly the Germans living in England who were now under suspicion:

> As we almost daily hear of the plight of various Americans, we cannot help but think how lucky we are to even have passage engaged although we have to wait over a month for it. As far as I can see the American Line is the only one which is going on its way unaltered. But let us hope that this almost useless war that Europe has been dragged into will soon be over and that the people can return to their peaceful occupations once more. Being at Woodbrooke for so long with so many different nationalities has made us much more in sympathy with the people and we think now more of the individuals than of a spot on the map. We often wonder about the Dutch and Germans we know, and how this trouble is affecting them. For there are so many people in all the countries who look upon it with as much horror as the rest of us. As Miss Kelman (an Edinburgh Woodbrooker) said the other day, it made her want to write to Mr. Hartmann, just to send her sympathy and good fellowship toward him, even if she was not able to help him materially. He is a German clergyman in Birmingham, and we have wondered how he is being treated. Even though many of his nationality have lived here for years and are in perfect sympathy with the English attitude they have to report themselves to the authorities

and in some cases have been confined almost as ordinary prisoners. We met an English woman the other day on the train who was quite disturbed because her husband (a German & teaching school in Glasgow & Folkirk) had been detained in the smaller town. He could not go back to his home without risking being taken again as a prisoner of war, so his poor wife had to go all the way to the smaller place. This means closing their own home in Glasgow, finding another in Folkirk, and also giving up his school in the former place. Doesn't it all seem perfectly absurd? To think of such things being done in this generation. When we were up at Portree someone expressed a wish to get back nearer civilization, but we wondered if that term could still be applied, or if it ever has been applied correctly.

Susanna gave her mother an account of their sightseeing excursion to Melrose, the Lammermoor hills, the valley of the Tweed, Abbottsford "and over Sir Walter Scott's favorite drive to Dryburgh. The view from Bemersyde out over the winding Tweed, surrounded with beautiful trees and farm land, to the Eildon Hills beyond was one of the finest views we had." Susanna closed the letter by thanking whoever sent her additional funds. Although she had not anticipated receiving any more money because of the uncertainty of wartime, she was very glad to open a "cablegram enclosed in an envelope from the American Express Co. which told of $200 coming over in gold for me by way of U.S. Treasury. Anna & I both had agreed that we wouldn't need more but it is a very nice feeling to know that we can get it as soon as we reach London . . . thanks so much to whoever sent it." In 1914, $200 was worth about $5,000 in today's money, quite a comfortable cushion.

Susanna's August 16 letter to Beulah described a monument in Edinburg which I missed on my visit there and would certainly look for on a next visit. "Anna & I went out for a walk, first to the Calton Hill burial ground, where we saw the Abraham Lincoln monument which was erected in memory of the Scottish-Americans who died in the Civil War. It is a bronze figure of Lincoln on a high granite pedestal on which is seated a figure of a colored man with his hand up-raised begging for emancipation."

Like all Americans abroad, our Quaker travelers waited anxiously for passage home. Signs of war were everywhere: battleships in the harbor, soldiers encamped on the outskirts, thousands watching them drilling, our Susanna among them. To escape the chilly sea wind, the girls took a shortcut back to the hotel through the slums. They were shocked at the horrid living conditions of the slumdwellers, the dark side of industrialism. The war had worsened the condition of the poor as many factories had closed. Susanna looked at the scene of wasted humanity with the compassionate eyes of a progressive Quaker activist:

> We did not linger long on account of the brisk sea wind, as well as the time. In order to get back quickly we came through some of the slum streets and the poverty down there is terrible. Anna says she has seen some pretty bad sections in our cities but nothing to compare with the filth and dejectedness of these people. At one place the soldiers were having their evening meal in an open field and lined up in back of an iron fence were great rows of women with babies in their arms and other children sitting along the curb, waiting for the few loaves or other leavings from the supper. We went down to visit the shelter of the S.P.C.C. the other day and they say that so many factories have been closed on account of the war that people are more in need than ever, and besides this everyone is spending all their energy in giving to help the army, while the poor are nearly starving. Doesn't it seem awful that they have to spend all this money for war when it really could be put to some use and benefit in this section to clean up the streets & houses if nothing more. But there is one thing especially we have noticed and that is that nearly every house even in the little alleys, or closes as they call them, have their window boxes of bright colored flowers. They add so much brightness to the dingy houses.

Susanna and Anna made their way south and stayed in York for several days in anticipation of their return home. They didn't want to arrive in London too quickly as it was overcrowded with Americans who managed to escape the Continent and were awaiting passage home. Luckily, Susanna and Anna were among the few who had secured reservations.

Susanna's August 21 letter thanked her father for the extra money that was on its way. She and Anna had been unable to procure passports from the American consulate in Edinburgh, but they did get certificates of citizenship. Americans abroad did not previously need passports, but things had changed in wartime, and they wanted to be sure nothing would keep them from sailing home. The American consul "said he had not heard of ladies being questioned or stopped, but . . . now we have those papers to show that we are Americans, although they will probably not be needed." She told her father not to worry.

Susanna wrote her next letter from York, dated August 23, to her Auntie Sue. Apart from sending birthday wishes and describing some tourist excursions, the letter mostly recounted the German atrocities in Belgium, acutely felt by our peace-loving Quaker who had friends in the war zone:

> The herring fisheries, although getting good prices, are losing all they usually get for their export trade to Germany. But these are small discomforts of the war compared to the great and almost unbearable distress of the Belgians who have fallen in the path of the invading German army. I was looking at yesterday's pictorial section of the paper, and some of the scenes are certainly terrible. It is bad enough to have to endure the battles, but to turn out the poor innocent inhabitants and burn their homes as well as killing many of them. It is really too horrible to think of. Then to realize that it is not only the outlying districts, but that Brussels, that beautiful city we visited such a short time ago, is now in the hands of the enemy, who may do almost anything at any time. We have thought so much about the lovely young girl who lodged us during Miss Neef's illness, and what has happened to them all. The impersonal side is bad enough but how much worse when we think of people we really know, and what they are probably being forced to endure.

Susanna's next letter, written on August 28 from Cambridge, gave her mother her remaining itinerary. She and Anna would go to London the next day for several weeks, then north to Oxford for two days, then to Woodbrooke near Birmingham for a day, then to Liverpool the day before they were scheduled to sail. Most of the letter discussed the war. Susanna expressed frustration that press reports were censored, with news of battles and casualties not reported until days after. (There was no radio or television coverage of the war; radio broadcasts would not start until 1920, and the first public demonstration of television would not occur until 1934.) "The first of the wounded soldiers have been brought back to England yesterday, and we have been reading their accounts of the fighting around Mons. A special Press Bureau has been appointed to censor all war news and the consequence is that we get very little news, except days late. . . . This town is just running over with soldiers; they say about 45,000 are quartered here and as soon as these get their marching orders, the Canadians from London are coming here to be trained."

By the next letter dated August 30, Susanna was in London, which was teeming with Americans who had arrived from the Continent and were trying to obtain passage home. She still expected to sail from Liverpool on September 23. The letter is thick with clippings from *The Times* about the war: a map showing the position of troops in Germany and Russia; a summary of the German atrocities in Belgium; a report of mass evacuations from Calais and Dunkirk in anticipation of the arrival of the Germans, while Lille and Boulogne had declared themselves *villes ouvertes*, or open cities, not resisting the advancing army in order to escape bombardment; and the story of hundreds of English tourists who had been stranded in Switzerland finally arriving in Boulogne and clamoring to get on the Folkestone ferry back to England.

The war news was indeed awful, but Susanna lightened the mood by giving an amusing account of an eccentric old lady at her boarding house who was seated next to her at the dinner table:

> We attended church this morning at St. Paul's where the minister admonished his congregation to love their enemies, but a funny old lady here at the house says that is better in theory than practice. This lady lives here most of the time, and therefore quite a fixture of the place. When Helen Waller Sterm and Emily Poley were here earlier in the year and occupying this same room we have on the "3rd floor

back," they called this woman the Duchess, and a fine name it is for her too. She sits at the head of the table in her light-colored gowns which all possess trains at least a yard long. Rings of all types and styles cover her fingers, but the most distinctive thing about her is her snow-white hair which is a most peculiar contrivance, downed we suppose only in the daytime. It rises in a high peak at least six or eight inches above her head and has a big black ornament of tulle on one side. She certainly looks as though she had just stepped out of a picture book of about three or four generations ago. I rather unfortunately was given the seat next to her deaf ear which makes me screech out while the rest of the table stops to listen. But we all think she is quite a joke and the others rejoice that A. & I are having our turn now.

An August 4 letter from London to Beulah enclosed a copy of the *American Bulletin* published at the Savoy Hotel, gathering central for Americans in London. Susanna and Anna had both registered there. The *Bulletin* listed sailings and availability, Americans registered in London and Amsterdam, information regarding passport applications, etc. Passports weren't necessary for returning Americans, but our travelers had the consular certificate they procured in Edinburgh just in case. Susanna told Beulah all the typical tourist outings she and Anna had done, including an enjoyable visit to the Tate Gallery and Madame Tussaud's waxworks. She also let Beulah know that after many formalities at American Express, she collected the forty gold pieces her father sent her as security funds. Susanna, Anna, and several other American boarders had gone to the theatre to see "*Grumpy*, an English play which was in New York last winter. It was quite good and kept us laughing most of the time, especially when Grumpy, the old grandfather, had such a time with Bradshaw the large time-table of all the trains on all the R.R. in England & Scotland & Wales & Ireland. We have had our troubles too and could appreciate his difficulties."

Susanna also sent Beulah several newspaper clippings. The one most interesting to me was an account of the renaming of St. Petersburg, now known as Petrograd, on September 1. "By Imperial order the city of St. Petersburg will henceforth be known as Petrograd. The termination 'grad' is the Slavonic equivalent of the German 'burg', which means town. The decision to rename the Russian capital is significant not only of the hatred of everything German, but of the intense patriotic feeling that is sweeping through Russia." With the same Germanophobia, once America entered the war, sauerkraut would be called "liberty cabbage."

In her next letter, Susanna tried to calm Auntie's fears about her niece's being so close to a war zone:

> Your letters sound as though you are still rather anxious about us, but again I can assure you it is quite unnecessary, for we are having a very nice visit in London, and are really seeing more than if the war had not broken out, for now the Suffragettes and Irish are all working with the government for the good of the nation, and are not thinking about their own petty grievances. Therefore all the galleries are open more than they have been for years. We have seen most of both the Wallace and Tate collections, and have visited two sections of the National Gallery. . . . Tomorrow we are going to the British Museum which is only about two or three blocks from here.

A bit surprising that Susanna considered the suffragettes' fight over not having the vote a "petty grievance"; I'm sure the Pankhursts and our Alice Paul would have disagreed. There is no evidence in the collection that Susanna and Beulah were actively involved in the suffrage movement. Participation in any public demonstration would probably have been prohibited by their father and certainly by Auntie—far too unseemly for respectable Quaker ladies.

At Quaker meeting, Susanna and Anna ran into acquaintances from Woodbrooke, including Catharine Albright, whose independent lifestyle Susanna had so admired in the spring. Together they toured a settlement in a London slum, after having seen the slums of Birmingham and Edinburgh:

> Yesterday we went to Hampstead meeting, and saw both Jack and Miss Catharine Albright (whom we visited over a week-end while we were at Woodbrooke). It seemed very nice to see them again. Jack came around in the afternoon and took Anna, Miss White and

me down to Toynbee Hall, a settlement where he is staying just at present. There are a great many (perhaps a hundred) young university boys working there trying to improve the neighborhood. They have all sorts of classes, and it is primarily an intellectual center, although gymnasium and other work is also carried on. Then we walked through the dirty slum streets, in and out between the carts, people, dogs and children which filled the street between the stalls of the Sunday market. They were bartering all sorts of goods from food stuffs to lace curtains. . . . Finally we reached Hoxton Hall where Ted Bigland is working so hard in the Friends mission, which is only one of a series of nine centers known as the Bedford Institute. A young Friend, Miss Fox, showed us over the buildings, class rooms, etc. including a large lecture room which had once been the very worst kind of a music hall and had been shut down by the authorities. Now they have big evening meetings, concerts, etc.

Susanna's September 10, 1914, letter to her mother enclosed a clipped article from that day's edition of *The Times*, calling London "the City of Refuge" for Belgian victims of the war, as well as for French and Russian refugees, offering them accommodation and hospitality. At the same time, England was sending shiploads of food to Belgium to help those who remained; numerous relief funds had been established to help the victims of war. Susanna was full of compassion for these suffering people: "The poor Belgians, little do we know what they have passed through in the last month, for it is almost impossible to understand & realize that many of the reports are probably true, and the poor people have lost everything they ever possessed."

In a fascinating coincidence, Susanna and Anna attended a benefit at the London Opera house to raise money for the refugees—a benefit organized by the suffragette Christabel Pankhurst, daughter of Emmeline, who had just returned to England from a two-year exile in France and was now helping with the war effort:

> Miss Pankhurst has just returned from a 2½ year exile in Paris, and so they took the big London Opera House for the evening and it was

packed to overflowing. We got there ¾ of an hour before the doors opened and then were on the side and four rows from the front of the balcony. It was interesting to see how devoted the people were to Miss P. as soon as she came into the box, nearly everyone stood and waved and cheered. Then someone started "For she's a jolly good fellow" and they all joined in, and then for a second time they cheered and waved again. She and all other prisoners have been released during the war on promise of good behavior and are trying to help as best they can in the war. All profit from that big meeting as well as the proceeds of a collection taken just before the close was to go to help the refugees of the Allies who are flocking to this little island by the hundreds and thousands.

Homesick Susanna closed her letter with a touching account of the previous night's dream, longing for the affection and embraces of her family. "Last night in my dreams I had a good hug and hope before long I won't be disappointed when morning comes. Anna and I have to take it out on each other and really we get quite squishy sometimes. Lots and lots of love and kisses but don't tell Beulah (I said that for she pretends she doesn't like such actions)."

There are only two more letters from Susanna in England, the first from London, the second from Liverpool, mostly concerning setting sail on the *Merion* on September 23. Their ship crossed the Atlantic without incident and arrived at its destination of Philadelphia. Susanna was finally safe at home again.

Only two more items in the Susanna Collection for 1914. The first is a stateside newspaper clipping dated October 2 about Dr. Battin, the guide of the 1908 Swarthmore trip to the Continent. "Andrew Carnegie and other friends of peace are greatly interested in the mission to Europe of Professor Benjamin F. Battin, who has been given a year's leave of absence by Swarthmore College to go abroad as the special diplomatic envoy of the Church Peace Union." The Church Peace Union, now known as the Carnegie Council, was established in early 1914 by the Carnegie Council for Ethics in International Affairs with an endowment of $2 million, about $50 million in today's money; its goal was uniting diverse churches and faiths, including the Quakers, for the work of abolishing war and establishing peace internationally. President Wilson wanted to keep the United States out of the war in Europe and did what he could on the diplomatic front, along with the efforts of the Church Peace Union and other groups such as Jane Addams' and Henry Ford's "Peace Ship" to Europe in December 1915, which Ford was sure would end the war and which was much derided because it didn't. Despite all the protests and peace efforts, the Germans continued to develop new horrific tools of war—poison gas and the U-boat (submarine), bringing America closer to engaging in the conflict.

The second and last entry from 1914 is the announcement of the December wedding of another of Susanna's friends. Susanna and Beulah would never have wedding announcements of their own.

CHAPTER 14

WAGING WAR

After all the engaging letters from Susanna about her travels on the Continent, her studies in England in 1914, and the drama of being so near to the war zone while so far away from home, the Susanna Collection dries up after her return home to New Jersey. The bundle of envelopes for 1915 disappoints: wedding invitations, wedding announcements, and birth announcements. The year must have disappointed Susanna as well. She remained with her family while her friends left their childhood homes to get married and start their own families. Yesteryear's chatty, gossipy, carefree letters exchanged between schoolgirls were tied up and put away in the wooden box with all the other epistolary bundles of her life. Knowing Susanna, she must have struggled with depression after her return from Europe, when her days quieted down to the old housekeeping-and-Quaker-meeting routine.

There are only three entries in the Susanna Collection for 1916. The first two are wedding announcements sent to Susanna and Beulah. The last is a letter to Susanna's Auntie Sue from a cousin at a boarding house in Hope, New York. The cousin began the letter by asking Sue for her recipe for elderberry jelly. The letter got interesting, however, when she mentioned outbreaks of infantile paralysis, now known as polio. "I was shocked to hear of those cases of Infantile Paralysis at Moorestown. We had an extremely sad case here in Hope—a little boy came from Brooklyn with his father, mother & sister & after being here 3 weeks was stricken with this dreadful disease & died in 3 days. Then the little sister had it very lightly—indeed some of the doctors say she did not have it.

There were 60 boarders at this place & a number of children—all under quarantine, but no other case has developed."

There was an epidemic of poliomyelitis, or polio, in the summer of 1916 in New York and elsewhere, with over 27,000 cases in the U.S. and 6,000 deaths nationwide, 2,000 of them in New York. Outbreaks of polio continued every year, usually in the cities and in the summer, peaking in the 1940s and 1950s when it claimed over a half million lives each year worldwide. Perhaps the most famous victim was Franklin D. Roosevelt, who was stricken in 1921 at the age of 39 and paralyzed from the waist down. His battle with polio did not keep him from serving four terms as president, victoriously fighting against the economic depression, or helping to lead the nation and Allies to victory in World War II. Roosevelt had great compassion for children stricken with polio, creating a hydrotherapy center in 1924, using the mineral-rich waters at Warm Springs, Georgia, and creating the National Foundation for Infantile Paralysis in 1938, later renamed the March of Dimes. The search for an effective vaccine began in the 1930s. Jonas Salk developed his vaccine in 1955, and a mass immunization took place in 1957, funded by the March of Dimes. Albert Sabin developed his oral vaccine in 1962 when another mass immunization took place.

There is nothing in the Susanna Collection from 1916 until 1924. I wondered what Susanna was doing all those years when America was fighting in World War I and recovering for years after the war. At least some answers would be given when the correspondence began again: she was fighting a personal battle.

We know little about Susanna's activities from 1915 to 1924, but we know much about Alice Paul's fight for women's equality, beginning with her war with President Wilson over women's constitutional right to vote. Although Alice was famous—infamous—in her own day, far too many women today don't even know who Alice Paul was, the enormous sacrifices she made to procure their right to vote, and her attempt to obtain full equal rights for them. Luckily, there is a growing body of fascinating and well-written research about the suffrage movement and Alice Paul in particular; I am indebted to the works of these many scholars and urge those interested to read them to learn more about the suffrage movement, the Nineteenth Amendment, and the Equal Rights Amendment, which Alice authored.

At the end of 1914, Alice was head of her own organization, the Congressional Union (CU), whose goal was to obtain suffrage via constitutional amendment, unlike its parent association, the National American Woman Suffrage Association (NAWSA), which continued to struggle to obtain the vote state by state. Despite the CU's efforts to pass the suffrage amendment and the growing popular support for it, no vote had been taken, so the CU undertook a new strategy of holding the party in power—the Democrats—responsible for the lack of suffrage.

In January 1915, the CU opened an office in Manhattan in rent-free space provided by socialite-turned-suffragist Alva Belmont. Alice renamed the suffrage amendment the "Susan B. Anthony Amendment." On January 6, delegates from fifteen states met with Wilson about the federal amendment, but Wilson still insisted that suffrage was a state issue. Nonetheless, on January 12, the amendment was debated and voted on in the House for the first time, although it lost by a vote of 204 to 174. Some congressmen argued that the vote would degrade women and make them less desirable as wives.[1]

That spring, Wilson deflected the CU's repeated attempts to meet with him, considering the group nothing more than an annoyance. Wilson ordered the press to destroy the newsreels of the CU's rejected requests for a meeting, raising suspicions about the president's attempts to control the press and silence dissidence. Wilson's attempts would intensify when the country engaged in the war, which was fast approaching: On May 8, 1915, the Germans sank the *Lusitania*, killing 1,198, including 128 Americans.

In the summer of 1915, Alice sought to expand the CU chapters westward to the states where women were enfranchised. To raise awareness of suffrage, in a stroke of marketing genius, Alice organized a Women Voters Convention at the San Francisco World's Fair—the Panama-Pacific International Exposition, whose nineteen million visitors, thanks to the CU, were educated about the cause of suffrage and the need for a federal amendment. In addition to suffrage exhibitions, Alice thrilled the crowd by engaging Hazel Hunkins to fly in a plane over San Francisco Bay and drop thousands of leaflets about suffrage onto the crowd below.² Moreover, Alice persuaded officials to declare the final day of the Women Voters Convention "Congressional Union for Woman Suffrage Day", and several renowned speakers rallied the crowd: Helen Keller and Annie Sullivan, former progressive powerhouse President Theodore Roosevelt, and Italian educator Maria Montessori.³ After the fair, a delegation crossed the country with a pro-amendment petition to present to pro-suffrage congressmen, after which they planned to meet with President Wilson at the White House in December.

In contrast to the CU's successes, the rival state suffrage group NAWSA suffered defeat in the elections as state suffrage was voted down in New York, New Jersey, Massachusetts, and Pennsylvania.

In January 1916, the CU moved into its new headquarters at Cameron House, 21 Madison Place, NW, in Lafayette Square near the White House. Alice and Lucy moved there, renting their rooms. Dora Lewis also rented one of the large bedrooms where she could stay on her visits to Washington; she encouraged Alice to use her nicer room. Cameron House became known as "the Little White House." To increase awareness of the CU, Alice opened a tearoom on the ground floor for passers-by as well as staff workers.⁴

Early in 1916, Harriot Stanton Blatch, daughter of Elizabeth Cady Stanton, joined her New York Women's Political Union with Alice Paul's Congressional Union after the defeat of state suffrage in the last election.⁵ In April, Alice announced to her CU Advisory Council that she wanted to create a woman's political party.⁶ Her call was answered in June: Alice, Harriot Stanton Blatch, and Alva Belmont launched the National Woman's Party (NWP), whose platform was the passage of the Susan B. Anthony Amendment and whose membership was limited to voting women in the suffrage states. Membership grew to 40,000 by the end of the year.

Because Alice did not live in a suffrage state, she could not be a member of her new party, but she ran the show behind the scenes, fast becoming the Greatest Show-Woman in American political history, bringing suffrage to center stage in American politics with informative and entertaining suffrage productions. Following her inaugural spectacle in 1913 and her events at the San Francisco World's Fair in 1915, she and the NWP created a new traveling suffrage show before the 1916 election: a five-week "Suffrage Special" train which called on women voters in the western suffrage states to denounce all elected Democrats as personally responsible for denying women the vote. With this confrontational train tour, the NWP emerged as a progressive party of non-violent female protest and suffragist rebels. The press ate it up. The NWP was lauded by the *San Francisco Bulletin* for its "'vigorous action . . . quite in the spirit of the revolutionary patriots, though without destruction of property or effusion of blood.'"[7]

The NWP hoped to coerce the Democrats to pass a suffrage amendment before the election, with the four million women in the suffrage states threatening to vote for the Republican candidates if they didn't. The suffragists faced growing opposition. When the NWP demonstrated in October at a speech given by President Wilson in Chicago, unruly men opposed to suffrage scuffled with the demonstrators, destroying their banners and injuring a few.

The NWP and CU received several blows in the fall. First, after long years fighting for suffrage at Alice's side, Lucy Burns was burned out and resigned from her full-time suffrage work on the road. Second, the Democrats didn't act on suffrage before the election, although they did pass other progressive legislation: restricting child labor, limiting the workday of railroad workers to eight hours, getting workers' compensation for government contractors, imposing the first estate tax, and appointing progressive judges to the Supreme Court. Third, Wilson was re-elected, although by a narrow margin. Fourth, and saddest of all, Inez Milholland, the beautiful, iconic, and hard-working suffrage protester, collapsed of fatigue on stage in California and died in November. Alice organized a demonstration at the Capitol on January 9, 1917, memorializing the suffragist martyr, after which three hundred women marched to the White House, where a delegation met with President Wilson. Wilson told them that although he personally supported suffrage, it was up to his party to initiate the amendment process.

The NWP met this stalemate with a change of strategy. Inspired by the effectiveness of union picket lines, Harriot Stanton Blatch suggested that NWP picketers protest in silence for suffrage in front of the White House. The morning of January 10, 1917, the first dozen suffrage picketers, who became known as the Silent Sentinels, marched from Cameron House to the White House, carrying banners striped with the NWP colors of purple, white, and gold, signifying dignity, purity, and brilliance[8], and a banner confronting President Wilson with Inez Milholland's impassioned plea: "Mr. President, how long must women wait for liberty?" The morning picketers were replaced by afternoon picketers who stayed until early evening, and the routine began the next day, continuing every day but Sunday for eighteen months thanks to the devotion of thousands of volunteers.

Although peaceful picketing by unions had been declared legal by the 1914 Clayton Act, this public display of protest by previously respectable women engendered much criticism. Although the Silent Sentinels didn't break windows or start fistfights, they did force their way through gender and social barriers, therefore seen by many as rebellious and undignified. *The New York Times* called them "silly" and "monstrous."[9] Even Alice's mother, Tacie, implored her to stop the pickets, which offended the president and disgraced the family. Alva Belmont, however, was delighted with the strategy and sent Alice a $5,000 check of support.

Silent Sentinels with protest banners in front of the White House, 1917. (Library of Congress Prints & Photographs Division)

At the March 2, 1917, CU/NWP Convention, the two groups officially merged and became known simply as the National Woman's Party, with Alice elected as chair.

As Wilson's March 5, 1917, inauguration approached, American participation in the war in Europe seemed inevitable, and Alice was bombarded with demands that she set aside her suffrage work to help with the war effort, as the Pankhursts had done in England. Alice, however, continued the Silent Sentinel pickets, arguing that women needed to cast their votes more than ever in time of war. As she told her recent convention: "Our organization is dedicated only to the enfranchisement of women. . . . We must do our part to see that war, which concerns women as seriously as men, shall not be entered upon without the consent of women."[10]

When the House convened on April 6 to finalize the vote on American participation in the war, the Silent Sentinels demonstrated at the Capitol as well as the White House. After the affair of the intercepted Zimmerman telegram in March revealing Germany's plot for Japan and Mexico to wage war on the U.S., on April 2, Wilson called for American participation in the war because the "world must be made safe for democracy." As America engaged in the World War, progressive dreams of a new and better world were challenged. Alice, however, would not relinquish her dream of women's enfranchisement and liberation and did not give up the fight. She published an article in *The Suffragist*, criticizing Wilson's call for democracy in the world when there was none in the United States because women could not vote.

Alice's patriotism came under increasing attack because of her relentless criticism of Wilson. Alice and the NWP, however, persisted in the fight for the vote. The Sentinels, including Lucy Burns and Dora Lewis, enraged the crowd during a June 1917 visit of the Russian delegation when their banner claimed that America was not a democracy like free Russia and called on Wilson to liberate his citizens. The crowd ripped down the banner but could not deter the Sentinels, the NWP, and certainly not Alice.

CHAPTER 15

PRISONERS OF WAR

With the country now at war, it became increasingly dangerous for anti-war and anti-government groups to voice their dissent. The Espionage Act, passed by Congress on June 15, 1917, permitted the police to shut down socialist headquarters and socialist publications such as *The Masses* and attack members of the Industrial Workers of the World. In this effort to silence all dissenters, Alice and the Silent Sentinels were targeted, and the Wilson administration attempted to stop the pickets and their attacks on the president. When the police told Alice that NWP pickets would be arrested, she protested that peaceful picketing was protected under the Clayton Act. The police countered by arresting the Sentinels for obstructing traffic. They were released pending their court appearance, and the Silent Sentinels defiantly continued picketing.

In June 1917, six Sentinels led by Mabel Vernon were arrested and fined, and this time they were imprisoned, becoming the first suffragists imprisoned in America. When the six refused to pay their fines, they were sentenced to three days in jail. On July 4, another eleven Sentinels were arrested, including Lucy Burns. At this early stage of the imprisonment of NWP protesters, their prison conditions were tolerable: the women were allowed to wear their street clothes and received edible food brought in from the outside. Conditions, however, would soon worsen for imprisoned Sentinels.

Alice, whose physical and emotional health had been permanently weakened by her multiple incarcerations and forced feedings in England, refused to pace herself in her fight for the vote and collapsed at Cameron House. She was sent to recover in a Washington sanitarium, where she was misdiagnosed with Bright's Disease. NWP co-founder Dora Lewis intervened and had her transferred to Johns Hopkins in Baltimore and put under the care of her brother, Dr. Howard Kelly, who corrected the misdiagnosis, prescribing two months of rest for severe exhaustion and digestive problems. Alice recovered at home in Moorestown for a while, then stayed with Dora in Atlantic City until returning to Washington in mid-August.[1]

While Alice was recuperating, NWP Sentinels continued protesting and getting arrested, and their punishment worsened. On July 14, sixteen were arrested, including Doris Stevens, and sentenced to sixty days in the horrific Occoquan workhouse in Virginia. The severity of this punishment aroused sympathy for the Sentinels. Help for the imprisoned suffragists came from two men close to President Wilson. Dudley Field Malone, who had represented Doris Stevens when she was arrested on July 14 and would later become her first husband, resigned in protest from his position as the Wilson administration's Collector of the Port of New York[2] and vowed to help the beleaguered suffragists. Even more compelling, an old friend of Wilson's, J. H. Hopkins, who had recently dined with his wife at the White House, asked the president to release the prisoners because one of them, Alison Hopkins, was his wife; moreover, Hopkins asked Wilson not only to release the women but also to pass the Susan B. Anthony Amendment.[3] Wilson was probably lying when he claimed that he was not involved in the arrests, but he ceded to the pressure and pardoned the group on July 19.

However, the attacks on the suffragists continued. Not long after Alice returned to Washington from her convalescence, she was injured by an angry mob gathered in front of Cameron House because of an NWP banner criticizing the president for not granting universal suffrage to women: "Kaiser Wilson: Have you forgotten how you sympathized with the poor Germans because they were not self-governed? Twenty million American women are not self-governed. Take the beam out of your own eye." The "Kaiser Wilson" banner so enraged the crowd that they tore it down and threw eggs, tomatoes, and stones at the building.

A shot was fired into the building. Alice was knocked over and dragged down the street by someone trying to rip off her purple, white, and gold NWP sash. Although the police finally arrived, they arrested only a few of the attackers.[4]

The National Woman's Party refused to be deterred by these attacks, and the police continued their punishments. On August 17, six Sentinels were arrested, sentenced to thirty days at Occoquan, and forced to endure prison garb, bed bugs, rats, dangerously unsanitary conditions, and maggoty food. In early September, another twelve Sentinels were arrested, including Lucy Burns, and sentenced to sixty days in Occoquan. These longer sentences did not stop the Sentinel volunteers; on the contrary, their ranks swelled.

In addition to growing sympathy in the press for the incarcerated Sentinels, several congressmen spoke out against the harsh treatment of the suffragists, especially since their peaceful protests were entirely lawful. On September 24, the House voted to create a committee to consider the issue of women's suffrage. However, Wilson's war on the NWP continued, and the punishment intensified. On October 6, twelve Silent Sentinels, including Alice, were arrested for obstructing traffic but given suspended sentences.

On October 20, 1917, Alice and three others were arrested. When Alice appeared in court two days later, she was unapologetic and said she would not be bound by laws in which she had no voice because she could not vote.[5] The judge sentenced her to seven months in the horrific Washington Asylum and Jail ("District Jail")[6]. Once there, Alice was restricted to solitary confinement for protesting the inhumane conditions. She went on a hunger strike when her jailers refused to grant her political prisoner status and was then subjected to forced feeding three times a day, which worsened her already fragile digestive health. After three weeks of forced feedings, her jailers increased their torture: committing her to the psychopathic ward, restraining her in solitary confinement, submitting her to daily psychiatric interrogations, and depriving her of sleep by shining a light in her eyes periodically each night. Help came to Alice from her strong faith, her belief in her cause, a few of the psychiatric nurses who on the sly assured her that she was not at all insane[7], and from psychologist

Dr. William White who examined Alice and refused to declare her insane, saving her from being permanently committed to an insane asylum.[8]

Although Alice was denied visitors, her sister Helen stood outside her window and took dictation from the suffrage leader who demanded political prisoner status.[9] Dudley Field Malone managed to see Alice; outraged at her confinement, he obtained a writ of *habeas corpus* to have her removed from the psych ward. Meanwhile, the public and the press protested the abuse of the Sentinels, many of whom were now suffering physical ailments because of their mistreatment. In November, another thirty-one Silent Sentinels were arrested, including Lucy Burns and Dora Lewis, and sentenced to Occoquan, where they were horribly rough handled in what was referred as the "Night of Terror": one woman was denied immediate medical care by her jailers when she suffered a heart attack, and Lucy Burns was shackled with her hands over her head all night. Dora and Lucy were then transferred to the District Jail where Alice was held, to be force-fed.[10]

In response to a scathing article by David Lawrence following a visit with Alice, all the Sentinels were released, their charges of obstruction of traffic having been dismissed for insufficient proof. Alice was in such a weakened state that she needed to recover for three weeks at Cameron House. Several of the imprisoned Sentinels filed lawsuits for damages of $800,000 against district commissioners and wardens, alleging physical abuse, alienation from friends and family, and damaged reputations. (For those with strong stomachs, Doris Stevens' *Jailed for Freedom* (1920) documents in vivid detail the sickening physical and psychological abuse inflicted upon Alice Paul and the Silent Sentinels whose peaceful and lawful protests repeatedly landed them in jail. Today's precious right to vote has been paid for with tears and blood.)

The October Revolution of 1917, when Bolshevik leader Vladimir Lenin seized power in Russia, triggered the "Red Scare" in the U.S., which would intensify after the murder of Tsar Nicolas and his family in July 1918. As if the Espionage Act of 1917 weren't harsh enough, the Sedition Act of 1918 would expand the government's ability to attack the left. Socialist leader Eugene Debs would be arrested for an anti-war speech in 1918 and sentenced to ten years in prison. Not surprisingly, the

NWP's membership included increasing numbers from the progressive left. "The Socialist presence in the NWP was always significant, especially among the organizers."[11] The growing socialist element in the NWP surely accounted for the continuing persecution of NWP members, in particular its leader Alice Paul.

In November 1917, the state suffrage game of whack-a-mole continued: suffrage passed in New York, but Maine and Ohio rescinded their previous approvals.

In December, the NWP officially honored all the Sentinels who had been imprisoned, each "prisoner of freedom" awarded a brooch of a cell door, reminiscent of the silver brooch in the form of a grated prison door the Pankhursts had given Alice after her first imprisonment in Scotland. During the NWP's Silent Sentinel campaign, 500 women had been arrested and 168 imprisoned, for the most part in the monstrous Occoquan workhouse.[12]

The sacrifice of the imprisoned Sentinels had certainly not been in vain. In January 1918, President Wilson informed a delegation of Democratic congressmen that he supported the Susan B. Anthony Amendment even though he had not made his endorsement public. A vote was therefore taken in the House, and the suffrage amendment passed. However, the Senate was not scheduled to vote until September.

In February 1918, the NWP moved from Cameron House to nearby 14 Jackson Place, the owners of Cameron House having cancelled the NWP's lease when it sold the building to the Cosmos Club. A converted outbuilding in the back of the new building became the NWP's tearoom, "The Grated Door."[13]

The police had not lately granted permits to the NWP for street gatherings, but the suffragists demonstrated without a permit anyway. On August 6, 1918, suffrage martyr Inez Milholland's birthday, they gathered in Lafayette Square, carrying the American flag and banners quoting Inez's famous call to action: "How long must women wait for liberty?" Forty-eight suffragists were arrested, including Alice, but they were released for insufficient charges.

Similar arrests and releases occurred on August 12 and 14. Finally, twenty-six were arrested, including Alice, and sentenced to a reopened workhouse prison for periods of five to fifteen days; Alice was sentenced for ten days. The conditions were even worse than usual. All the prisoners became ill from contaminated water and air. Hunger strikers were refused medical treatment. After five days, all prisoners were released, and the NWP was granted permission for park demonstrations, which probably would have continued without permission.

In September 1918, the Anthony Amendment came up for a vote in the Senate. With the November election looming, Wilson did not publicly endorse the amendment because he didn't want to lose southern support. Southern Democrats still didn't support suffrage, and the amendment lost but by only two votes. However, the Senate had until March 4, 1919, to pass the amendment. With this deadline in mind, Alice focused the NWP's pressure on Democratic senators by urging voters to vote against Democrats for their refusal to enfranchise women. The NWP surely contributed to the Republican victory in November, the Republicans winning a majority in both the House and Senate. The passage of the Anthony Amendment seemed guaranteed with the new 66th Congress to be sworn in in March. Alice's war for women's suffrage seemed to be ending. Concurrently, World War I came to an end on November 11, 1918.

To keep the fires of enthusiasm burning, Alice initiated a new campaign in Lafayette Square near the White House: a perpetual flame she called "Watchfire of Freedom." At dusk, hundreds of suffragists, many of them carrying torches, burned copies of Wilson's speeches about freedom in a stone urn containing wood supposedly from Independence Square in Philadelphia. They intended to keep the fire burning until the next Senate vote was taken on February 10, 1919.

On February 9, 1919, the day before the Senate vote, Alice took a step too far: sixty suffragists burned a paper effigy of Wilson. Thirty-eight were arrested. Alice's audacity sparked a great deal of backlash in the press and even in the NWP. The Senate vote lost by one vote, and the 65th Congress ended on March 4. This burning of Wilson's effigy, which many perceived as disgraceful and unpatriotic, was one of the rare mistakes Alice made. Even if the amendment passed next time around, Alice would still need ratification by three-quarters of the states. She needed to do some damage control to recover from this *faux pas*.

CHAPTER 16

THE BEST AND WORST OF TIMES

*I*t was a time of victory in war but also a time of death and unrest. The end of World War I on November 11, 1918, was certainly cause for celebration and relief, the end of a hellish conflict that had killed an estimated sixteen million people, more than 115,000 of them Americans. However, a new attack began when the soldiers returning home in November and December brought with them the deadly Spanish influenza, which killed more people than the war did, with estimates of worldwide deaths as high as fifty million. In America alone, 675,000 people died of the flu.

Returning soldiers brought not only the deadly disease but also frustration and social unrest when they couldn't find jobs. Postwar unemployment combined with a soaring cost of living led to the country's worst period of labor unrest, with 3,600 strikes in one year.[1] One result of this social discontent was the expansion of the Socialist Party from 80,000 to 104,000. Moreover, the Communist Party emerged from the Socialist left, as well as the American Communist Labor Party supported by charismatic political activist and "Red" journalist Jack Reed and by the Industrial Workers of the World (IWW) whose founder, Eugene Debs, was now in prison, sentenced to ten years for an anti-war speech in 1918.

At the beginning of 1919, Alice shook off the February 10 defeat of the Susan B. Anthony Amendment in the Senate, which occurred after her NWP burned Wilson's effigy. Confident that the amendment would be passed in a few months after the new Republican Congress was sworn in, Alice rolled out a new campaign to maintain public and congressional support of suffrage: a coast-to-coast "Prison Special" train tour reminiscent of the 1916 "Suffrage Special" tour, this time featuring NWP Sentinels in prison garb describing the horrors of prison they had endured in their struggle for the vote. Of the 2,000 suffragists who picketed, 500 were arrested, and 168 were jailed.[2] The tour ended with a spectacular fundraiser at Carnegie Hall.

At long last, victory arrived for the NWP and all suffragists: the House passed the Susan B. Anthony Amendment on May 21, 1919, with a vote of 304 to 89; the Senate passed the amendment on June 4 with a vote of 56 to 25. Suffrage for all American women had now been federally guaranteed, pending ratification of the amendment.

The victory was sweet and joyous for the NWP and other suffrage groups, but Alice refused to rest on her laurels and immediately began lobbying for ratification. Three-quarters of the states needed to ratify the Nineteenth Amendment by the fall of 1920. Alice elicited the help of all the NWP chapters she had established nationwide, asking each to participate in the push toward ratification. Alice came up with a public relations ploy of her own to change the recent negative and unpatriotic image of suffragists: a new spokeswoman. No longer was America to picture the suffragist as angry, outspoken, audacious, unwomanly, and worthy of a jail cell. The new face of suffrage was now a beloved American icon, a lovely, feminine symbol of patriotic rebellion: Betsy Ross, sewing a star on the American flag when each state ratified the amendment:

> "The Betsy Ross of Suffrage" appeared on the cover of the July 19 *Suffragist*. Alice herself posed as the legendary seamstress of the American flag, taking an uncharacteristic turn in the spotlight as she embodied the American Woman waiting for suffrage.... Appropriating a national icon allowed her to construct ratification as quintessentially American, following the path hacked out by the founders. Alice became the incarnation of watchful waiting, patiently sewing on star after star as the process of ratification unfolded.... Such a conventional image seems an odd pose for assertive suffragists.

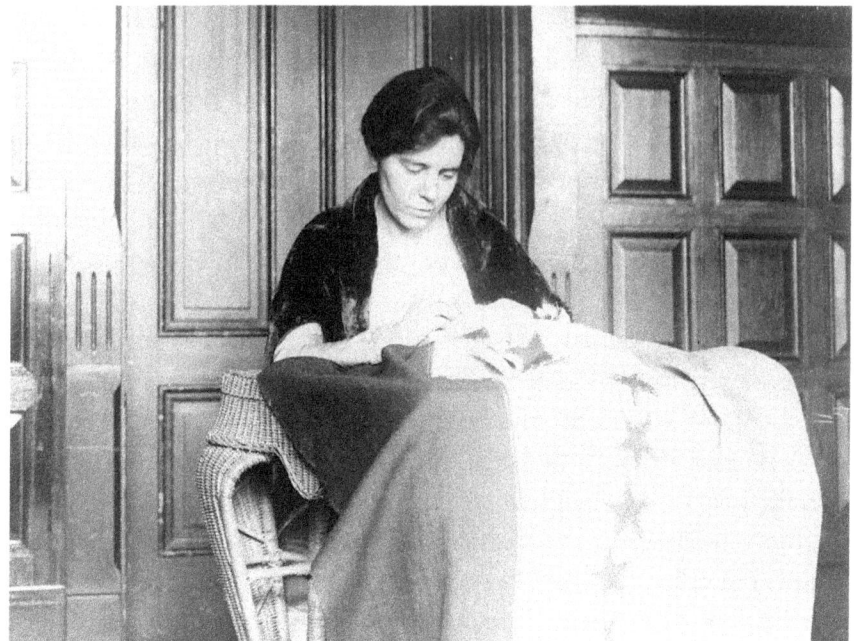

Alice Paul as the Betsy Ross of Suffrage sewing the 36th star on the ratification flag, 1920. (Library of Congress, Prints & Photographs Division)

> Do not fear, the photograph seems to say: women, satisfied with their approaching victory, now return to their age-old parlor pursuits, never again to irritate.[3]

Alice posing as Betsy Ross was a brilliant stroke of marketing in the campaign to ratify the suffrage amendment, but it must have enraged her cousin and my grandfather, Edwin S. Parry and his family. His mother, Lydia Satterthwaite Parry, was a direct descendant of Elizabeth Griscom Claypoole (Betsy Ross), and he was extremely proud of this heritage, evidenced in his book *Betsy Ross Quaker Rebel*. As strict Hicksite Quakers, the Parry family supported the principle of women's suffrage but disapproved of Alice's unladylike, confrontational tactics. Many thought she had brought shame to the family. I can only imagine the family discussions that ensued when radical, iconoclastic Alice marketed herself as a modern-day Betsy Ross. This could well explain why Alice was rarely spoken of by my branch of the Parry family tree. My mother always told me, if you don't have anything nice to say, don't say anything at all. They didn't.

In the summer of 1919, while Alice and the NWP pushed for ratification of the Nineteenth Amendment, President Wilson crossed the country trying to drum up support for his beleaguered League of Nations. He was exhausted by the tour, suffered a massive, debilitating stroke, and never returned to health. He would be replaced in the 1920 election by Warren G. Harding, whose corrupt administration would be marked by the Teapot Dome Scandal. The country, like Wilson, was unwell, sick with lynchings, race riots, strikes, and government violations of civil liberties in reaction to the "Red Scare." Elected Socialist officials were removed from office, and young J. Edgar Hoover arrived at the government's Bureau of Investigation and began his enforcement career by pursuing, arresting, and deporting Communists.

As Wilson's dream of a League of Nations died after World War I, the dreams of many social activists died when postwar reactionism attempted to undo prewar Progressive advances. Coincidentally, former President Theodore Roosevelt, champion of the Progressives, died in 1919. What remained in the wake of the Progressives' prewar dreams of a better, fairer, more peaceful world was their disillusionment in the face of the war's death and destruction, widespread unemployment, slums, corruption, and government repression. Gertrude Stein called these once hopeful, now disillusioned Americans "the Lost Generation", and T. S. Eliot called their world "The Waste Land."

Unlike many of her fellow Progressive activists, Alice never lost hope and finished victorious: on August 18, 1920, Tennessee became the thirty-sixth state to ratify the Nineteenth Amendment. Alice unfurled the NWP flag with thirty-six stars from the balcony of her headquarters. Suffrage, the dream of millions of American women, had been guaranteed by the Constitution. Alice closed the NWP's Washington headquarters and moved with Maud Younger to a small apartment, taking on the task of raising money to pay off the party's ratification debt. In November 1920, Alice and millions of American women cast their first vote.

It must be noted that although the dream of millions of American women was realized as they cast their votes in 1920, black women in the discriminatory South were denied this right, which would not be given to them until the 1960s. (Not that voting in today's America is completely fair, with whitewashing tactics such as gerrymandering and voter suppression.) Alice has been criticized for not including black women in her fight for suffrage. It was not an easy decision for Alice, but a tactical one: she needed Southern votes to achieve the Nineteenth Amendment. Alice the Quaker considered black women equally deserving of the vote; Alice the politician chose not to specify this right in her platform, leaving that battle to future activists.

After women's votes were cast in November 1920, Alice organized a ceremony at the Capitol on February 15, 1921, presided over by Quaker social activist Jane Addams and attended by over 100 women's groups. NWP's rival NAWSA did not attend, although they, too, had worked hard to obtain ratification. The ceremony honored the original suffragists, and Congress was presented with a marble sculpture of suffrage pioneers Susan B. Anthony, Elizabeth Cady Stanton, and Lucretia Mott.[4] The memorial, sculpted by Adelaide Johnson, intentionally left the bust of a fourth suffragist unfinished. It remains unfinished to this day. With my mind's eye, I see Alice Paul as the fourth face of American suffrage.

The day after the ceremony at the Capitol, February 16, 1921, Alice convinced the NWP convention that its new goal should be full equal rights for women. Alice, wanting to pursue a law degree, took a leave of absence from the NWP. Alva Belmont was elected president, with Doris Stevens serving as her personal assistant.[5] Elsie Hill was elected the new chair. Alice attended the American University Washington College of Law and was awarded an LLB in 1922. She would put her legal expertise to good use: In her lifetime, Alice would draft 600 pieces of legislation and get 300 of them passed.[6]

The NWP established new Washington headquarters in 1922 in four row houses between 21-25 First Street, NE, behind the Capitol. The NWP was still active, but its ranks had dwindled. Many of the women who fought so hard for suffrage as members of groups such as the NWP and NAWSA (now the League of Women Voters) were tired of fighting. Content at having the vote, they happily returned to their families and their traditional lives of domesticity. Alice, however, was not at all a traditional woman. She was a more radical New Woman, and she continued the fight. Obtaining the vote had always been simply the first step in her master plan of full political, economic, and social equality for women. In 1923, Alice penned the Lucretia Mott Amendment, which was first introduced the same year, appropriately on July 20 in Seneca Falls, New York, on the seventy-fifth anniversary of the first women's rights convention.[7] The Lucretia Mott Amendment would become known as the Equal Rights Amendment, and the New Woman would become known as a feminist.

CHAPTER 17

BATTLE IN THE SHADOWLANDS

*T*he epistolary void in the Susanna Collection from 1917 through 1923 stands in stark contrast to Alice Paul's many accomplishments in the years following her founding of the National Woman's Party in 1916: organizing the campaign of Silent Sentinel pickets in front of the White House in 1917; suffering multiple arrests, incarcerations, and forced feedings for the cause of suffrage; pushing the Susan B. Anthony (Nineteenth) Amendment through the halls of Congress to a victorious vote in 1919 and lobbying for its successful ratification in 1920; earning her law degree from American University in 1922; and writing the Lucretia Mott (Equal Rights) Amendment in 1923. Her astounding achievements in these seven years testified to her courage, determination, focus, stamina, and self-sacrifice. She was undeniably heroic.

Susanna, on the other hand, seemed to have disappeared from public life. When her letters resumed in 1924, they revealed that she had, in fact, been forced to withdraw from her family and the world at large for years. Her March 23, 1924, letter to the family was postmarked in Loomis, New York. At first, it sounds as if she were at a health farm taking an extended cure, and she seemed primarily concerned about Beulah's health and wanted her to take a rest cure as well:

> What a beautiful spring morning! Temperature nearly 50 degrees and perfect here on the porch. It is lovely in the sunlight, and I have

even taken off my hat to get the full benefit. . . . Mrs. Charlton, our occupational therapy teacher, also starts on her three-week vacation today, and Jesse is going to keep the shop open but don't believe he will do much teaching. . . . I have been thinking a lot about Beulah and want her to plan to take a vacation <u>immediately</u> . . . I want her to take a full month if not longer . . . and learn how to relax . . . I need a chance to do a little bossing, so please humor me, and see how well the home & community can get along without her.

As the letter continues, it is clear that this was no spa where Susanna was staying but some sort of hospital where its patients received visitors. Thirty-nine-year-old Susanna was one of the patients: "The visitors such as husbands, sweethearts, etc. have arrived so guess I will go and look up Betty and take our walk to the Annex. Dr. Peters says I must exercise & I guess he is right so good-bye." Her next letter written on March 30 reveals that Loomis was, in fact, a tuberculosis clinic:

> Mary D. has been having so much trouble to sleep since being here & had planned to go home next week, but her husband is taking her home tomorrow instead. She doesn't seem to have any T.B. & why stay here & get all upset nervously. She may go to Wernersville for a while instead. Why would not that be a good place for Beulah to go for her month of rest? I am anxious that she take me seriously in regard to it. . . . I am glad B. has been to a specialist, it certainly pays when there is any doubt as to treatment. And I certainly hope she will be much better, but know a good rest will help the cure along. . . . Helen is beginning to pack up & has given me her big cushions for the cure chair. Betty says I never will exercise now.

With a bit of investigation, I discovered that Loomis, New York, in the Catskill Mountains, was the site of the Loomis Memorial Sanitarium for Consumptives, named after its founder Dr. Alfred Loomis. Consumption, or tuberculosis, was one of the leading causes of death at that time. Although the BCG vaccine against TB was first used on humans in 1921, it was not widely used until after World War II. Loomis was an upscale and expensive facility in this resort area. The Loomis treatment was based on natural food, exercise, and the fresh mountain air. Although located in the town of Liberty, the Loomis Sanitarium was a town in itself, with its own water, sewage system, and bakery—isolated from Liberty because of the possibility of contagion.

Susanna had indeed gone missing from home, fighting her own battle with one of the world's deadliest diseases. The letters don't indicate where or when Susanna contracted her tuberculosis, but perhaps it was in one of the slums she visited in Birmingham, London, and Edinburgh while at Woodbrooke in 1914. However, my cousin Lee recalls hearing that Susanna's and Beulah's next-door neighbor in Riverton died of TB, so the disease was widespread. Yet another lesson in the Susanna Collection about vaccinations, the lack of which contributed to the spread of this deadly disease.

An April 6, 1924, letter reveals that Susanna had been at Loomis for many months, if not years, funded by Beulah's regularly depositing money into her bank account. Beulah had taken over the administration of the family finances. "Tonight as I was writing my check for Loomis for the last month, I wondered whether I had properly thanked her (B.) for putting all that extra money to my credit in the bank. It certainly comes easily to me and I am afraid I don't show proper appreciation of all that has been & is being done for me." Susanna is grateful for not having to worry about money to pay for her stay as her family was blessed with significant wealth from both the Parry side and the maternal Haines side. Title records on 809 Main Street reveal that mother Lizzie and Auntie Sue, on April 26, 1923, "conveyed to Susanna H. and Beulah H. Parry, of same place, the major part of the farm, in two adjacent tracts of 190 and 88 acres." Even if the family investments might suffer in the coming Depression, their extensive land holdings—278 acres—would protect them from want.

There is no further correspondence in the collection until September, but we know from a copy of his obituary in the Parry Family Records and his headstone in the Westfield Friends Burial Ground that, sadly, Susanna's father, Howard, died at his home in Riverton on July 21, 1924, at the age of sixty-nine. It is no wonder that chatty communications stopped while the family grieved. But life continued, as it must, and the letters recommenced.

On September 1, 1924, "Sue" received a letter from Emmie, a friend from Loomis who seemed quite attached to Susanna, calling her "honey" and "dearie," showing somewhat jealous curiosity about Susanna's new friend Agnes. Her letter also revealed that Beulah had to endure not only the loss of her father but also a setback with surgery; that her mother, Lizzie, was apparently recovering from the loss of her husband; and that Susanna had been able to leave Loomis and go home to Riverton for the mourning period. "Who is new chum Agnes—tell her I surely do envy her muchly. Was so glad honey to hear about your dear Mother. I certainly thought of her and do hope that Beulah is better—poor kid it was so hard on her and right after her operation but a comfort to have you with them—give them my love when you write and how is Auntie? Well dearie do please write again soon for I do love my letters from you. . . . All love for you honey, Devotedly, Emmie."

Susanna's September 2, 1924, letter to her family revealed how much smaller her world had become, with the former world traveler confined to her bed, her canvas chair, and a jigsaw puzzle, envious when other TB patients received visitors, not very optimistic about their return to health or her own, battling for her life in the shadowlands:

> Right after breakfast I went out to my canvas chair under the tree and sat there all morning long in a gingham dress with no coat. It was lovely and I had so much fun working out a picture jig-saw puzzle. Haven't had so much fun for a long time. It has a picture of Geo. & Martha Washington in the Mt. Vernon Garden. . . . Myrta has a friend visiting her & she is positively silly about it. Instead of staying quietly in bed as she should she has been to the phone innumerable times, talking when she should whisper, phoning for flowers to put in her room, candy to feed her, ice for a cold drink when she arrived, etc., etc., etc. until we are sick of it. You might suppose she was trying to entertain the Queen. . . . Dick & Molly left yesterday morning, with a very pressing invitation to me to be sure and visit them! I wonder if I ever will! They are such a lovely couple, it is a shame they

don't have better health and strength to make the happy home theirs should be.

In her September 4 letter to Beulah and family, Susanna described watching friends at the sanitarium coming and going but showed optimism about her own upcoming discharge. She also thanked Auntie Sue for sending her a check:

> This morning right after breakfast we were weighed & reported. I seem to be holding my own pretty well, no great changes in weight either one way or the other. Then I went down to Liberty to do some shopping & get my hair shampooed & treated. When I returned found the nice Mrs. Tanner I had liked so much in the hospital had moved in the room Molly had, right next to Agnes. So naturally I am delighted. Isn't it always the way? Just let things work out as they will, and everything comes out all right. Now I expect she will soon be out to meals and I will have found another chum almost immediately. . . . The first day or so after Agnes goes will be the loneliest, so am glad to keep busy. Got some materials to make birthday presents with today, so guess I can keep out of mischief. The part I dislike most is sitting alone at the table, but know it won't be for long. . . . There are certainly a lot of people leaving this next month, and I am so glad my time also will soon be up. . . . Tell Auntie this letter should be addressed to her to thank her for that lovely check which came in her last letter. . . . I felt too 'flush.' But at least half of what I spent was for other people so I wasn't selfish with it, and I thank her so much for it, so that I <u>can</u> do for others as I know she would want me to.

Susanna's September 21 letter is a bit depressing, concerning mother Lizzie's having to have her teeth pulled, many people returning to Loomis with relapses, and Beulah's continuing health problems: "I am so sorry to hear about Mother's teeth, but if they were in that condition she is much better off without them. . . . There are so many coming back now for their second attempts. . . . This is a gay life isn't it? . . . I must write Molly & Agnes at least, and have one ready for Emmie. Guess you might enjoy her last letter, so will send it instead of copying her message. . . . How is

Beulah these days? You haven't mentioned her health lately. Does she still have to take those sleeping pills?"

Susanna's mood was much more upbeat in her September 28 letter, showing signs of her old lightheartedness: "I had a case of good old fashioned giggles at the supper table, even got Myrta going too. We were almost a disgrace and for no apparent cause." Susanna continued her joy when she raved about a new entertainment device—the radio: "As I started out for my walk I went around by the hospital, but long before I got there, heard something which sounded like a Victrola but much louder. One of the boys had it on the north porch, and I found out later it was a Radio. I never heard such a loud one before and can understand now how people might dance to the music, for you might have supposed the whole orchestra was there. I even heard it away up by the Chapel." Although radio technology began at the end of the nineteenth century, it was not until 1920 that Americans received broadcasts of news, sports programs, and musical entertainment. The same year, the first licensed radio station, KDKA in Pittsburgh, began broadcasting. It would take another fifteen years to link the nation together with a network of radio transmitters.

Susanna seemed to have developed good friendships at Loomis that made her stay tolerable, but she was looking forward to leaving the sanitarium if her upcoming fluoroscope found no more shadows in her lungs:

> Companions can make such a difference to one's happiness. I am so thankful every day that I have Marie. She is such a dear. But can't say as much for the rest of the cottage. But it won't be much longer now. I expect they will fluoroscope me this week and then maybe I can consider a date . . . I am going to discard lots of my curing garments. The big carriage blanket I will leave, but my steamer blanket & the wool one Auntie sent me, I will mail direct to the cleaners and in that way they will be perfectly all right to use at home.

Susanna wrote her last letter from the Loomis sanitarium on October 3, 1924. She thanked her Auntie and family for the money they had forwarded to see her through her last days away from home. Her family was very excited about her homecoming, but Susanna was anxious about having to adjust to a new routine at home after years at the sanitarium, like a soldier facing the difficulties of adjusting to his old way of life after years of war away from home. "Your letters yesterday all make me feel that my home coming will be an event, but I am wondering whether I am worthy of such a fuss. I only hope I won't be an anxiety to you. It will take a while to get adjusted to a new routine and be hard to keep to my own rather than yours. But many of the other girls have managed it and I guess I can too. Here's hoping, anyway!"

Susanna indeed left the Loomis Sanitarium to rejoin her family in Riverton: the next letter in the collection, dated June 9, 1925, was addressed to "Sue" at 809 Main Street and written by Jim, a friend from Loomis in Walterboro, South Carolina. From the letter, we learn that Susanna's home doctor had given her a good report and that she was planning a final follow-up at Loomis. He, however, might not have been so well, having decided to return to Loomis for an examination. "Well I know you all have everything all straightened out at home and I suppose it is very hard for you to realize how long you were away, isn't it? . . . I have decided to go back to Loomis in the near future for an examination."

The next letter is also from a Loomis friend, Marie from Cannondale, Connecticut, whose company Susanna had enjoyed so much in her final days. It is such a sad letter—pages about how poorly she'd been feeling. Consumption was an appropriate name for this disease, which consumed every thought of many of the patients afflicted with it. Their lives became the story of their illness, the only story they told: "My dear Sue: What there is left of me will surely endeavor to scratch a few lines . . . since the last of May everything has gotten so far beyond me & I think when I pick up a pen it is almost beyond words. And now we are settled here for the summer. At least I hope you'll come up & see us—as I'll need company while I sit stretched out—for I don't think if my present weary feeling has anything to do with it that I'll be able to move for the rest of the summer." Just about all of Marie's hope had been consumed by consumption.

The only other items in the collection for 1925 are an announcement of a September marriage in Germantown, Pennsylvania, and an invitation to a September wedding in Riverton. Similarly, 1926 entries begin the same way, with two announcements of June weddings.

The remaining 1926 correspondence is between Susanna's mother, Lizzie, and Auntie Sue. On December 7, Lizzie wrote Auntie Sue from The Hollywood in Southern Pines, North Carolina, where she, Susanna, and Beulah were vacationing. Auntie Sue was at a favorite home-away-from-home, the Chalfonte Haddon Hall in Atlantic City, which, unlike today's honkey-tonk stretch of casinos, was a posh resort at the turn of the century. Lizzie wrote that Beulah was ailing and also seemed concerned about her sister's reclusion: "I do hope thee will mingle with the people. Thee will enjoy thy stay much more." Beulah wrote her Auntie Sue on December 29; Beulah, Susanna, and their mother were still at the Hollywood Hotel in Southern Pines, and Auntie was still at the Chalfonte in Atlantic City. Beulah said they'd been playing golf and taking bridge lessons, enjoying their beautiful room, and having such a good time that they'd decided to stay until the fifteenth. In Lizzie's December 31 letter to her sister, she said she and Beulah planned to go on to Camden and Pine Ridge Camp in South Carolina, while Susanna would take the train to visit her friend from Loomis, Emmie L., in Jacksonville, Florida. Interesting to me, she mentioned my grandfather, mother, and aunts: "Had a very nice letter from Edwin Parry. Children have all had chicken pox."

Beulah wrote Auntie Sue on January 6 and 9, 1927, with an update of financial matters: checks and taxes and investments. She had taken control of the family's finances since her father's death, under Auntie's auspices. With the real estate holdings now in the hands of Susanna and Beulah and Beulah overseeing the cash flow and investments, the younger generation had taken control of the helm. Steady hands would certainly be needed to guide the Parry family ship in the rough waters that lay ahead in the 1930s.

Except for an April 1927 letter from Alice to the Parry women, to be mentioned shortly, the only items in the collection for the rest of 1927 and all of 1928 and 1929 are occasional marriage announcements.

During this time, Alice had transitioned from the first part of her plan for the liberation of women—federally mandated enfranchisement—to the second and larger part—federally mandated equal rights. The Susan

B. Anthony Amendment was ratified in 1920, and the Lucretia Mott Amendment for equal rights, written by Alice, was introduced in 1923. Although this second amendment was rejected on the first go-round, Alice would never relent and would fight for women's equality for the rest of her life. This second war would be lonelier than the first for Alice because her NWP army had dwindled. After the exhausting seven-year war for the vote ended in victory in 1920, many battle-weary suffragists left the NWP to return to their homes and families. Many encouraged Alice to do the same—an impossibility for Alice, for her true home was

Alice Paul and Alva Belmont, 1923. (Library of Congress)

her party, her true family the feminists at her side. Many left the NWP because they opposed its focus on an equal rights amendment, fearing the loss of protective legislation for women already in place (the reason Eleanor Roosevelt opposed the amendment). Some of the faithful remained to fight for equal rights, including Harriot Stanton Blatch, Alva Belmont, Doris Stevens, and Elsie Hill, but by 1925, the NWP ranks had fallen from 60,000 to 20,000.[1]

After earning her first law degree in 1922, an LLB from The American University Washington College of Law, Alice pursued and obtained two more degrees from American University: a Master's in Law in 1927 and a Doctorate in Civil Law in 1928. A staggering accomplishment. Alice had been a perpetual student all her adult life, first earning her Bachelor's in Biology from Swarthmore then a Master's and Doctorate in Sociology and Economics from the University of Pennsylvania. Her advanced degrees, particularly the law degrees, armed Alice with the legislative tools she needed to pursue her goal of equality for women under the law.

The Susanna Collection contains an April 18, 1927, letter from Alice to her Parry cousins and aunt. She had moved to temporary quarters at 117 B. Street, SE, away from NWP headquarters to allow her to concentrate on her coursework. She apparently hadn't heard the door knocker when they tried to visit and was sorry to have missed them:

> Dear Aunt Lizzie, and Susanna and Beulah,
> When I went down to lunch to-day I found your card and am so sorry to have missed you. Why did you not send up the card. I wanted so much to see you. Next time that you plan to come to Washington you must be sure to write me beforehand so that I can meet you and show you around the city.
> I have moved over to this address so as to be undisturbed in preparing for my examinations and in working on a book I am trying to write, but you can always reach me by addressing me at the Headquarters.
> Parry writes that he and Helen are coming down this week to see the cherry blossoms. I hope that you saw them while you were here.

Again regretting so much that I missed you,
                                    I am affectionately,
                                    Alice Paul.

Alice and the NWP would be on the move for a while after 1928, when she finished her third law degree. In 1929, when the building housing NWP headquarters was scheduled for demolition to make way for a new Supreme Court building, Alva Belmont bought the Sewall House behind the Capitol at 144 Constitution Avenue, NE. When renovations were finished in December 1930, the building was officially dedicated as the Alva Belmont House, which housed NWP headquarters as well as Alice and other NWP leaders. In 1972, the Alva Belmont House would become the Sewall-Belmont House and Museum, and in 1974 designated a National Historic Landmark. In 2016, President Barack Obama designated the site as a National Monument: the Belmont-Paul Women's Equality National Monument, honoring and documenting the contributions of Alva Belmont, Alice Paul, and the National Woman's Party, which was headquartered at the building from 1929 to 1997, when the NWP stopped its lobbying activities. The monument is open to the public.

The timing of the purchase of Alva Belmont's house in 1929 was auspicious, for, at the end of that year, the financial world would collapse, and the world at large would fall into economic crisis for a decade. At least the NWP and Alice would have a roof over their heads during the Great Depression.

CHAPTER 18

THROUGH DEPRESSION AND WAR

*B*y the end of the 1920s, Susanna had fought and won her battle with tuberculosis and survived the mourning period after her father's death. Susanna's life had regained a sense of normalcy at the Riverton homestead with her mother, Auntie, and Beulah. Her cousin Alice had celebrated the ratification of the Susan B. Anthony Amendment for suffrage, written and introduced her Lucretia Mott Amendment for equal rights, earned three law degrees, and was about to move into the new NWP headquarters at the Alva Belmont House. She was poised to resume her continuing fight for women's equality: for her, normalcy.

On the political front, in 1923, Warren G. Harding, known primarily for his corrupt administration, died of a heart attack and was replaced by Calvin Coolidge. After guiding the American ship for the next six years through a dangerously unregulated economy, Coolidge refused to run in 1928 and was replaced by Herbert Hoover, who was inaugurated on March 4, 1929.

Then came the darkest week in America's economic history from October 24 to 29, 1929—Black Thursday through Black Tuesday: The Great Crash of 1929, the start of The Great Depression in the United States, which rippled across the world and lasted for a decade. By 1933, about half of the banks in America had failed, and unemployment had climbed to 30%. Across America, depression and despair: ruined bankers jumped out of windows to their deaths, houses and farms repossessed, millions of jobs lost, the dejected unemployed in long soup-kitchen lines, tent cities, and dust storms from the barren Dust Bowl. John Steinbeck would be awarded the Pulitzer Prize in 1940 for *The Grapes of Wrath*, his poetic novel about the Great Depression which chronicles the struggle of the Joad family, repossessed tenant farmers who flee from the Oklahoma Dust Bowl to California, hoping to find a better possible life as migrant farm workers, suffering inconceivable adversity and starvation, struggling to maintain their dignity while fighting for their very lives.

The lives of millions of Americans were crushed in the decade of the Great Depression. Luckily for cousins Susanna and Alice, they were not as affected as most because their families possessed extensive landholdings, including farms, and as fiscally conservative Quakers had not been tempted to squander their treasure on material extravagance or risky stock market speculation. I would wager that they showed great compassion for and generosity toward others in this decade of suffering and want.

There is nothing in the collection from 1929 to 1933, dark years of depression in America that Herbert Hoover was incapable of confronting, resulting in his overwhelming defeat by Democrat Franklin D. Roosevelt in the 1932 election. Roosevelt would lead the country slowly out of The Great Depression with his "New Deal" initiatives, including the Social Security Act and monumental engineering and building projects such as the Hoover Dam, Mount Rushmore, and the Tennessee Valley Authority, which would provide jobs and transform the American landscape. Looking ahead, industrial mobilization for World War II would be the country's final step out of the Depression and into full employment for women as well as men.

The only item in the Susanna Collection in 1933 is a New Year's greeting card from William P. Gest, the Chairman of the Board of Fidelity-Philadelphia Trust Company, offering words of encouragement to his clients in a time of adversity. He could well be talking to our current age of wasteful, selfish greed:

> Adversity is the test of friendship, the challenge of courage, the touchstone of our professions, the opportunity of sympathy, a stimulus to reform, a school of patience, a teacher of faith, hope and charity. We

have learned again that there is nothing stable in human affairs, and those who have avoided undue elation in prosperity should be free of undue depression in adversity. Let us, therefore, in the coming year, seek to build anew the palace of our social structure, though on lower levels in physical value, yet to greater heights in ethical attainment.

On the top of the New Year's card, Susanna penned words of faith and hope from Elizabeth Barrett Browning: "There are nettles everywhere/ But smooth green grasses are more common still./The blue of heaven is larger than the cloud."

The next five years in the collection are void, silent. The Depression years were further darkened for the Parry family on September 22, 1936, by the death of Susanna's, Beulah's, and Alice's Aunt Lydia Satterthwaite Parry (my great-grandmother), mother of their cousin and my grandfather Edwin S. Parry. Unimaginably, Edwin himself died of pneumonia on December 9, 1936, shortly after the death of his mother.

Edwin S. Parry, c. 1926.

Edwin's mother-in-law, Charlotte Bond, wrote the collection's next item, a hand-delivered card addressed to Mrs. Haines (Auntie Sue), dated August 23, 1938. Charlotte Bond (my great-grandmother) is the mother of my grandmother Mary Bond Parry, widow of Edwin S. Parry, who died two years earlier. Mary Parry and her mother, Charlotte Bond, still lived in the Parry house at 804 Main Street in Riverton, across the street from Susanna, Beulah, their mother, and Auntie Sue, who lived at 809 Main Street. When she wrote the card in a very legible hand, Charlotte Bond was eighty-eight years old; she would die in 1952 at the age of 102. The card was a birthday poem she had composed for her friend Sue, words of good wishes from one aged friend to another:

> We are growing old together
> The years are passing by.
> How many more can we weather?
> Don't they really seem to fly!
> The saying says "Grow old with me
> The best is yet to be."
> The birthdays come, the birthdays go
> Just how many we do not know.
> This day I hope will be
> A happy anniversary.
> Full of joy and all things sweet
> Love from your friend across the street.

Sadly, shortly after this 1938 card to Auntie Sue Haines, Elizabeth (Lizzie) Haines Parry, Susanna's and Beulah's mother, died. Yet another mourning to endure. In May 1939, Susanna and Beulah received a letter of condolence from a friend from Coral Gables, Florida, who now lived in Mexico: "Many months ago I wanted to answer your Xmas card, but found it so difficult to say what was in my heart, that I kept putting it off. To-day finds me no more capable of adequately describing the loss all of us have suffered, than it finds me capable of paying the tribute to the good it has done me to have had your mother as my dear friend."

Alice Paul also had reasons to mourn in the 1930s. Her mother, Tacie Parry Paul, died on May 24, 1930, and was buried at Westfield Friends Burial Ground. After recovering from the loss of her mother, Alice had to endure another loss in 1933, the death of her long-time friend, benefactor, and fellow NWP leader Alva Belmont. Alice made the funeral arrangements, honoring Alva's contributions to women's suffrage. Generous to the end, Alva left the NWP the Alva Belmont House, headquarters of the NWP, as well as $100,000, worth about $1,900,000 in today's money.

Just as Alice did not stop her work for women's rights during World War I, she did not stop her work during The Great Depression. Knowing that she wouldn't make progress on equal rights in America with the country in the throes of the Depression, she turned her attention in the 1930s to women's rights internationally. She served as chair of the Woman's Research Foundation of the League of Nations from 1927 to 1937.[1] From 1930 to 1933, she was a member of the Nationality Committee of the Inter-American Commission of Women, a part of the Organization of American States.[2] In 1930, Alice and NWP principal Doris Stevens compiled an extensive report for the Inter-American Commission of Women on how laws in various countries affected women's nationality, addressing the widespread injustice of women losing their citizenship if they married someone from another country.[3] Alice, Doris, and Alva Belmont attended the League of Nations meeting in September 1931 to present the findings of their report.

After lobbying for women at the League of Nations headquarters in Geneva, Switzerland, in 1938, Alice founded the World Party for Equal Rights for Women, known as the World Woman's Party (WWP). Headquartered at Villa Bartholini on Lake Geneva, Alice's WWP became a conduit to help Jews escape from Europe. With Hitler on the rise and war in Europe inevitable, the WWP gave asylum to an estimated dozen persecuted Jewish activists and intellectuals and helped them obtain passports and passage to the United States.[4] One of the families Alice helped escape from the Nazis was the Mullers: Felix and Alice Muller and their two children from Karlsruhe, Germany. The Mullers would have their chance to help Alice in turn decades hence.

Terror spread rapidly throughout Europe. Germany invaded Poland in 1939, resulting in Britain and France declaring war on Germany. The Germans then invaded Denmark, Norway, Belgium, the Netherlands, Luxembourg, and France in 1940. Alice moved the WWP headquarters from Geneva to Washington in 1941, shortly before the United States joined the conflict on December 7, 1941, when the Japanese attacked Pearl Harbor. Back in Washington again, Alice was elected Chair of the National Woman's Party in 1942. By this time, the NWP's influence had shrunk, its membership having fallen to 4,000. Alice rewrote the ERA in 1943. She continued her international lobbying efforts beginning in 1945 when she and Elsie Hill attempted to introduce equality provisions in the United Nations' Universal Declaration of Human Rights. They succeeded in 1948 when language about gender equality was included in six sections of the U.N. Charter, which recognized "the equal rights of men and women and of nations large and small." Once again, Quaker Alice had not participated in America's war effort, but by the time the war ended in 1945, she had made a positive difference, helping Jews escape from Nazi persecution in Europe and fighting for women on the international stage.

Alice's cousins Susanna and Beulah, now heads of the Parry household, also made a difference during the war years, albeit on a smaller scale. On October 4, 1941, Susanna and Beulah received a letter from L. Calvin Robbins, just beginning his studies at George School, a Hicksite Quaker boarding school in Newtown, Pennsylvania, whose curriculum included both college preparatory courses and community service. Calvin was the son of Susanna's and Beulah's Floridian cousin Ida Parry. In a very sincere letter of thanks to the sisters, he acknowledged the significant opportunity they had given him in financing his education. "I feel that George School is a wonderful opportunity for anyone. The main asset is its preparation for college and also the great ideals which it upholds. The living together in a democracy with the mutual cooperation of all helps make what George School stands for./ I am greatly indebted to both of you for giving me the opportunity of attending such a fine school. Your generosity was appreciated by our whole family and especially myself. I hope I shall be worthy of such a gift in time to come./Your loving cousin, Calvin."

On November 2, 1942, Calvin wrote another letter of heartfelt thanks to Susanna and Beulah for their generosity in financing his education at George School. "As I commence my second year here I become more aware than ever what a wonderful opportunity and asset has been given to me. . . . These things I have mentioned before have been made possible by both of you in your financial support. Your kindness has been appreciated from the bottom of my heart and it shall never be forgotten. This goes not only for myself but for the rest of my family."

Susanna and Beulah received two more thank you letters in 1942 from other Quakers for smaller acts of kindness—from the mother of a newborn baby thanking them for the gift of a pink afghan and from a mother whose daughter had been married in "the beautiful setting" of Susanna's and Beulah's house. Susanna saved these letters because they were meaningful to her and her sister. There is no replacement for a well-written, sincere thank-you letter, a dying art form in today's world of dashed off electronic tweets.

The next letter of note in the collection is addressed to Susanna at 1202 Granada Boulevard in Coral Gables, Florida, one of America's first planned communities developed in the 1920s. Susanna and Beulah had a winter home there, as did other Quaker snowbirds who regularly gathered for meeting at their place. I found a reference to the two sisters on the website of miamifriends.org's history of Friends in Miami: "Although there are reports of periodic gatherings, the Miami Meeting is the result of efforts of Barnard and Jesse Walton, Philadelphia brothers whose yearly journeys to Florida gathered Friends. Winter residents Susanna and Beulah Parry held First Day worship in their Coral Gables home beginning in the 1940s."

The January 30, 1943, letter sent to Susanna in Florida was written by Mary Parry, my grandmother "Nanna", widow of Susanna's late cousin Edwin and daughter of Charlotte Bond who had composed the birthday poem for Auntie Sue five years previously and who was now ninety-three years old. The two Parry women used to live across Main Street from Susanna and Beulah but had recently downsized to a house they shared

Lizzie (left), Susanna (center), and Beulah Parry in Coral Gables, Florida, c. 1938.

with two friends. She referred to the group as "the four old ladies at 622 Thomas Avenue." It was lovely to see Nanna's bold handwriting again and strange to picture her as a fifty-seven-year-old woman, over a decade younger than I am now. Gazing out her window, she described the wintry scene in Riverton in the aftermath of a blizzard:

On Thomas Ave., from my window I can see four sleds tied together with children on them being pulled by two boys. Evidently the sleet which has fallen steadily for twenty-four hours has made an icy surface for a girl is on skis and a boy skating on it. I also have seen one sleigh drawn by a pony with a gentleman and two little children on it. I can't even remember when I last saw that! I think you chose a good winter to go to Florida.

Mother and I have certainly been enjoying your jams and jellies and as we do we talk about you and say how much we both miss you! . . . Charlotte & Bill were not able to come home for Christmas which of course was a keen disappointment to them as well as to us. They seem to enjoy it where they are, and Charlotte is so hoping Bill will not be transferred although he has been there longer than most seem to be.

I was moved to read this last paragraph, because Charlotte & Bill were my mother and father. Charlotte was Mary's daughter, and her husband, Bill, was Dr. William P. Mulford. They married on August 16, 1940, just after his graduation from the University of Virginia Medical School. After the war began, the newlyweds moved to Pensacola, Florida, for the young doctor's training as a medic in the Navy Medical Corps. The imminent transfer my mother dreaded was to the California coast; from there her husband would be deployed to the Pacific, where he would earn the Bronze Star "for heroic service as medical officer, attached to the Fourth Marine Division, in action against enemy Japanese forces at Saipan, Marianas Islands, on June 15 and 16, 1944." I am so very grateful that my father returned home from the war; if he hadn't, I wouldn't be here telling this story.

CHAPTER 19

LITTLE STAR, NORWEGIAN EYES

*N*ever think the story is over.

It's now 1946 in the collection. After the death of FDR in 1945, President Harry Truman ordered atomic bombs dropped on Nagasaki and Hiroshima, forcing the surrender of Japan. World War II had finally ended, claiming the lives of an estimated sixty million people, including 420,000 Americans. Susanna was sixty-one years old. She had survived tuberculosis. Her parents were gone. She still lived with Beulah and her Auntie Sue. Her circle of friends was composed primarily, if not exclusively, of Quaker Friends and family. Her heart had been broken in her youth when her beloved E. married and had children, but she had recovered and carried on. She had traveled extensively and studied in Europe: one could say she had her fair share of adventures. With the arc of her life on its downward turn, her correspondence had dwindled down to wedding and birth announcements for the children of her childhood friends, thank-you letters for kindnesses she and Beulah had shown to others, and occasional birthday wishes. I wasn't expecting any surprises from the collection now.

Then came the February 28, 1946, letter from Oslo, Norway, from Dagny Tischendorf, whom Susanna had met in England at the Woodbrooke Quaker Study Centre thirty-two years before in 1914. Other letters from Dagny would follow over the next eleven years—letters among the most interesting in the collection. Intriguing, poetic letters. Love letters, perhaps. From this first letter, we see that Dagny and Susanna had not been in touch for decades, perhaps since their days at Woodbrooke. It was Dagny who had compared Susanna to a twinkling star. She told Susanna that she had often thought of her but didn't have the courage to write, but that she had received news about Susanna from Anna Griscom Elkinton, Susanna's roommate at Woodbrooke, who had kept her informed about Susanna's illness and recovery. My guess is that Anna had asked Susanna to get in touch with Dagny, knowing of the hardships she had suffered in Norway because of the war. Dagny was delighted to have received a letter from Susanna and told her distant friend about her life in Norway since their youth. (Note: Because English is not Dagny's native language, I have made occasional corrections in grammar and spelling, but for the most part, her English is impressive.)

> Dear Susanna!
>
> What a joy to get a letter from you!! I rejoiced when I saw your handwriting!! Upon the very instant I was back to Woodbrooke where we all strolled along the garden—young and gay people. Much water has run into the sea since those happy days and life has shifted for most of us with lights and shades. But bright memories never fade and the memories of Woodbrooke and friends there have always been fresh in my mind.
>
> Often I have thought of you. I didn't dare to write to you. I wrote to Anna and got news about you from her. I knew you were friends. Once she wrote and said you were ill and I felt very sorry about it and thought of writing to you, but I dropped it. Later on she wrote and told that you had quite recovered and I rejoiced in hearing so. —And I'll tell you—Perhaps you still remember that I called you: Little Star?!—For many years I was an eager stargazer. Armed with big star maps on dark nights I strolled along with crowds of friends and people and told them about the stellar sky and the Greek mythology which is so interwoven with the stars. —on such expeditions I always sent you a thought. It was a matter of course because I in years gone by had given you the star name!! —You see, in that way you have long had a corner in my heart together with the stars of heaven. —

... I live together with a friend. She has held high social offices here in Oslo and has done brilliant social work during many many years. We bought this flat in 1927 and since we have kept together through good and evil days. It is said about our home that the hall bell is never at rest and I have felt the truth of it now when I am writing to you because I have been interrupted several times. —

You write that you have sent me 2 boxes—and I thank you ever so much for your kindness and care. It is exceedingly good of you and I am deeply touched. —Florida—so far away! I fancy soft and warm winds, blue ocean and the firmament studded with stars—and from that land of wonders the boxes are coming to me. I'll look at them with awe—and they will let me feel a wave of air from that fairy land and from your goodness! But I feel ashamed to accept so much. —

Well, I must bring this letter to a close and try to get it off by air mail. So you'll get it quicker. I myself have been in the air more than 150 times and I loved to fly until the aeroplanes started to carry bombs. —Then my air enthusiasm was bombed, smashed!!!!

With much love to you
and also please give my love to your sister
Your friend
Dagny Tischendorf.

What an interesting addition to the collection, something completely different: Dagny for twenty years had been living with another woman, a well-known social worker, in an apparent Boston marriage: what Susanna had dreamed of doing with E. and what, it seems, that Dagny might well have hoped Susanna would do with her when they were young students of social reform. Unrequited hope and longing, perhaps, explain her unwillingness to reach out in writing to Susanna. Unfortunate for Susanna that the two classmates had been out of touch for decades because Dagny had had a fascinating life and her letters were transcendental, full of imagination and poetry. Years ago, she had acquired enough expertise in social reform to be on the lecture circuit, and she had published a book of poems in 1938. Moreover, she was a rare female pilot, with over 150 flights on record. Although well beyond middle age, she and her friend lived a busy and engaged life, with their doorbell never silent.

On April 17, 1946, Dagny thanked Susanna for her gift of two boxes of coffee and goodies from Florida:

> I took the contents in my hand and let the thoughts run. —Products ripened by the sun, —grown up from the soil of a far-away country. They flashed forth to me a glimpse of Florida!!!!
>
> In the evening Ragna Bugge (my friend) and I were sitting by the fire speaking of you, and on the table before us we had the most delicious drink: coffee—your coffee. How we enjoyed it!! —
>
> And the boxes! chocolate, tea, peas, raisins, rice, etc. —things we haven't seen during the whole war time. . . . Dear Susanna, thank you ever so much for your goodness!! —But I feel ashamed to accept so much. I think of so many people in other countries who are in need of food. The food conditions in Norway are not so bad any longer. Of course we haven't plenty, but we have enough. Fate has been good to us in many ways. . . .
>
> With love
Yours
Dagny.

Dagny's November 25, 1946, letter described her rugged vacation on the wild island of Ulvoy and showed her to be a remarkable free spirit and a poet:

> Fancy an island (not an island! Too small to be called so) only a rock, —a fist against the blue ocean, —weather-beaten, abrupt, with shores cut up by the washing of the sea, —wild and lonely!!! There my friend and I stayed for several weeks. What a paradise! What a lavish and gipsy life!! Gales and dangers! Yachting, fishing, climbing. Always and always surrounded by sky, ocean, surfs and spray. And in August, moonlight and stars. . . . I wonder if you would have liked to go with us yachting on the high seas—for instance a night in August—in moonlight with the phosphoric light sparkling on the keel line. —

We didn't return home before September, —arrived in Oslo brown as bronze with cheeks stiffened by salt.

Thus passed the summer. Now like a fairy dream. But tunes from the ocean are still echoing in my mind and I am longing to be back to the island and to the plain, brave and honest fisherfolk. —

I, too, wonder if Susanna would have liked to go adventuring on the high seas with Dagny and Ragna. My guess is Susanna would have found it far too wild, even when she and Dagny were young women back in 1914. However, perhaps Susanna did have regrets; if so, she surely kept them to herself.

Dagny's February 11, 1947, letter thanked Susanna for her Christmas presents which she had shared with others:

Dear Susanna!

How wonderful you are!! A letter, a calendar and a parcel—what shall I say? How can I thank you—I was overjoyed to get your letter—your calendar does not only show me the days and ask me to take care of them, but it beams like a sun on the wall with the deep truths written on it, and every day I go to it to find something which gives wings, light and perspective.

Your parcel has given joy to more than me. A young girl got the sportsdress. You should have loved to see her joy. She danced around the room and felt in full feather. It fitted her as hand in glove. I promised to send you her most heartfelt thanks. —The pullover went to another girl. She caught her violin and played a piece of music! And said that when she next time played in the broadcasting she would play a most pretty piece of music in honour to and in thought of you.

The stockings and the shawl went to me. —when cold and snow have left us and spring is beautifying earth and air I'll put them on and go out in nature and sing you a song. —You think it'll reach you? Air is so passing, so movable, so filled with waves and mystery, —Perhaps some of the rhythms I'll trouble it with are able to gasp their last breath into your rooms!! And all the other things you sent—coffee, fruit, chocolate, sugar. . . . How delicious! And how all is sweetening my existence!

The next letter from Dagny arrived almost a year later, January 10, 1948, once again thanking Susanna for her Christmas package:

> My friend, Ragna Bugge, and I rejoiced like children when we unpacked it and caught sight of all the nice and fine things. My warmest thanks to you, not only for the contents but also (and not least) for your kind thoughts. Like gentle trade winds they blew out of the parcel!! And I am happy to feel trade winds in our cold climate!! But, dear friend, I must tell you again . . . that we can really get many articles in Norway now. Conditions are no longer so bad. —I should rejoice if you would send me some words. You have often and often been in my thoughts and I want so much to know if you are well. Your parcel was sent from Riverton, I noticed, not from Florida . . . and now I am anxious lest the hurricane I read about in October has destroyed your home there.
> . . . In July last summer Ragna and I left town and went to the island I told you about in my last letter. Summer was dry, weather too hot but the sea breeze was always there brisk and cold. Ocean mostly calm. We often pulled along far away on the open sea. Wonderful life! Shining the waves—in sunshine, in moonshine and in Northern lights. In September we returned to civilization (which means) the struggling world. . . . We Norwegians are very glad that the Nobel Peace Prize was given to the Society of Friends. —Really, if peace will ever return to the world I feel sure that it shall be due to the work of the Quakers. We do admire their ideas, their spirit and greatness of mind.

Dagny told Susanna that she and her partner, Ragna, had spent the weeks before Christmas working to give the poor a better Christmas, an annual custom for them, as was fixing sheaths of grain around their windows to feed the birds. As always, she sent her love to both Susanna and Beulah.

As referenced in Dagny's letter, in 1947, the Nobel Peace Prize was awarded to the Quakers' Friends Service Council in London and the American Friends Service Committee in Philadelphia. The Quakers had been previously nominated in 1912, 1923, 1924, and 1936 for giving relief without political discrimination to victims of war and famine. Nobel Peace Prize Chairman Gunnar John, in presenting the award, praised the Quakers' long-standing service to humanity: "The Quakers have shown us that it is possible to translate into action what lies deep in the hearts of many: compassion for others and the desire to help them—that rich expression of the sympathy between all men, regardless of nationality or race, which, transformed into deeds, must form the basis for lasting peace. . . . they have given us something more: they have shown us the strength to be derived from faith in the victory of the spirit over force."

A year later, on February 20, 1949, Dagny thanked Susanna for her Christmas letter and photos of the Florida house, revealing the previous year's storm damage:

> Best thanks for your Christmas letter. I rejoiced in getting it. Because letters from you always bring with them a gleam of sunlight! Often I have wondered how—if your sunny Florida is the fountainhead or if the light waves come from yourself. Surely they do! You must be a sunny girl reflecting the air and beauty of your country!! —I looked with great interest at your house and the big cocoas. How naughty of them to smash the roof! But I suppose they deny fault and cast the blame on storms and gales. Proud of their strength they'll sing you a whistling laughter through their leaves!!

Dagny then described the birthday celebration for her partner, Ragna Bugge:

> We have had our own home together for more than 20 years. In February last she completed 70 years (she is much older than I am) . . . She is known up and down Norway as a social worker. And she is called "The Mother of Oslo". On her birthday nearly half the town was on foot to do homage to her. A constant stream of

visitors came all day long. Our home was transformed into a floral kingdom. In June last year our King bestowed on her his "Medal for Merit" in gold.

In July Ragna and I went to the island south in Norway. I have told you about the island in previous letters. We returned in September. I love that jungly place. The large wavy ocean with blaze of leaping flames in remote skylines is a source of constant joy. And in spite of often deafening thunder from the surfs it is the most quiet spot I know. —Weather was up and down. —Two big steamships broke down on the half-tide rocks somewhere near the island. The crews were saved by our friends, the fishermen. Fancy, Susanna, S.O.S. in a dark stormy night. Lives ventured to rescue lives. Strong brave men doing their duty. Hopes answering hopes across the roaring seas!! In a time of restrictions and written laws (all of which I try to revolt against) it gives hope to realize that unwritten laws still are listened to—laws that take their rise in the best qualities of the human soul. — ...

Perhaps I am going to Holland soon—only to stay for a short time. My "adopted mother" is not in good health. Have I never told you about her? She lives in the country in her magnificent house. She is a well known painter and was a very great friend of my mother. She is very old but still a woman of wit and great intellect. Her home is a center of culture, science and art. Before she got ill she used to visit Norway almost every year and we had the most happy days together. But sorry to say, I never feel happy in her home. I am too democratic, a vagabond, a rambler, an obstinate barbarian, a revolter against luxury, titles and people with stars on their breasts if not a human heart is beating underneath the brilliant surface. How I long for my country, my own plain and happy home when I stay in Dutch castles surrounded with drawbridges, ditches, canals—and almost get choked by the breath from the middle age!! ...

Please give my love to your sister. I'll never forget how kind you two have been to me.

Much love
from your friend Dagny.

The next Dagny letter in the collection is dated November 12, 1951. While Susanna and Beulah were in the sunny warmth of Florida, she and Ragna were in the cold of Norway:

> But I like the winter, love the starry nights and the beautiful northern lights!! I even love the ice-roses on my windows. The frost sometimes draws them so beautifully—that glorious ice-blooded imp of an artist who breathes beauty on everyone's windowpanes! And outside he flings his diamonds generously around him—for the moon to shine on. Susanna have you ever been on skis, pursued your way over the moonlit vastness? In the solitude there you'll ask yourself What is earth? What is heaven? . . .
>
> I'll tell you about my summer ramble this year. A very great friend of mine, Baroness Van Till (Dutch) and I had a glorious travelling together. She had never been in Norway but all over the world and now she wanted so much to see my country. So she left her husband and children in Holland and came to us for some weeks. She and her husband are great friends of Queen Juliana and Prince Bernhard's, so when they heard of her plan of going to me Prince Bernhard offered to bring her to Oslo in his lovely Dakotafly. You know he is a very clever pilot. They landed at Fornebo aerodrome (near Oslo) and I went to meet them. A rather lovely meeting!! She stayed a week and then she and I went away—to Jotunheimen—the wildest and tallest mountains of Norway, and we had a glorious time roaming and roaming along in that realm of beauty! She is a well-known painter, aged only 43, keen on all sports and champion both in tennis, golf and hockey—very tall and very handsome—an excellent climber accustomed to roam and go hunting in the jungle and mountains of Java and Ceylon. We enjoyed immensely to be together. . . . We let the wonderful nature sink into us, didn't mind if weather was fine or bad. We reached the highest peaks (about 2,400 m.) even in stormy weather, enjoyed listening to all the various callings and warnings from the mountain-world: avalanches sliding down, blue and green waterfalls running out of the glaciers, and the eagle's voice sometimes telling us from his nest that we were intruders in his realm—we had

to take care—and all the flowers, the white mountain queen, the various kinds of ranunculi and heather—everyone like wonderful eyes beaming against the sky!

Free-spirited Dagny wished Susanna and Beulah a merry Christmas "and a new year of happy days!!—The world situation is in such a chaos, we are all wondering what the future holds for us—but always, let us always pray and hope for peace. Much love to you/Your friend Dagny/Greetings from my friend Ragna Bugge." The chaos in the world that Dagny referred to was, at least in part, the Korean War, which had begun in June 1950 and would end in July 1953, a war which would claim an estimated 35,000 lives, more than 3,000 of them Americans.

Dagny wrote Susanna on February 1, 1952, to thank her for her Christmas present—a picture book about Florida which had sent her dreaming:

> I have walked along the glittering Florida beaches in hot sunshine, looked at shells and waves, waves from the open sea, bluish green—they topple over like white ostrich feathers,—looked at seabirds flying away with the sun on their wings and sailing majestically on the waves—they are rocking on the huge waves like in a sea-cradle. . . . I have steered my boat on idyllic water ways and lakes, looked at water hyacinths and tropical vegetation, felt the mysterious charm of the moonlit tropical night where fantastic silhouettes are standing out against the sky—Thank you for the lovely book from your exotic country—so beautiful and so varied in its beauty—thank you—I'll keep it as a treasure.
>
> As for me I am freezing a little after having dreamed about your warm and sunny land!! We have degrees of frost here (and a lot). Norway is snowclad, nature is resting. Northern lights are sparkling, stars are twinkling, lakes are covered with ice. Trees growing on their beaches mirror their white beauty in their shiny ice surfaces. You meet the frost everywhere when you go out and he loves to jar you to the roots of your hair!!—Oslo is busy preparing everything for the winter-olympiad. The games are going to start on the 15th of February.

Expectancy prevails in the town and it does its best to pretty up itself with arches, flags and lights. We all hope for a success—and of course many gold medals for Norway!! —

Ragna Bugge (my friend) sends her greetings to you, and she asks me to tell you that she too has enjoyed your book immensely. All is well with us. Luckily we have not yet joined in that coughing-and-sneezing choir which for a long time has been singing in nearly every home here!! — . . . Please do write some lines again when you have got time. I am so thrilled when I get some words from you. My best greetings to your sister. —

Lovingly,
Dagny.

Dagny wrote her next letter to Susanna almost two years later, on December 1, 1954. We learn from Dagny that Susanna and Beulah had torn down their old homestead in Riverton and built a smaller, more practical house in its place:

> I looked in my little Woodbrooke album some days ago, and realized that 40 years have passed since that lovely term we spent together at W. We were all in those days in our spring of life—now we are in the autumn—but I can't feel that—maybe because I have still not got snow in my hair! Strange that this showery weather during all my years has not crooked me like an old birch on the hillside! Very good for man to be thoroughly blown through. That removes dust—sweeping wind is always a cleaner!
>
> You wrote in your last letter that you then went on with the building of a new house. I think the house stands nicely in your garden now and that you have already enjoyed many happy days within the walls of your new home. You tell you had to pull down the house where 3 generations had lived because it was too big for you. That must have been quite a job, and a job that caused some heartbreaking too because that which has been established of old always is painful to disturb. Oh our forefathers lived in a happier time than we do!

. . . I made a little journey, went up to some mountain-lakes and lived there for a short time in the most complete and wonderful solitude and peace—far away from the busy world but near to nature and heaven. Lakes are designed to mirror heaven. They catch and hold the majesty of sky, record the journey of a truant cloud, reflect the sunlight and mark the peregrinations of an aimless moon. Lakes are like scratch pads on which the winds scribble idle messages. They grow dark and troubled announcing the coming storm. Sometimes they are like sheets of blue silver because the day is still and the sky clear. The lake reflects evening's quiet, becomes a part of a peaceful night's symphony. By the lake-side one finds the hallowed reverence of a cathedral and if its stillness is broken by the splash of a fish staying up late, the sound is not profane. I felt the eternal silence of night accentuated by the lake, but the lake with curious acoustics reflects also the whispering of the night, the hum of the insects, the noises of night's creatures, the murmuring of the wind in the trees, bushes, all sounds of the night gently breaking the silence so night is not dark silence at all, but is sound and music that you cannot understand until you have been part of it by a lake at night. . . .

How nice that you remember that we called you 'Little Star', but you don't know why? Why didn't you ask us then? It was because your eyes were like the stars we saw twinkling in the night. . . .

Christmas is approaching. I'll think of you when I light the lights of our Christmas tree and see the star on its top. All good wishes to you and your sister for a happy Christmas—and health and happiness in the coming year! —and thanks to Little Star for all the rays she so faithfully has beamed against me during now 40 years.

As ever your friend,
Dagny.

Dagny's seeing Susanna's—Little Star's—eyes as twinkling stars reflected her love of Susanna's spirit, which lit up her eyes. Susanna's cousin Alice Paul also had eyes which glowed with her bright spirit. Feminist author Inez Haynes Irwin wrote lovingly of Alice's eyes, "big and quiet and dark as moss-agates. When she is silent they are almost opaque.

When she talks they light up—rather they glow—in a notable degree of luminosity"[1] Mabel Vernon also waxed poetic about the powerful charisma of Alice's eyes: "She's no bigger than a wisp of hay, but she has the most deep and beautiful violet-blue eyes, and when they look at you and ask you to do something, you could no more refuse—"[2] Hazel Hunkins was similarly enthralled by Alice's gaze: "She had such blue eyes, no they were so dark, they were purple. One didn't disobey Alice Paul. She was such a compelling person."[3]

On January 21, 1955, Dagny sent a thank-you note to Susanna for her Christmas card and calendar, uncharacteristically short but poetic nonetheless. The note on Susanna's Christmas card had mentioned problems with the building of the new house:

> Dear Susanna!
>
> Thank you very much for your Xmas card and the most beautiful calendar "Our America" which arrived yesterday. Good heaven how beautiful it is. Every day when I look at it and think of you I'll also get a wonderful picture printed in my eye and mind. This is also America—a land so varied, so rich in marvelous sceneries, quite another America than we foreigners fancy when we think of it. We mostly think of big towns, big buildings and cars running so quickly that we would hardly dare to cross the streets. After this day I'll not any more think of the towns and big buildings—I'll think of the idylls, the charm and beauty of big America—revealed to me by your calendar.
>
> I hope you are in Florida now and enjoy the sun. I am afraid you'll shiver with cold when I tell you about our cold degrees—for some weeks we have had from minus 10 to minus 15. We all look like smokers when we walk in the streets—our breath follows us like white clouds lingering in the air. Not so much snow this winter. We'll get more I hope in February. I like snow—it is so clean, so pure, so soft—takes away all noises. It is wonderful.
>
> What troubles you have had with the rebuilding. I hope you got everything all right before you went to Florida. How lovely to live in a house on the edge of the woods—be able to look at birds, squirrels and other nice creatures. Sometimes some squirrels pay me a visit, sit

on the railings and look at me. I know they want food then and I give them heaps. They are quite tame.

       Happy New Year!
       My greetings to your sister.
       Love
       from Dagny.

I learned from my cousin Ed that the problem which delayed the construction of the new house was deciding what to do with the huge stone foundation of the old house; they finally decided to use the stones on the façade of the new house, linking it with the old homestead.

The next item of note in the collection is the announcement of the marriage of Josephine B. W. to Walter R. J., Jr. on June 23, 1957. This was surely the marriage of E.'s son: E. had married Walter R. J. in 1910.

Susanna and Beulah Parry's new house in Riverton, New Jersey, c. 1955. (Courtesy of the Alice Paul Institute, www.alicepaul.org)

The next item is not from the collection but from the "Report of the President and of the Treasurer" of Swarthmore College, 1957: "In January 1956 Susanna H. Parry ('08) and Beulah H. Parry ('09) of Riverton, New Jersey, conveyed to the College contiguous parcels of land in Delran and Cinnaminson townships, Burlington County, New Jersey, totaling 248 acres." Imagine the value of the gift of 248 acres of developable land in South Jersey bordering Route 130. In 1923, Susanna's and Beulah's parents and aunt had transferred two parcels of land totaling 278 acres to the sisters, so they had kept thirty acres and given the rest to Swarthmore College, their alma mater founded by their grandfather Judge William Parry.

Susanna's and Beulah's philanthropy extended to individuals as well as institutions. My cousin Ed told me that the sisters had given some of their land to his newly wedded parents to enable them to build a home in the 1940s. They also financed Ed's and his sister's education at Moorestown Friends School and Ed's tuition at Gettysburg College in the 1960s. Ed said he knew from family discussions that the sisters had helped pay for the education of other Quakers, but the specifics were never disclosed. From thank-you notes in the collection, we know that, in the 1940s, the sisters financed the tuition at George School of another child of one of their cousins: L. Calvin Robbins, son of Ida Parry.

On Swarthmore College's website, I discovered that Susanna's will established a scholarship fund in her and Beulah's names to make awards to deserving students based on academic merit and financial need. Swarthmore's Department of College Advancement informed me that the initial value of the scholarship in 1979 was about $800,000. As of June 30, 2020, it was valued at $8,513,474; it has helped Swarthmore students every year, providing student financial aid of over $400,000 in 2020. Susanna and Beulah never married or had children, but they made an enormous difference in the lives of many young Quakers by helping to give them a quality education; their generosity continues to this day, long after their deaths. Their philanthropy is inspiring.

Dagny wrote her last, heartbreaking letter to Susanna on December 13, 1957. She was following up on a calendar she sent to Susanna for Christmas without a note:

So it doesn't say much—it only tells that you are in my thoughts and that I am still a living creature on this globe which infernal human science strives so eagerly to destruct! So do forgive my silence. Heaps of times I have thought of you and sunny Florida during these last years and felt you like a Little Star far very far away. —But really I had no good news to tell and I've always thought it right not to write to friends when shadows and troubles make the days dark and sad. During such periods I leave correspondence to the thoughts in the hope that they'll find their way across every ocean. —

And now let me start to tell: many dear friends died during the last years—some were old, some young. I have many young friends maybe because I feel young myself in spite of old age (not yet grey hair!) and let them fly like birds out and in in my home and share their interests and help them in many ways. —In 1955 my only sister died and I had to sell our villa near Bergen because I could not live in two places. What a sorrow to do so! It was my childhood's lovely home! And now not more than a month ago Ragna Bugge died. She was called "The mother of Oslo"—big necrologies were written about her in newspapers all over Norway. She and I had our home together for 30 years. Good heaven how I miss her and grieve her. I feel quite forlorn here in our big flat now. She was so good and so clever, a prominent social worker who had held high social positions and got the medal of merit in gold from King Haakon. I am alone now and terribly unhappy. I knew her health was not so good any longer but I always hoped we would be allowed to be together still some years. Well we must all one day pass away, life and death are followers—they are not opposed to each other, they go quietly together. We only seldom think of that, don't realize that death is a link in life's big chain, is a step on the mighty life ladder of development. Death is a law in our existence and all laws of nature give an exponent of the will and voice of God. —

It is Xmas time, but no snow . . . I hope we'll soon get snow—snow makes everything so beautiful . . . snow so deep that you can jump into its softness and disappear!!

I hope all is well with you and your sister and send you both my best wishes for a happy Christmas and a happy New Year.

> As ever your friend
> Dagny Tischendorf.

This was Dagny's last letter. She was profoundly depressed after her sister's death, followed shortly thereafter by the death of her partner of thirty years. She sounded lost, longing to jump into the snow's softness and disappear. And disappear she does from the collection. I tried to find out from the internet when she died, fearing that she committed suicide. All I could find definitively was her date of birth—1888, daughter of Norwegian organist Gabriel Tischendorf. No confirmed date of death, except for one notation of 1964 qualified by a question mark. Nothing else except for an article she had published in 1914, which showed her as a social reformer with strong leftist leanings. The *American Journal of Sociology* (Vol. 20, 1914, p. 564) gives a synopsis of the 1914 article, probably written after her stay at Woodbrooke. The article is entitled "The Upper Class and the Workingman's Idealism":

> Strangely enough, it is not the so-called upper-class which originated the motto "all for one and one for all." This ideal comes from those liberal minds who have seen the depths of life and whose spirits have risen to the height of idealism and have found a response to this idealism in the masses of workingmen. The great awakening among these masses the upper class knows little about, other than as the rumbling of a dangerous volcano. This class, which attaches so much importance to its psychological and philosophical spirit, should build its theories on knowledge of life from actual experience. If one carefully studies the workingmen in their daily life, one will find them to be more faithful, sincere, God-fearing, patriotic, and honorable than many of those in the higher stations of life. Their aspiration is to secure for themselves a better present and for their posterity a better future. Hence the agitation for hygienic factory and housing conditions, shorter hours, and higher wages. This movement, which has unity, discipline, order, enlightenment and efficiency as its

foundation, and struggles for "freedom, equality, and brotherhood," demands a great deal of perseverance from its adherents in its struggle against conservatism, egoism, and the gregarious animal instincts.

I often wondered why Susanna was not drawn to Dagny. Both wrote with passion about the beauties of nature: the colors of sunsets, the variety of flowers around them, the crashing of waves. Susanna, as a Quaker, shared Dagny's interest in social welfare and reform in trying to make the world a better place: after all, they met at Woodbrooke. Both shared emotional ties with other women and refused to submit themselves to what Susan B. Anthony called a "man-marriage." Dagny's article, however, shows a sharp point of difference with Susanna: her disdain for the upper class and preference for the working class, even though she was born into wealth. Susanna, on the contrary, was by no means a Marxist and felt quite at home in her comfortable world of privileged Quakers. If I were writing a work of fiction here, I would have Susanna leave her world and inhibitions behind in the autumn of her life and join Dagny for wild adventures in Norway. Dagny could have been the "other E." that Susanna once hoped to find. This, however, is not a work of fiction, and the story of Dagny and Little Star ends here.

With Dagny gone, Little Star Susanna remained alone in the night sky, as she had been for so long: removed, solitary, silent, steadfast, shining.

Friends sent Susanna and Beulah a 1957 Christmas letter which closed with their Quaker hope for a troubled world: "In spite of Sputniks, missiles, fear, and world tension which seems to mount daily, we still believe that Love can conquer, for 'perfect love casteth out fear'. May we wish you all a joyous Christmas and Happy New Year." The world certainly must have seemed new, strange, and frightening to Susanna and her generation. The "Space Race" had begun: Russia had launched Sputnik, the first satellite, on October 4, 1957; the United States would soon follow with Explorer 1 on January 31, 1958; and the National Aeronautics and Space Administration would be established in June 1958. The Nuclear Age had also progressed since the bombing of Hiroshima and Nagasaki. In December 1957, America's first commercial nuclear power plant was put into service at the Shippingport Atomic Power Station in Pennsylvania. In addition, there was a new, horribly contested war erupting, with President Dwight D. Eisenhower having deployed the first military advisers to Vietnam in 1955. The Quakers had good reason to pray for the world then. They have just as much, perhaps even more, reason to pray for the world now.

In March 1958, Susanna and Beulah received a note of thanks from Miriam D., an old friend of the "Girls." Miriam was in Zurbrugg Hospital in Riverside, New Jersey, recovering from yet another procedure for what seemed to be cancer. Although Susanna and her sister, wintering in Florida, couldn't visit their friend personally, they did send her a generous check, for which Miriam was very grateful: "I think, mess that I am, that I am the luckiest person as far as friends go. Everyone has been wonderful, doing all they can for me, but when I received that little envelope from you, I was just about overcome. It is much, much more than I deserve. . . . However, it makes my bank balance feel much more comfortable to have a fat check like that added to it. . . . You are most thoughtful, considerate and wonderful friends and I love you dearly and have for many years, you must know." Once again, Susanna and Beulah had responded generously to a Friend in need.

There are no more items of note in the Susanna Collection, whose last entry is a March 1971 postcard to Beulah wishing her a happy birthday. Beulah died three years later, in May 1974. Susanna, now alone, moved to the Greenleaf Nursing Home in Moorestown, New Jersey. But the story is not over. Susanna's days with Beulah were now over, but not her days—and nights—with her cousin Alice.

CHAPTER 20

PASSING THE TORCH

By 1945, Alice had returned from Geneva where she had established the World Woman's Party (WWP) and helped a number of Jews escape from the Nazis; back in Washington, she had served once again as head of the National Woman's Party; and most recently she had been lobbying the United Nations to insert language concerning gender equality into the U.N. charter. Alice was sixty years old. NWP membership had declined significantly to under 4,000: many NWP suffragists had returned to their homes; some, like Lucy Stone and Mabel Vernon, had formed splinter groups of their own; and some had probably walked away because they had had enough of Alice's infamous authoritarian leadership style, which was good for getting things done but hard to take.

Knowing she had to pass the torch of leadership, Alice resigned as head of the NWP in 1945 and appointed Anita Pollitzer to take her place. Doris Stevens, who had been an influential leader with Alice since the CU days, protested the appointment of Pollitzer and complained about how Alice's internationally-focused WWP had influenced the national policy of the NWP. Stevens was ousted from the NWP in 1947 after an unsuccessful attempted coup and became the vice president of the Lucy Stone League in 1951, serving in that capacity until her death in 1963.[1]

Although Alice no longer headed the NWP, she was still an active principal, and the woman's party she founded continued to lobby Congress to pass the Equal Rights Amendment, pushing for the amendment to be introduced in each new session of Congress.[2] Alice and the NWP also introduced and passed a substantial body of legislation on a variety of women's issues. Two decades passed, then a major victory: Alice, the NWP, and black lawyer Pauli Murray, who saw the fight for Civil Rights and the struggle for women's equality as the same battle,[3] convinced President Lyndon Baines Johnson to include a prohibition against sexual discrimination in Title VII of the Civil Rights Act of 1964, which had originally been intended to prohibit employers from discriminating because of race or religion. An important victory for seventy-nine-year-old Alice, although not the complete victory she had hoped for and given her life to, for more than six decades.

In 1966, Betty Friedan, author of the landmark feminist treatise *The Feminine Mystique*, formed the National Organization for Women (NOW)—an enthusiastic, energized, well-organized, fast-growing community of feminist activists —the next generation, the so-called "second wave"—which grabbed the torch of equal rights for women from the NWP and ran toward victory.[4] With NWP membership now less than 1,000, Alice accepted NOW's invitation to join the new, rising group of feminists, as did many other NWP members. Congress was at last convinced to pass the ERA on March 22, 1972; however, opponents to the amendment attached a seven-year time limit for ratification, which would later be extended to 1982. Alice was eighty-seven when her amendment passed, but she would not live to see it ratified. At least she would not live to see it defeated when the ratification failed by three states. Friedan saw to it that the ERA, originally written by Alice and called the Lucretia Mott Amendment, would now be called the Alice Paul Amendment. The torch had been passed: from Lucretia to Alice, and from Alice to Betty. Who bears the leadership torch today?

After returning from Europe during the War, when not in Washington, Alice lived with her sister Helen, who died in 1961. After Helen's death, she lived with her close friend and NWP co-worker Elsie Hill, who died in 1970.[5] When the ERA passed in 1972, Alice lived full-time in the cottage in Ridgefield, Connecticut, which she had inherited from her sister Helen. In 1974, at age eighty-nine, she suffered a stroke and was hospitalized in a local nursing home. Her nephew Donald, son of her brother Parry (who had died long before in 1952), became Alice's guardian and plundered her estate before being removed as guardian:[6] "As Paul's health declined her only living relative, a nephew, Donald, came to care for her. Paul was not close with Donald and he ended up living off her money until concerned women stepped in. . . ." The court appointed feminist activist Peg Edwards as *ad litem* guardian to monitor Alice's health care and well-being. However, by this time Alice was without resources; with bills and taxes unpaid, Alice risked being placed under state care.[7] (I found the last footnoted reference in Clark Edwards' "Unpacking the Suitcase: The Real Last Chapter of Alice Paul and Peg Edward's Activism, and Why These Stories Matter", a fascinating treatise written by the granddaughter of feminist Peg Edwards, Alice's court-appointed guardian. Clark's adventure began when she unpacked her grandmother's suitcase, just as my epistolary journey began when I untied the dusty bundles of Susanna's letters.)

When things seem hopeless, miracles sometimes happen. On November 4, 1975, *The New York Times* printed an article about ninety-year-old Alice Paul: "Mother of U.S. Equal Rights Measure Nearly Penniless in Nursing Home at 90." The article reported that Ernestine Powell, Alice Paul's personal lawyer who was once Chair of the NWP in Washington,[8] had just asked the NWP to provide a loan for Alice's care; although Alice had been well cared for in the nursing home until then, the money was now gone. The NWP, which had dwindled to several dozen active members, rejected this request for charity to aid the very founder of the organization—which should have been an easy yes for them. The article was an appeal for funds to help this aged and destitute icon of suffrage and women's rights.

By a lightning stroke of coincidence and grace, the *New York Times* article was reprinted in *The International Herald Tribune* and was read abroad by the sister of Alice Muller, whose family Alice Paul helped escape from the Nazis. She sent a copy of the article to her stateside sister Alice Muller, who got to work to try to save the woman who decades before had helped save her. Alice Muller asked her son, a lawyer, to approach a Quaker judge in New Jersey about procuring help for Alice Paul, granddaughter of the venerable New Jersey Quaker Judge William Parry and daughter of the late William Mickle Paul, Quaker President of the

Moorestown Bank. The judge asked the Quakers in Moorestown to help Alice Paul, and they did. Alice was moved to the Greenleaf Extension Home in Moorestown, an extension of the Quaker Greenleaf Nursing Home. The Mullers visited her there.[9]

In another amazing coincidence, the Greenleaf Extension Home, Alice's new residence, was originally endowed by her cousin Beulah Parry[10] to help aged Quakers without resources. Even more jaw-dropping: Alice's roommate when she was moved to the Greenleaf Nursing Home was her cousin, our Susanna.[11] So our cousins, our Quaker rebels, who began their lives as childhood playmates and college classmates, ended their lives as roommates. My guess is they kept each other entertained with many a story.

When Alice turned ninety-two in 1977, Pennsylvania and New Jersey proclaimed January 11, 1977, as "Alice Paul Day", and First Lady Betty Ford personally congratulated her over the phone. Alice died later that year of pneumonia on July 9, 1977.

Susanna died in October 1979 at age ninety-four. Upon Susanna's death, her estate agent held an estate sale open to the surviving relatives mentioned in the will. All items in the house at 809 Main Street in Riverton were priced and tagged. The Parry beneficiaries selected their desired household items that once belonged to Susanna and Beulah, and the value of those items was deducted from their monetary distribution upon the settlement of the estate. On the day of the estate sale, something told my cousin Ed to go up to the attic; he obeyed, walked up the stairs, and found the dusty box of Susanna's correspondence which had not been valued because they were, after all, just old letters. The agent let Ed have the collection for free. He took it to his home, put it in his attic, and brought it out at a family reunion almost four decades later. The rest of the story has been told in these pages.

EPILOGUE

LOOKING BACK

So caught up in our daily routines and the demands of the moment, we rarely take the time to stop and consider the complete sweep of our lives, not only looking forward to what lies ahead—the where-we're-going, but also looking backward at our past to what lies behind—the where-we've-been. My cousin's discovery of a dusty box of letters and memorabilia—the Susanna Collection—has led me to experience the sweep of Susanna Parry's life, from her birth to her death and study the sweep of her favorite cousin Alice Paul's life. Although far too many people don't know anything about the Quaker heroine of women's rights, Alice Paul, there is now a substantial body of research about her (and some very good reads) available to those who want to learn more. Almost nothing is known, however, about Susanna Parry—until now. The Susanna Collection discloses the details of the life of an educated, privileged, compassionate Quaker woman from a past century, whose rebellion in her youth reflects the fascinating phenomenon of the Progressive Era's New Woman.

Looking back at the lives of these Quaker cousins, the differences between the two are obvious. Because Alice's father died when she was just beginning college in her mid-teens, she did not have masculine control over the decisions of her adulthood. Moreover, Alice's mother, Tacie, who used to take young Alice to her suffrage meetings, financially supported Alice in all her efforts—from her higher education to her work for the vote and equal rights. Unlike Alice, Susanna long remained under the tight control of her father, who died when Susanna was thirty-nine.

Howard Parry, the masculine head of a strict Quaker household, with full support of her mother and controlling aunt, kept Susanna reined in when she fell in love with her college roommate and wanted to break with tradition as a New Woman living with E. in a so-called Boston marriage. The respectable Quaker families of both Susanna and E. saw to it that the two young women were separated and closely monitored. The roommate was quickly married off to a suitable man. Susanna, however, refused hypocrisy and never married. She shook off her depression and stoically carried on in her Quaker lifestyle, becoming a generous philanthropist supporting higher education in her later years.

Alice and Susanna also differed in how they focused their energy and time. Alice's focus was outward. She was a celebrity, always in the public eye and in the news, known everywhere for her aggressive, unflagging fight to advance the cause of all women politically and legally, both here and abroad. Susanna's focus, on the other hand, was inward. She lived privately, known for the most part only to her family and members of her community, the Society of Friends.

The cousins, at least in their adulthoods, had very different personalities. Alice was serious-minded, all about the job at hand—first suffrage, later equal rights. Ironically, in this regard, she was much like her busy, distant father, who didn't devote much time to relationships with his children. Finding passion only in the struggle for full equality, Alice gave no time to establishing friendships, let alone more intimate relationships. Despite being on fire for women's rights, she was often cold with others. "Unlike Mabel Vernon . . . who was warm, good-humored, and always interested in the lives of her friends, Alice was a 'dedicated leader to whom you couldn't possibly sit down and tell a funny story, who wouldn't enjoy just something that had no relation to her work.'"[1] On the other hand, Susanna had an impish sense of humor, prone to giggling, acting silly with friends, and giving hugs. Susanna, unlike Alice, was delightful to be around—funny, affectionate, warm. Willing to waste a little time having fun with a friend.

Alice's devotion to her cause of full equality for women, her all-consuming obsession, came at a high price: the total sacrifice of her personal life. As a result, Alice never shared a grand passion with another, as far as we know. Although Alice inspired passion in quite a few devoted workers at her National Woman's Party, it appears she never fully returned the sentiment. The NWP was a burgeoning feminist community, fostering some same-sex relationships, such as Mabel Vernon, who lived with her companion Consuelo Reyes in Washington from 1951 until Mabel's death in 1975. Alice, however, did not have such a dedicated and close relationship.[2] Alice "never married, nor did she maintain the Boston marriage of an enduring relationship with any woman. Nor did she have the kind of passionate brief love affairs with other women as Susan B. Anthony and Frances Willard experienced."[3]

The big surprise in the collection, unknown to any of my living family members, was that Susanna, unlike Alice, experienced real love for another woman—her college roommate—her one-and-only E., her "Wifie." Their relationship was painfully brief, cut short by their controlling Quaker families. Although they dreamed of gazing on the azure blue of the Bay of Naples on their honeymoon, they never made it there together, although they saw it separately traveling with their families. The second big surprise in the collection: in her sixties, Susanna received over a decade of letters from a Norwegian sociologist and dreamer whom she last saw forty years before when they were students in England, letters wonderful to read, at times pure poetry, between the lines expressing Dagny's love for Susanna. Perhaps Susanna didn't reciprocate Dagny's desire, or perhaps she did but knew her family would have forbidden such a relationship. However, she knew that she was appreciated and loved, and she maintained an epistolary connection with her close but distant friend.

Despite these differences, our two cousins shared some similarities. They came into the world in the same year, 1885, born into almost identical circumstances, both the oldest children of well-to-do Hicksite Quaker families, both in their prime at the height of the Progressive Era, both New Women with dreams of a new way of life.

As happens to most of us, neither Alice nor Susanna realized all their youthful dreams. Alice was not as strong or successful as she would have liked to be. She suffered multiple spells of mental and physical exhaustion due to all the censure, incarcerations, forced feedings, and relentless battles for the rights of women. And although she obtained the vote, she did not see her Equal Rights Amendment ratified. Similarly, Susanna's life was not as she had envisioned. Her family and community prevented her from living with her beloved in an alternative "new" lifestyle. This broke her heart, and she suffered periods of deep depression. Moreover, she had to endure unforeseen illness in her middle age, battling tuberculosis for years. However, both cousins carried on in the face of their disappointments and setbacks and managed to make a positive difference in the lives of others. This is the stuff of heroines.

Alice effected enormous change on behalf of women, most notably in getting the Nineteenth Amendment passed and ratified, securing the vote for women. She also participated in passing much legislation to improve the lives of women, worked to protect the nationality of women marrying foreigners, convinced the U.N. to include the rights of women in its charter, and persuaded President Johnson to give women equal protection in employment under Title VII of the Civil Rights Act. What politician today has accomplished as much as Alice Paul or has even half her courage or devotion to the cause of helping others? She is an inspiring, impossible role model for anyone, male or female.

Although Susanna's contributions were smaller than Alice's, her generosity was enormous compared to me, and I dare say, most of us. She and Beulah, advocates of a Quaker education that teaches social responsibility and academics, financed the education of several young Quakers in their lifetime and continue to do so today, decades after their deaths, through their scholarship fund at Swarthmore College. They also gave a monumental gift of developable land to Swarthmore College, which was founded by their grandfather, Judge William Parry. They also, in their daily lives, performed frequent acts of kindness to meet the needs of family and Quaker Friends, whether sending a check to a struggling Friend in hospital or a box of food and clothing to an old friend in war-torn Norway. The world would be a far better place if more of us emulated Susanna's compassion and generosity.

Both of our Quaker cousins were rebels, like the original Quaker rebel, Betsy Ross. Alice's rebellion was active, bordering at times on militant. The Alice who smashed every window in her London jailhouse cell also broke through social and political conventions in America, creating the first woman's political party, organizing the first non-union pickets in front of the White House, standing firm with fists raised in the face of President Wilson and his Democratic Party until a constitutional amendment was passed giving all women their inalienable right to vote—the Nineteenth Amendment which celebrated the centennial of its ratification in 2020. I hope that this book will introduce Alice to those who never read about her in their history books and change the story of scandal that has circulated about Alice in my family for generations: the facts prove that Alice was far more heroic than scandalous.

Susanna's rebellion in her adulthood, unlike Alice's, was passive. In her youth, however, she actively rebelled. Susanna was a New Woman who experienced reciprocated love with her college roommate. The parents of Susanna and E. shut the relationship down, separating the girls and keeping them on different, socially acceptable paths. Susanna and E. relented, fearing ostracism from their families and religious community, as well as the loss of their significant family fortunes. This story happened over 100 years ago, when a woman's ability to earn a living was primarily limited to teaching, factory work, and prostitution. My guess is that, had Susanna and E. fallen in love 100 years later, in a world far more accepting of alternative lifestyles and offering far more career opportunities to women, they may well have lived together happily. But their world was not our world. E. reentered the Quaker mainstream, marrying and bearing children. Susanna, however, refused to marry, having no interest in becoming a man's partner. She remained single, imprisoned in the confines of social convention and Quaker propriety. A stoic rebel standing her ground, alone, her invisible fist raised in silence.

Until now. I hope I have finally given Susanna a voice. Susanna chose not to tell her story in her lifetime, but she saved the letters, fragments of her life, dusty bundles in an old wooden box, long unopened and unread. The task was given to me to piece together the story of her life's puzzle, a story which she, in her time, could not tell. But I, in my time, have a voice, and the story of Susanna, the story not of a heroine but of Everywoman in her struggle to live an authentic life, has now been told.

ACKNOWLEDGMENTS

To my grandfather, Edwin Satterthwaite Parry, who inspired this work. I figured if he could write a book about his great-great-grandmother Betsy Ross, I could write one about his cousins Susanna and Alice.

To other relatives: To my cousin Ed Graff, who was led by the spirit to go into the attic at Susanna's estate sale, find the box of her correspondence, and decades later pass it along to me to discover her story in the dusty pages. To my cousin Lee Shubert for encouraging me to write Susanna's story and to add her cousin Alice Paul to the mix. To my sisters, Susan Gantly and Charlotte Marlis, for their interest in Susanna's story and their guidance about safeguarding the identity of "E." And to all these relatives for their love of family history and each other.

Many thanks to all those who helped me put the pieces together: former Executive Director of the Alice Paul Institute, Lucy Beard, who generously shared materials about Alice and the Parry family; Jim Davis, Archives Associate at Friends' Central School of Philadelphia for digging through old yearbooks and files in search of Susanna and Beulah; Peggy Seiden, Swarthmore College Librarian; David Obermayer, Swarthmore College Archivist; Wendy Chmielewski, Curator of the Swarthmore College Peace Collection; Nikki Senecal, Director of Donor Relations at Swarthmore; and b. p. dandelion, Programmes Leader at Woodbrooke's Centre for Research in Quaker Studies, for his kind encouragement and for putting me in touch with Hans Eirik Aarek, who provided useful information about Dagny Tischendorf.

To Lawrence Knorr, my editor and publisher at Sunbury Press, for taking a chance on an unknown writer and pushing me to make the hard changes needed to make this a better book and reach a wider audience. And to Sarah Peachey at Sunbury, who skillfully and quickly cleaned up the text after the heavy lifting was over: her ability to find a flaw and improve a turn of phrase is humbling.

Great thanks to my long-time friend and mentor Dr. Kinley Roby, who gently encouraged me for years to write this book. I never would have begun or finished this daunting task without his golden rules: "write a page a day" until the book is finished, "send a query a day" until it finds a publisher, and "whatever your editor wants you to do, do it"—advice I pass on to all aspiring writers.

And most of all, *un grand merci* to my husband, Laurent Denis, who supported my spending countless hours with deceased relatives while dust gathered in the corners of the house and weeds grew in the garden, and who himself spent many an hour helping me navigate through online tasks. *Je t'aime.*

BIBLIOGRAPHY

THE SUSANNA COLLECTION

The author is caretaker of Susanna Parry's papers, which were found at Susanna's estate sale by the author's cousin Ed Graff. The author has given the originals of all items from the Collection written by Alice Paul to the Alice Paul Institute in Mt. Laurel, New Jersey.

SOURCES

"Alice Paul American Suffragist." The Editors of Encyclopedia Britannica. Last edited July 5, 2018. Britannica.com, Biography & Facts.

"Alice Paul Biography." Women in History Ohio. Last updated February 13, 2013. womeninhistoryohio.com.

Baker, Jean H. *Sisters: The Lives of America's Suffragists*. New York: Hill and Wang, 2005.

Colman, Penny. *The Vote: Women's Fierce Fight*. Penelope M. Colman, Kindle Edition, 2019.

"Doris Stevens." Wikipedia.

"Dudley Field Malone." Wikipedia.

Edwards, Clark. "Unpacking the Suitcase: The Real Last Chapter of Alice Paul and Peg Edward's Activism, and Why These Stories Matter." Scholarly and Creative Work from Depauw University. 2014.

Frost-Knappman, Elizabeth and Kathryn Cullen-Dupont, eds. *Women's Suffrage in America: An Eyewitness History*. Updated ed. New York: Facts on File, 2005.

Fry, Amelia R. "Conversations with Alice Paul: Women Suffrage and the Equal Rights Amendment; Alice Paul. An Interview Conducted by Amelia R. Fry." Suffragists Oral History Project. Calisphere, University of California. Content.cdlib.org/view?docId=kt6f-59n89c&doc.view=entire_text/.

Fry, Amelia R. "Sara Bard Field: Poet and Suffragist. An Interview Conducted by Amelia R. Fry." Suffragists Oral History Project. Calisphere, University of California. 1979.

Gates, Bill. "The Wright Brothers." *TIME. Scientists & Thinkers of the 20th Century* 153, no. 12, (March 29, 1999: 72-73.

Goodwin, Doris Kearns. *The Bully Pulpit: Theodore Roosevelt, William Howard Taft, and the Golden Age of Journalism.* New York: Simon & Schuster, 2013.

"Inter-American Commission of Women." Wikipedia.

"Isadora Duncan." Wikipedia.

Kane, Katherine Conger. "Hazel Hunkins Hallinan." *The Washington Post*, August 21, 1977.

Kops, Deborah. *Alice Paul and the Fight for Women's Rights*. Honesdale, PA: Calkins Creek, 2017.

Lunardini, Christine. *Alice Paul: Equality for Women*. Lives of American Women, edited by Carol Berkin. Boulder, CO: Westview Press, 2012.

McCarter, Jeremy. *Young Radicals in the War for American Ideals*. New York: Random House, 2017.

Miller, Marla R. *Betsy Ross and the Making of America*. New York: Henry Holt and Company, 2010.

The New York Times Guide to Essential Knowledge. Rev. and Expanded 2nd ed. New York: St. Martin's Press, 2007.

Neuman, Johanna. *Gilded Suffragists: The New York Socialites Who Fought for Women's Right to Vote*. New York: New York University Press, 2017.

Parry, Edwin Satterthwaite. *Betsy Ross Quaker Rebel*. Philadelphia: The John C. Winston Company, 1930.

Rupp, Leila J. "'Imagine My Surprise': Women's Relationships in Mid-Twentieth Century America." In *Hidden from History:*

Reclaiming the Gay and Lesbian Past, edited by Martin Baume Duberman, Martha Vicinus and George Chauncey, Jr., 395-410. Markham, Ontario: New American Library, 1989.

The San Francisco Lesbian and Gay History Project. "'She Even Chewed Tobacco': A Pictorial Narrative of Passing Women in America." In *Hidden from History: Reclaiming the Gay and Lesbian Past*, edited by Martin Baume Duberman, Martha Vicinus and George Chauncey, Jr., 183-194. Markham, Ontario: New American Library, 1989.

Smith-Rosenberg, Carroll. "Discourses of Sexuality and Subjectivity: The New Woman, 1870-1936." In *Hidden from History: Reclaiming the Gay and Lesbian Past*, edited by Martin Baume Duberman, Martha Vicinus and George Chauncey, Jr., 264-280. Markham, Ontario: New American Library, 1989.

Stevens, Doris. *Jailed for Freedom*. New York: Boni & Liveright, 1920. Reprinted by Schocken Books, 1976.

Traxel, David. *Crusader Nation: The United States in Peace and the Great War: 1898-1920*. First Vintage Books Edition. New York: Random House, 2007.

Vicinus, Martha. "Distance and Desire: English Boarding School Friendships, 1870-1920." In *Hidden from History: Reclaiming the Gay and Lesbian Past*, edited by Martin Baume Duberman, Martha Vicinus and George Chauncey, Jr., 212-229. Markham, Ontario: New American Library, 1989.

Walton, Mary. *A Woman's Crusade: Alice Paul and the Battle for the Ballot*. New York: St. Martin's Griffin, 2016.

Zahniser, J. D. and Amelia R. Fry. *Alice Paul: Claiming Power*. New York: Oxford University Press, 2014.

NOTES

CHAPTER 1: THEIR AMERICA
1. *New York Times Guide*, 399–400.

CHAPTER 3: NEW CENTURY, NEW WOMEN
1. Traxel, *Crusader Nation*, 10.
2. Gates, "The Wright Brothers," 72–73.
3. San Francisco Lesbian and Gay History Project, "She Even Chewed Tobacco," 192.
4. Smith-Rosenberg, "Discourses of Sexuality," 264–265.

CHAPTER 4: COMING OF AGE
1. Zahniser, *Alice Paul: Claiming Power*, 14.
2. Ibid., 13.
3. Ibid., 13–14.
4. Ibid., 18. Zahniser's source: "Conversations with Alice Paul," Paul/Fry Oral History, 27.
5. Ibid.
6. Ibid., 18–19. Zahniser's sources: Babbidge, "Swarthmore College," 144; Bond, *Journal, 1901–1903*, Bond Papers, Series 1, Friends Historical Library.
7. Vicinus, "Distance and Desire," 215.
8. Zahniser, *Alice Paul: Claiming Power*, 21. Zahniser's source: D'Emilio and Freedman, *Intimate Matters*, 189–94.
9. Ibid. Zahniser's sources: D'Emilio and Freedman, 189–94; *AP Journal*, 24 and 27 September, 21 October and *passim*; Giesecke interview, 5; "College Girls' Larks and Pranks," Ladies Home Journal, March 1910, 8.
10. Ibid, 21–22.

CHAPTER 5: YOUNG HEARTS TAKE FLIGHT
1. Baker, *Sisters*, 192.
2. Zahniser, *Alice Paul: Claiming Power*, 28–29.
3. Ibid, 23.
4. Baker, *Sisters*, 192.
5. Ibid., 75. Baker references Lillian Faderman, *Surpassing the Love of Me*n (New York: Morrow, 1981), 157–77; Carol Smith-Rosenberg, "The Female World of Love and Ritual: Relations between Women in Nineteenth Century America," *Signs 1* (Autumn 1975): 1–30.
6. Ibid., 77.
7. Vicinus, "Distance and Desire," 266.
8. Zahniser, *Alice Paul: Claiming Power*, 31.

CHAPTER 6: ALL THINGS MUST PASS

1. Vicinus, "Distance and Desire," 215.
2. Zahniser, *Alice Paul: Claiming Power*, 36. Zahniser references Fry, "Conversations with Alice Paul," 23.
3. Parry, *Betsy Ross Quaker Rebel*, 28–32.

CHAPTER 10: PARIS

1. Zahniser, *Alice Paul: Claiming Power*, 54. An error in Zahniser has been corrected: Zahniser says Alice's aunt wrote Tacie, but the note cites Beulah Parry's letter to Tacie, and Beulah (Susanna's sister) was Alice's cousin, not her aunt.

CHAPTER 11: COMING HOME

1. Walton, *A Woman's Crusade*, 14.
2. Zahniser, *Alice Paul: Claiming Power*, 59. Zahniser's source: AP to TP, 14 Jan 1909.
3. Walton, *A Woman's Crusade*, 16.
4. Ibid., 22.
5. Zahniser, *Alice Paul: Claiming Power*, 93.
6. Walton, *A Woman's Crusade*, 32.
7. Ibid., 104. Zahniser's source: Votes for Women, "Miss Paul," 7 January 1910.
8. McCarter, *Young Radicals*, 32.

CHAPTER 12: A NEW CHAPTER

1. Zahniser, *Alice Paul: Claiming Power*, 112. Zahniser's source: AP, "The Woman Suffrage Movement in Britain," in "Significance of the Woman Suffrage Movement," Supplement, *Annals of the American Academy of Political and Social Science* 35 (July 1910): 23–27.
2. Ibid., 117. Zahniser's sources: AP, "The Church and Social Problems," *Friends' Intelligencer* 20 (August 1910): 513–15; Benjamin, *Philadelphia Quakers*, 176–84.
3. Miller, *Betsy Ross*, 207.
4. Ibid., 201.
5. Kops, *Alice Paul*, 41–42.
6. Lunardini, *Alice Paul*, 55. Lunardini quotes article in *New York Times*, March 4, 1913.
7. Ibid., 57.
8. McCarter, *Young Radicals*, 35.
9. Zahniser, *Alice Paul: Claiming Power*, 165.
10. Walton, *A Woman's Crusade*, 85–86.
11. Lunardini, *Alice Paul*, 61.
12. Zahniser, *Alice Paul: Claiming Power*, 188.
13. Lunardini, *Alice Paul*, 63.

CHAPTER 13: 1914

1. Lunardini, *Alice Paul*, 83–84.
2. Ibid., 91. Lunardini quotes *New York Tribune*, August 30, 1914.

CHAPTER 14: WAGING WAR

1. Zahniser, *Alice Paul: Claiming Power*, 212.
2. Lunardini, *Alice Paul*, 100.
3. Ibid., 101.
4. Zahniser, *Alice Paul: Claiming Power*, 231.
5. Ibid., 235.
6. Lunardini, *Alice Paul*, 105.
7. Zahniser, *Alice Paul: Claiming Power*, 243. Zahniser quotes *San Francisco Bulletin*, 26 April 1916.
8. Walton, *A Woman's Crusade*, 103.

9. Lunardini, *Alice Paul*, 115.
10. Ibid., 117–18. Alice Paul to State Chairmen, February 8, 1917, NWP Papers.

CHAPTER 15: PRISONERS OF WAR

1. Zahniser, *Alice Paul: Claiming Power*, 270.
2. Walton, *A Woman's Crusade*, 185; Wikipedia, "Doris Stevens"; Wikipedia, "Dudley Field Malone".
3. Lunardini, *Alice Paul*, 124–25.
4. McCarter, *Young Radicals*, 197–98.
5. Zahniser, *Alice Paul: Claiming Power*, 280.
6. Walton, *A Woman's Crusade*, 180.
7. Lunardini, *Alice Paul*, 129. Lunardini's reference is: Fry, Amelia R. *Alice Paul Oral History*. Bancroft Library, 208.
8. Fry, "Alice Paul Oral History," 208.
9. Zahniser, *Alice Paul: Claiming Power*, 289.
10. Lunardini, *Alice Paul*, 130; Kops, *Alice Paul*, 107–11.
11. Zahniser, *Alice Paul: Claiming Power*, 277.
12. Lunardini, *Alice Paul*, 133.
13. Kops, *Alice Paul*, 118.

CHAPTER 16: THE BEST AND WORST OF TIMES

1. McCarter, *Young Radicals*, 261. McCarter references Diggins, *Up from Communism*, 22; Robert K Murray, *Red Scare: A Study in National Hysteria* (Minneapolis: University of Minnesota Press, 1955), 9.
2. Walton, *A Woman's Crusade*, 235.
3. Zahniser, *Alice Paul: Claiming Power*, 317.
4. Lunardini, *Alice Paul*, 144.
5. Wikipedia, "Doris Stevens."
6. Walton, *A Woman's Crusade*, 247.
7. Kops, *Alice Paul*, 140–41.

CHAPTER 17: BATTLE IN THE SHADOWLANDS

1. Lunardini, *Alice Paul*, 142.

CHAPTER 18: THROUGH DEPRESSION AND WAR

1. Britannica.com, "Alice Paul."
2. Frost-Knappman, *Women's Suffrage in America*, 445.
3. Wikipedia, "Inter-American Commission of Women."
4. Lunardini, *Alice Paul*, 159–60; Walton, *A Woman's Crusade*, 249.

CHAPTER 19: LITTLE STAR, NORWEGIAN EYES

1. Walton, *A Woman's Crusade*, 60. Walton references Inez Haynes Irwin, *Uphill with Banners Flying*. Penobscot, ME: Travesty Press, 1964), 14.
2. Fry, "Sara Bard Field."
3. Kane, "Hazel Hunkins Hallinan."

CHAPTER 20: PASSING THE TORCH

1. Wikipedia, "Doris Stevens."
2. Lunardini, *Alice Paul*, 165.
3. McCarter, *Young Radicals*, 313.
4. Lunardini, *Alice Paul*, 168.
5. Women in History Ohio, "Alice Paul Biography"; Rupp, "Imagine My Surprise," 403.
6. Walton, *A Woman's Crusade*, 250.

7. Edwards, "Unpacking the Suitcase," 81.
8. "Ernestine Powell," Worthingtonmemory.org.
9. Walton, *A Woman's Crusade*, 251; Lunardini, *Alice Paul*, 170–71.
10. Women In History Ohio, "Alice Paul Biography."
11. Walton, *A Woman's Crusade*, 251.

EPILOGUE: LOOKING BACK

1. Walton, *A Woman's Crusade*, 168. Walton references Rebecca Hourwich Reyher, *Working for Women's Equality*, 1978, oral history by Amelia R. Fry and Fern Ingersoll, Suffragists Oral History Project, The Bancroft Library, University of California at Berkeley, 201.
2. Rupp, "Imagine My Surprise," 402.
3. Baker, *Sisters*, 193.

INDEX

Addams, Jane, 29–31, 128, 131, 172, 190
Albright, Catharine, 149, 152, 154, 169
Alice Paul Amendment. *See* Paul, Alice: Equal Rights Amendment and
American Equal Rights Association for Universal Suffrage, 4
American University Washington College of Law. *See* Paul, Alice: education
Anthony, Susan B., 3, 4, 31, 53, 190, 229, 237
Anthony Amendment, Susan B. *See* Nineteenth Amendment
art, modern era changes in
  "Ash Can School," 37
  Expressionists (Munch), 37
  Impressionists (Monet, Degas, Pissarro, Renoir), 36
  Picasso (Cubism), 37
  Post-Impressionists (Cezanne, Van Gogh, Gaugin), 37
Atlantic City, New Jersey, 133–34, 156, 181, 199

Baltimore, Maryland, 6, 49, 120, 181
Battin, Benjamin, 71, 77, 79, 87, 96, 102, 105, 171
Belgium: Bruges, 143–45; Brussels, 71, 110, 143–44, 166
Belmont, Alva Vanderbilt, 32, 132, 141–42, 175–76, 178, 190, 200–203, 207
  "Marble House," 132, 142
Belmont, Oliver, 32, 132
Belmont-Paul Women's Equality National Monument (also Belmont House), 202, 207
Betsy Ross Quaker Rebel, viii, 66, 188, 243, 246
Blatch, Harriot Stanton, 176, 178, 201
Boissevain, Inez Millholland. *See* Milholland, Inez
Bond, Charlotte, 206, 209
Bond, Elizabeth, 44
Bond, Mary. *See* Parry, Mary Bond
Bostonians, The, 55–56
Boston marriage, 56, 155, 214, 236–37
Braithwaite, Isaac, 139, 159
Bugge, Ragna, 215, 217–18, 221–22, 227
Burns, Lucy, 121–23, 126, 128, 131–32, 141, 176–77, 179–80, 182–83

Cadbury family, 30, 64, 153–54
California, 17, 39
  Panama-Pacific International Exposition, 38, 138, 175
  San Francisco, 38, 55, 60, 138, 175, 177
Cameron House, 176, 178, 181, 184
Canning Town Settlement, London, 69
Carnegie, Andrew, 32, 109, 171
Carnegie Hall, 141, 187
Catt, Carrie Chapman, 131
Churchill, Winston, 122
Cinnaminson, New Jersey, 7, 153, 226
Claypoole, Elizabeth. *See* Ross, Betsy
Claypoole, John, viii, 42
Close, Ethel, 45, 57–58
College Settlement (New York City). *See* settlement houses
Columbia University. *See* Paul, Alice: education
Communist Party of America
  Communist Labor Party, 186
  Debs, Eugene, 29, 31, 33, 183, 186
  Industrial Workers of the World (IWW), 32, 180, 186
  Reed, Jack, 186
  Socialist Party in America, 29, 31, 186
Congressional Committee. *See* Paul, Alice: Congressional Committee and
Congressional Union. *See* Paul, Alice: Congressional Union and
Cook, Laetitia Haines, 18, 59, 60
Coral Gables, Florida, 16, 206, 209–10
Cunard Line, *Slavonia*, 71–72, 74, 76–80, 82

Dale, Arthur, 17
Dale, Francenia Haines, 17
dance: modern era changes in
  Castle, Irene and Vernon, 36
  Duncan, Isadora, 36
  Nijinsky, Vaslav, 36
  Stravinsky, Igor, 36
  tap, 36
"Declaration of Rights and Sentiments," 4
Democratic Party, 21, 43, 142, 175, 177, 184–85, 239

Depression, The Great, 194, 202–205, 207
Dickinson, Anna, 53
District Jail (Washington, D.C.), 182–83
Dorr, Rheta Childe, 130–31
Douglass, Frederick, 4
Dyer, Mary. *See* Quakers

"E". *See* Parry, Susanna, relationship with E.
East Fryeburg, Maine, 60–61
Eastman, Crystal, 128
Eastman, Max, 32, 128
Edward VII, 23
Edwards, Peg, 233
elections, U.S.
    of 1868, 2
    of 1876, 3
    of 1880, 3
    of 1884, 3
    of 1888, 3, 20
    of 1892, 3, 20–21
    of 1896, 21
    of 1900, 24
    of 1904, 25, 27
    of 1908, 28
    of 1912, 29
    of 1916, 177
    of 1920, 189
    of 1928, 203
    of 1932, 204
Elkinton, Anna Griscom, 139, 143–51, 155–71, 213
Emancipation Proclamation, 4
Equal Rights Amendment. *See* Paul, Alice: Equal Rights Amendment and
Espionage Act, 33, 180, 183

Feminine Mystique, The. See Friedan, Betty
feminism, viii, xii, 34, 55, 126, 131, 191, 201, 223, 232–33, 237
film, development of the industry
    Jolson, Al, 80
    Great Train Robbery, The, 37
    Lumiere Brothers, 37
    motion picture camera, 21
    Thomas Tally's Electric Theater, 37
forced feedings. *See* Paul, Alice: forced feedings
Ford, Betty, 234
Ford, Henry, 38; "Peace Ship," 172
"Forest Home," Linwood, Maryland, 14–15, 63
Fox, George. *See* Quakers and Quakerism
Franz Ferdinand, Archduke, 142, 154
Friedan, Betty, 232
Friends. *See* Quakers
Friends Central School of Philadelphia. *See* Quakers

Gantly, Susan Mulford, ix, xiii, 240
Gardener, Helen, 128
Geneva, Switzerland, 207

George School, 137, 208–209, 226
Germany
    Alice Paul in, 65
    Susanna Parry and family in, 102–106
    in World Wars, 109, 166–67, 179, 207–208
Gilded Age, The, 20, 30, 34, 132
Gillette, Emma, 128
Gospel of Wealth, The, 32
Graff, Dora Parry, viii, xiii
Graff, Ed, ix, xiii, 15, 225–26, 234, 240, 242
Grapes of Wrath, The. See Steinbeck, John
Greenleaf Nursing Home (Moorestown, New Jersey), 230, 234
Griscom, Anna. *See* Elkinton, Anna Griscom

Haines, Elizabeth. *See* Parry, Elizabeth Haines
Haines, Joseph L., 14–16, 43, 48, 63
Haines, Susanna, 10–11, 14–16, 18–19, 43, 48, 61, 63–64, 70–71, 77–78, 86–88, 105, 115–18, 133–35, 149, 163, 166, 169, 206
Havemeyer, Louisine, 132
Haverford, S. S., 123, 140, 142–43, 150–51
Hicksite Quakers. *See* Quakers
Hill, Elsie, 190, 201, 208, 232
Holloway Gaol, 122–23
Holmes, Anne, 45
homosexuality, 40, 44–45, 53–54
    Anthony, Susan B., 53, 237
    Bond, Elizabeth, 44
    Bostonians, The, 55–56
    Boston marriage, 56, 155, 214, 236–37
    Duncan, Isadora, 36
    Ladies of Llangollen (Sarah Ponsonby and Lady Eleanor Butler), 54–55, 159
    lesbian relationships in the 19th century, 53
    "Passing Women," 40
    Stein, Gertrude, 55
    Toklas, Alice B., 55
    Wilde, Oscar, 40
Hooch, Pieter de, ix, 102, 106–107
Hoover, J. Edgar, 189
Hopkins, Alison, 181
Hopkins, J. A. H., 181
Hull House. *See* Addams, Jane and Quakers: settlement houses
hunger strikes. *See* Paul, Alice: forced feedings
Hunkins, Hazel, 176, 224, 243

immigrants, 30
Inter-American Commission of Women, 207

Jackson Place, 184
Johns Hopkins University, 181

"Kaiser Wilson" banner. *See* National Woman's Party: "Silent Sentinels"
Keller, Helen, 176

Kent, Elizabeth, 133
Korean War, 221

Labour Party (England), 23
Lafayette Park/Lafayette Square, 176, 184–85. *See also* National Woman's Party: "Watchfire(s) of Freedom"
League of Nations, 189, 207; Women's Research Foundation of, 207
League of Women Voters, 190
Lewis, Dora, 128, 141, 176, 179, 181, 183
Literature: modern era changes in
  Dreiser, Theodore, 33
  Eliot, T. S., 34, 189
  James, Henry, 34, 40, 55
  Lawrence, D. H., 34
  Naturalism, 33
  Norris, Frank, 33
  Sinclair, Upton, 26, 32–33
  Wharton, Edith, 34
  Zola, Emile, 33
London, England, 69, 71, 79, 114–17, 120, 122, 149, 152, 164–71, 194, 218, 238
London School of Economics. *See* Paul, Alice: Education
Loomis Memorial Sanitarium for Consumptives, 193–99
"Lost Generation," 189
Lusitania, 147, 175

Malone, Dudley Field, 181, 183
"Marble House." *See* Belmont, Alva Vanderbilt
Marlis, Charlotte Mulford, viii, xiii, xiv, 240
Married Women's Property Act of 1860, 4
Masses, The, 32–33, 128, 132, 180
McCloskey, Lydia Parry, viii, xiii
medicine, diseases and advances in
  antihistamines, 117
  aspirin, 1, 22
  asthma, 63
  cholera, 21
  Dick, George, 19
  DTP vaccine, 19
  Fleming, Alexander, 144
  Freud, Sigmund, 39
  Haffkine, Waldemar, 21
  hay fever, 116–18, 136
  Lister, Joseph, 20, 144
  Pasteur, Louis, 20, 144
  penicillin, 17, 19, 144
  polio, 173–74
  pneumonia, 1, 2, 17, 43, 205
  Reed, Walter, 39
  scarlet fever, 19, 59
  tuberculosis, 2, 193–95, 197–98
  typhoid fever, 11, 15, 21, 37, 39, 50, 63
  whooping cough, 19

Wright, Almroth, 21
Merion, 150–51, 171
Milholland, Inez, 129, 177–78, 184
Miller, Rena, 45, 53
Montessori, Maria, 176
Moorestown, New Jersey, 7, 41–42, 57, 124–25, 128, 132, 141, 173, 181, 226, 230, 234, 254
Moorestown Friends School. *See* Quakers
Moorestown National Bank, 7, 234
Mott, Lucretia, 3, 7, 190–92, 200, 204, 232
Mt. Laurel, New Jersey, viii, xi, 57, 242. *See also* Moorestown, New Jersey
Mulford, Charlotte Parry, viii, xiii, 133, 211
Mulford, Dr. William P., 211
Muller, Alice and Felix, 207, 233–34
Murray, Pauli, 232
Music, modern era changes in
  Berlin, Irving, 36
  Charleston, 36
  Joplin, Scott, 35
  Ragtime, 35
  Stravinsky, Igor, 36

Naples, Italy, 53, 71, 80–84, 86–87, 237
National American Women Suffrage Association (NAWSA), 125–33, 141, 175–76, 190
National Association for the Advancement of Colored People (NAACP), 30
National Organization for Women (NOW), 232
National Woman's Party (NWP), vii, xiv, 132, 176–77, 182, 189–90, 207, 231–33, 237
  arrests and imprisonments, including "Night of Terror," 180–85, 187
  colors of, 178
  founding of, 32, 132, 141, 176
  headquarters of, 176, 178, 184, 190, 202, 207
  membership of, 176, 184, 190, 200–201, 208, 231–33
  merger with Congressional Union, 179
  Alice Paul and. *See* Paul, Alice: National Woman's Party
  "Prison Special" train tour, 187
  ratification campaign for 19th Amendment, 187–89
  "Silent Sentinels," 133, 142, 178–84; "Kaiser Wilson" banner, 181
  "Suffrage Special" train tour, 177
  Suffragist, The, 130–31, 179, 187
  Title VII. *See* Title VII, Civil Rights Act of 1964
  "Watchfire(s) of Freedom," 185
"New Marriage," 40
"New Woman," xii, xiv, 36, 40–41, 44, 50, 53, 56, 62, 64, 131, 154–55, 191, 235–37, 239
"Night of Terror." *See* National Woman's Party, arrests and imprisonments
Nineteenth Amendment/Susan B. Anthony Amendment, xiv, 181, 238–39

passage of, 184, 186–87, 238
ratification by the States, 185, 187, 189, 238
suffrage debates, 130, 175
suffrage votes, 175, 184–85
Wilson's opposition to: *See* Wilson, Woodrow
Nobel Peace Prize, 30, 217–18
Norway, 208, 212–15, 217–22, 227
NOW. *See* National Organization for Women
NWP. *See* National Woman's Party

Occoquan Workhouse, 181–84

Panama Canal International Exposition. *See*
 California: Panama-Pacific International
 Exposition
Panic of 1873, 3
Panic of 1893, 15, 21
Pankhurst, Christabel and Emmeline, 31–32, 48,
 54, 72, 114, 120–23, 126–29, 131–32,
 169–70, 179, 184
Parry, Alice (daughter of Charles), xiii, 64, 68
Parry, Alice Stokes, viii, xiii, 7–8, 15
Parry, Anna Morrell, xiii, 8, 16, 19
Parry, Anna Sill, xiii, 8, 13, 64
Parry, Beulah, viii–xiii, 10–14, 16, 19, 33, 49,
 51–52, 59, 66–68, 70–71, 77–79, 82, 84,
 86–87, 89, 91, 93–94, 100, 104, 107,
 111, 113, 115–17, 119–20, 135–36, 140,
 143–45, 148, 150–53, 156–59, 162, 164,
 168–69, 171–73, 192–97, 199, 201, 203,
 205–206, 208–10, 212, 217, 220–22,
 225–26, 229–30, 234, 238, 240, 246
Parry, Charlotte. *See* Mulford, Charlotte Parry
Parry, Charles, xiii, 13
Parry, Dora. *See* Graff, Dora Parry
Parry, Edwin Satterthwaite, viii, xiii, 11, 13, 15, 17,
 43, 50, 123, 126, 133, 188, 199, 205–206,
 209, 240, 243
Parry, Elizabeth (Lizzie) Haines, viii, xiii, 7–8,
 10–12, 15–19, 43, 59, 63–64, 71, 117–19,
 194–96, 199, 201, 206, 210
Parry, Howard, viii, xiii, 1, 7–8, 10–11, 116–19,
 136, 194, 236
Parry, John R., xiii, 8, 16
Parry, Lydia. *See* McCloskey, Lydia Parry
Parry, Lydia Satterthwaite, viii, xiii, 8, 50, 118, 149,
 188, 205
Parry, Mary. *See* Turner, Mary Parry
Parry, Mary Bond, viii, xiii, 43, 133, 206, 209–11
Parry, Oliver, viii, xi, xiii, 8, 11, 15, 50, 63, 149
Parry, Sara, xiii, 16, 19
Parry, Susanna, viii–xv, 3, 14, 40, 48, 64, 69,
 117–18, 133–38, 198, 204–206
 and Alice Paul, 7, 9, 43, 46, 57–58, 68–70,
 114–15, 201–202, 230, 234–35
 childhood, 1–3, 10–13, 16–17, 42

correspondence with Dagny Tischendorf,
 213–29, 237–38
death of, ix, 234
philanthropy, 6–7, 33, 208–209, 226, 230
Quaker activities, 5, 9, 135–36, 139. *See also*
 Woodbrooke *below*
relationship with "E.", 45, 49, 51–53, 56, 58,
 60–63, 66–67, 72–73, 81–82, 86, 120,
 136, 138–39, 212, 236
Swarthmore years, 5, 41, 44–46, 48–50, 52, 54,
 56, 59–61, 63–68, 70–72
travels in Europe, 11, 70–72, 74–117, 139,
 142–171
 First "Susanna Tour":
 Italy: Bellagio and Lake Como, 96–97;
 Florence, 91–93; Sorrento, 77–78, 84–86;
 Venice, 89, 93–95
 Netherlands: Amsterdam, 104, 106–108;
 Hague, The, 108–110
 Paris, 110–114, 143–44
 Second "Susanna Tour":
 Edinburgh, Scotland: Scotland, 159,
 161–62; Edinburgh, 162–64
 Lake District, 159–60
 North Wales: Wales, 156–59; Betws-y-Coed,
 157–58; Carnarvon,157–58; Conwy
 Castle, 157–58; Llandudno, 157–58
as tuberculosis patient, 192–98
at Woodbrooke (Birmingham, England), 30,
 139–40, 145–56
Parry, Tacie. *See* Paul, Tacie Parry
Parry, William (Will), xiii, 8,18
Parry, Judge William, viii, xi, xiii, 1, 5, 7–8, 11, 15,
 41, 226, 233, 238
Paul, Alice, vii–viii, x–xv, 1, 7, 40, 65–66, 125–26,
 133, 174–75, 189–91
 and Susanna Parry. *See* Parry, Susanna, and Alice
 Paul
 appearance, 12, 42, 127, 188, 200, 224
 arrests: in United Kingdom, 122–23; in United
 States, 182–84
 childhood, 9–10, 12, 42
 Congressional Committee and, 128–30
 Congressional Union and, 130–33, 141–42,
 175–79
 death of, 234
 education: at Swarthmore, 5, 41–47, 50;
 at New York School of Philanthropy
 (Columbia University), 50–51, 57–58; at
 Woodbrooke, 30, 65–66, 68–70, 72, 114;
 at London School of Economics, 114, 120;
 at University of Pennsylvania, 5, 65, 126; at
 American University Washington College
 of Law, 5, 190, 201
 Equal Rights Amendment and, xiv, 175, 190–91,
 199–201, 208, 231–32

forced feedings: in United Kingdom, 123; in
  United States, 182
health, 123–24, 132, 141, 180–81, 232–33,
  237–38
National American Women Suffrage Association
  (NAWSA) and, 125–32, 141, 190
And National Organization for Women, 232
National Woman's Party and, vii, 50, 132, 141,
  176–191, 207–208, 231–33, 237
Pankhursts and (WSPU and), 48, 54, 72, 114,
  120–23, 126–28, 131
Quaker influence, 6, 41–43, 233–34
single-mindedness, 32, 45, 114, 236
social work, 50–51, 57–58, 69–70, 72, 114
1913 Suffrage Parade, 128–29
Title VII of Civil Rights Act, 232, 238
Wilson and. *See* Wilson, Woodrow: Paul, CU,
  and the NWP and
Women's Social and Political Union (WSPU)
  and. *See* Pankhurst, Christabel and
  Emmeline
World Woman's Party and, 207–208, 231
Paul, Donald, 232–33
Paul, Hannah, 57
Paul, Helen, viii, xiii, 11, 135–36, 141, 148, 183,
  201, 232
Paul, Mickle, 142
Paul, Parry, viii, xiii, 201, 232
Paul, Tacie Parry, viii, xiii, 1, 5, 7–8, 41–44,
  120–23, 125, 131, 178, 207, 235
Paul, William (Will), viii, xiii, 12
Paul, William Mickle, viii, xiii, 5, 7–8, 42–43,
  233–34
Philadelphia, Pennsylvania, 6, 46, 51, 65, 67, 102,
  123, 125–27, 130, 136–37, 141, 171, 185,
  204, 209, 218
pickets. *See* National Woman's Party: "Silent
  Sentinels"
Pollitzer, Anita, 231
Powell, Ernestine, 233
Presidential Elections. *See* elections, U. S.
presidents, American
  Arthur, Chester A., 3
  Cleveland, Grover, 3, 20–21
  Coolidge, Calvin, 203
  Eisenhower, Dwight D., 230
  Garfield, James, 3
  Grant, Ulysses S., 2–3
  Harding, Warren G., 189, 203
  Harrison, Benjamin, 20–21, 24
  Hayes, Rutherford B., 3
  Hoover, Herbert, 203–204
  Johnson, Andrew, 2
  Johnson, Lyndon Baines, 232
  Lincoln, Abraham, 2, 4, 109, 164
  McKinley, William, 16, 21–22, 24–25

  Roosevelt, Franklin, Jr., 174, 204
  Roosevelt, Theodore, 18, 20–22, 24–29, 34, 109,
    176, 189
  Taft, William Howard, 22, 26, 28–29, 123
  Truman, Harry, 212
Progressive Era and progressivism, xiv–xv, 18,
  23–33, 35, 152, 177, 189, 237

Quakers and Quakerism (Friends), x–xi, 30, 41–43,
  57, 60, 66–67, 121, 123, 125–26, 135–40,
  152–53, 165–66, 169–72, 204, 229–30,
  233–36, 238–39
Dyer, Mary, 6
Fox, George, 5, 159
Friends Central School of Philadelphia, 46–48,
  51, 240
"Great Separation," 6
Hicks, Elias, 6
Hicksite Quakers, 1, 3, 5–7, 9, 41, 44, 125, 135,
  151, 188, 208–209, 237
Moorestown Friends School, 41–42, 226
Nobel Peace Prize of 1947, 217–18
Penn, William, 6
and Ross, Betsy, vii–viii, 50, 66–67, 125–26,
  132, 188, 243
settlement houses, 30, 50, 56–58, 69, 72, 114,
  139, 152, 169
Westfield Friends Burial Ground, 194, 207

Republican Party, 2, 21–22, 24, 27–29, 43, 177,
  185, 187
Riverton, New Jersey, viii–ix, 7, 14, 16, 50, 59–60,
  63–64, 100, 116–17, 119–20, 134, 136,
  145, 151, 194–95, 198, 203, 206, 210–11,
  222, 225–26, 234
Robbins, L. Calvin, 208–209, 226
Rockefeller, John D., 26, 35
Rockefeller, John D., Jr., 32
Ross, Betsy (also Betsy Griscom, Betsy Ashburn,
  and Betsy Claypoole), vii–viii, 50, 66–67,
  125–26, 132, 187–88, 238, 240, 243
Russia: 20th century political changes
  Bolsheviks, 183
  Lenin, Vladimir, 183
  Red Scare, 183, 189

Sargent, Aaron, 4
Satterthwaite, Lydia. *See* Parry, Lydia Satterthwaite
Science, modern developments in
  atomic energy, 2, 21, 212, 230
  Becquerel, Henri, 21
  Curie, Marie and Pierre, 38
  Einstein, Albert, 38
  Geiger, Hans, 38
  Hale, George, 39
  Nuclear Age, 212, 229

radioactivity, 21, 38
Rutherford, Ernest, 38
Thomson, J. J., 21
sculpture of Elizabeth Cady Stanton, Susan B. Anthony, and Lucretia Mott, 190
"second wave" of feminism, 232
Sedition Act, 183
Seneca Falls, Convention of 1848, 3–4, 191
settlement houses. *See* Quakers: settlement houses
Sewall-Belmont House. *See* Belmont-Paul Women's Equality National Monument
Shubert, Lee, x–xi, xiii, 194, 240
Silent Sentinels. *See* National Woman's Party: Silent Sentinels
Sill, Anna. *See* Parry, Anna Sill
Spanish influenza, 186
Squirrel Inn, 7, 57–58
Stanton, Elizabeth Cady, 3–4, 31, 176, 190
Stein, Gertrude, 56, 189
Steinbeck, John, 204
Stevens, Doris, 181, 183, 190, 201, 207, 232, 244
Stokes, Alice. *See* Parry, Alice Stokes
Stone, Lucy, 231
suffrage for women. *See* voting rights for women
suffragette vs. suffragist, 31, 72, 114, 121, 127
Suffragist, The. See National Woman's Party: *Suffragist, The*
Susan B. Anthony Amendment. *See* Nineteenth Amendment
Swarthmore College, viii, x, 5, 7, 9, 31, 41, 43–46, 48–50, 52–53, 56, 58–59, 64–66, 68, 70–72, 76, 78–79, 83, 171, 201, 226, 238, 240

Technology: modern advancements in
  Bell, Alexander Graham, 1, 20
  Benz, Karl, 20
  Edison, Thomas, 1, 21
  gramophone, 20
  Kodak camera, 104
  radio technology and broadcasting, 1, 37–38, 167, 197
  Space Race, 229
  telephone, xiv, 1, 10–11, 18, 20–21, 37–38, 44, 61
  Wright, Orville and Wilbur, 37
Tischendorf, Dagny, 212–229, 237
Title VII of Civil Rights Act of 1964. *See* Paul, Alice: Title VII of Civil Rights Act
Turner, Mary Parry, viii, xiii, 13, 17, 43, 50, 119

University of Pennsylvania, 5, 65, 125–27, 201
United Nations, 32, 110, 208, 231

Universal Declaration of Human Rights. *See* United Nations

Vernon, Mabel, 50, 130, 141, 180, 224, 231, 236–37
Votes for Women, 121, 123
Voting rights for women: 31–32, 43–44, 50, 72, 114, 127, 131–32, 141, 176, 178–79
  federal amendment approach to, 31, 125, 127–30, 141–42, 174–77. *See also* Nineteenth Amendment, Seneca Falls Convention, and state power over voting rights

Washington College of Law. *See* Paul, Alice: education
Washington District Jail. *See* District Jail (Washington, D. C.)
Wellesley College, 56
Westfield Friends Burial Ground. *See* Quakers
White, Dr. William, 183
Wilson, Woodrow, 29, 129, 142, 177, 181, 184–85
  address to Congress, 179
  death of wife Ellen, 142
  Elections. *See* Elections, U.S.
  health of, 189
  inauguration, 128, 179
  League of Nations and, 189
  Paul, CU, and the NWP, 129–30, 174–82, 185–86, 239
  war stance, 29, 33, 172, 179
Women's Research Foundation. *See* League of Nations
Women's Rights Convention of 1854, 4
Women's Social and Political Union (WSPU), 72, 114, 120–23, 127, 129, 131–32, 170, 179, 184. *See* also Paul, Alice: Pankhurst and WSPU
Woodbrooke (Birmingham, England), x, 30, 64, 68, 126, 135, 153, 155–56, 159, 163, 212–13, 222, 240
  Alice Paul at, x, 30, 65–66, 68–69, 72, 114
  Susanna Parry at, x, 30, 139–40, 145, 148–49, 151–52, 155–56, 167, 194, 212–13
World's Fair of 1915. *See* Panama-Pacific International Exposition
World War I, 29, 142, 154, 161–72, 175, 179–80, 186
World War II, 19, 174, 204, 207–208, 211
World Woman's Party (WWP). *See* Paul, Alice: World Woman's Party

Younger, Maud, 189

ABOUT THE AUTHOR

(Photo by Maryline G. Ventura)

LESLIE MULFORD DENIS was raised in Moorestown, New Jersey, like her distant relative Alice Paul. She wore many professional hats before becoming an author: university instructor of English, public finance administrator, university financial officer, property developer, and B&B owner in Normandy. After a stateside decade in Kennebunk, Maine, and the Eastern Shore of Maryland, she and her husband Laurent recently returned to France and are restoring the house and grounds of a century-old manor. She is currently writing her memoirs as a cookbook: every recipe has a story. For more about Leslie, her book *Susanna and Alice: Quaker Rebels*, and her blog about her life in France, please visit lesliedenis.com.

www.ingramcontent.com/pod-product-compliance
Lightning Source LLC
Chambersburg PA
CBHW031432160426
43195CB00010BB/709